THE
CARAVAN MANUAL

John Wickersham

Author:	John Wickersham
Editor:	Jill Gough
Cover design:	Dave Hermelin
Photographs:	John Wickersham
Illustrations:	Paul Tanswell

© John Wickersham 2000

First published 1993
Reprinted 1993, 1994
Revised 2nd Edition 1996, Reprinted 1997, 1999
Revised 3rd Edition 2000, Reprinted with minor amendments 2001
Reprinted 2002 (twice), 2003 (twice), 2005 (with minor amendments) and 2007 (with minor amendments)

Published by:
Haynes Publishing, Sparkford, Yeovil, Somerset BA22 7JJ, UK

A catalogue record for this book is available from the British Library

ISBN 978 1 85960 333 8

Haynes Publishing, Sparkford, Yeovil, Somerset BA22 7JJ
Tel: 01963 442030 Fax: 01963 440001
Int. tel: +44 1963 442030 Fax: +44 1963 440001
E-mail: sales@haynes.co.uk
Website: www.haynes.co.uk

Haynes North America, Inc.
861 Lawrence Drive, Newbury Park,
California 91320, USA

Printed in Great Britain by J. H. Haynes & Co. Ltd

Gas Regulations

Gas Regulations and the way in which appliance manufacturers interpret them regarding the installation of their products are subject to continuing change. It is strongly recommended that anyone contemplating the installation of a gas appliance should consult the appliance manufacturer's customer service department before undertaking any work themselves. This may reveal different recommendations from those stated here, in which it is suggested that a competent amateur could consider tackling the preliminary carpentry and fitting work in accordance with the installation instructions. However, it is suggested in the chapters concerned with gas systems and appliances that work on the gas connection(s), flues and the final testing of an installation should always be entrusted to a competent and appropriately qualified gas engineer.

Contents

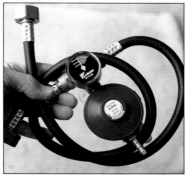

Foreword

This remarkable book covers just about all you will need to know to get the most from your caravan. It contains good advice for the newcomer to caravanning, but seasoned caravanners will also be sure to find masses of useful information as well, from battery life to sealant problems. The technical detail is comprehensive without being jargon-ridden or overwhelming, and the latest revisions bring matters right up to date on standards and industry practice. The Caravan Club has always stressed the importance of proper maintenance and servicing and The Caravan Manual will help those who can do some of the work themselves whilst pointing out clearly those areas best left to the professionals.

T A Watson,
Director General,
The Caravan Club

The Camping and Caravanning Club recognises the importance of a well maintained and regularly serviced caravan to ensure the safety of its members and other road users. We welcome this third edition of Haynes Caravan Manual as it will help the Club's 200,000 caravanners to keep their units well maintained and to ensure that they meet the latest regulations and European Standards for safe and enjoyable caravanning.

David Welsford,
Director General,
The Camping and Caravanning Club

Author's note

In 1990 I started taking photographs and preparing the text for a caravan manual. It was a huge job but I was fairly certain that many caravanners would be interested in a practical book.

One thing that helped in this endeavour was the support of a publisher whose name has always been long-associated with wheeled machines, their repair and maintenance. Little did we realise that many years and two editions later, *The Caravan Manual* would be one of the best selling practical books to bear the Haynes badge.

Much has happened in the ten years since the first manuscript was prepared and the black and white photographs were developed in my dark room. Caravans are now more sophisticated, technological innovations have helped the designers and unprecedented levels of creature comforts are provided as standard features.

Similar progress has occurred in the publishing process too. All leading caravan magazines are now printed in full colour and it was only right for *The Caravan Manual* to follow the trend.

To lead caravanners into the Year 2000 and beyond, the Third Edition of *The Caravan Manual* has been completely rewritten. Virtually all the illustrations have been updated, and reference is made throughout the text to the latest European Standards. It is sincerely hoped that you will find *The Caravan Manual* of great use, whether you buy it to carry out your own repairs and improvements, or whether you use it as a point of reference.

This project would not have been possible without the support of a notable team at Haynes Publishing, together with many people in the caravan industry who have given their time so generously. I am indebted to these knowledgeable and enthusiastic advisers who have helped so much in the production of this new version of *The Caravan Manual*.

John Wickersham
January 2000

Introduction and overview

A touring caravan provides the means for travelling far and wide. The aim of this book is to help you keep your caravan in tip top condition so your travels can be carried out in comfort and safety.

The statistical evidence is convincing. According to the National Caravan Council's research, there are over 500,000 caravans in regular active use. In Britain, caravanning is certainly very popular.

■ The caravanning clubs

Further confirmation of its popularity is reflected by the monthly distribution of the members' magazines from the two major caravan clubs. The combined circulation of the magazines sent to members of *The Camping and Caravanning Club* and *The Caravan Club* is huge. The figure in 1998, independently confirmed by the Audit Bureau of Circulations, amounted to a remarkable average monthly circulation of 443,495 copies! Add non-club members to this figure, and the number of keen caravanners in this country is undeniably large.

■ Caravanning in comfort

The reason for taking up caravanning is very personal. For some, a caravan provides accommodation for an annual summer holiday. Others use their caravans all-year round – sometimes for touring and sometimes to provide a base when attending major events. The diversity of opportunities for travel is a key attraction, but one element is common to all participants – the desire to caravan in comfort and safety. Herein lies the reason for writing this book.

■ Servicing and repairs

Modern caravans are very sophisticated and to ensure they provide comfortable accommodation with a safe set-up, they need to be serviced at regular intervals. Just as cars need servicing, so do caravans and their appliances. Needless to say, you also have to learn how to operate the appliances correctly and it may be helpful to have a rudimentary understanding of the way they work. Features like this are covered in the chapters which follow.

Occasionally, something might fail to function. When this happens it is always useful to know what the repair procedures are likely to entail. This is especially important for readers who want to carry out their own repairs. However, it is no less important for owners who prefer to take their caravan to a dealer. Having a broad understanding of what the repair involves helps you know if a job has been carried out correctly. Either way, guidance relating to many of the more common problems and the appropriate courses of action are provided in this manual.

■ Upgrading facilities

Some caravan owners also decide it would be desirable to *improve* the facilities in their caravan. Service items might be upgraded, for example, and new appliances installed. Depending on one's knowledge, skills and workshop equipment, many projects can be tackled. *The Caravan Manual* provides the appropriate guidance. To support this advice, Appendix C on page 168 lists manufacturers' addresses.

Since the First Edition of *The Caravan Manual* was published in 1993, hundreds of caravanners have successfully tackled their own repairs and servicing work. Needless to say, this has enabled them to save considerable amounts of money by using their own time and labour. However, a great deal has changed since the original publication.

■ New regulations and quality problems

Not only have many new products been introduced, European standards and new legislative measures have had an impact on this industry. Indeed some of the products previously in use are no longer deemed to be safe, and a number of familiar items have been withdrawn from the market. A short section in the Appendix records some of the new standards that have recently been introduced.

Other developments have been brought about by changes in car design and construction. The greater use of electronic systems in modern vehicles, for example, has certainly had an effect on matters like wiring a car for towing.

On a less pleasing note, the relatively high incidence of damp in caravans is a matter of considerable concern. For instance, *The Caravan Club 1999 Quality and Reliability Survey* learnt from the 5,500 survey participants, that 2% of caravans had dampness *at the time of delivery*. Furthermore, 11% of respondents experienced damp in their caravans during the first three years of use. One presumes that pleasure boats do not leak at the time of delivery and it is realistic to expect a caravan to achieve equal standards. Against this background, the chapter on body construction was researched with particular diligence.

■ The Third Edition

Taking all these changing circumstances into account, the Third Edition of *The Caravan Manual* is not merely an update of the original text. On the contrary, the book has been completely re-written and hundreds of new illustrations have been added as well.

Equally important is the fact that the book is now published in full colour which undoubtedly gives further clarity to the text. With its launch at the start of the new Millennium, it makes an important addition to previous caravanning literature.

It was mentioned in the First Edition that this manual is intended to be put to practical use. The author's objective has not changed. If some of the pages get marked by greasy fingers, don't worry! This is an indication that you are putting the ideas contained herein to full and practical use.

Please treat *The Caravan Manual* as a working document rather than a book for your coffee table. It has been written with the intention of making your caravanning experiences as enjoyable and safe as possible. Grubby finger marks are a small price to pay for the pleasure!

Towing advice

Safe towing is dependent on a well-matched pairing of car and caravan. The power of the towcar's engine, the weight-to-weight relationship and the load distribution are important matters. So too, is the driver's skill and experience.

The successful pairing of a towcar and caravan involves a number of elements. The aim here is to draw attention to the points you need to consider in order to obtain a well-matched outfit. It is an involved subject and sources of further help are also provided.

Sources of help

The Caravan Code

Some of the main considerations are given in a booklet entitled *The Caravan Code*, which is published by The National Caravan Council (NCC) in co-operation with *The Camping and Caravanning Club* and *The Caravan Club*. Information reproduced in caravan handbooks is usually based on *The Caravan Code* and copies of The Code are available directly from the NCC.

Further information can also be obtained from the caravanning magazines which are available from most newsagents.

Caravan magazines

On account of their monthly publication, caravan magazines are able to keep abreast of the latest models of cars and caravans. Towcar tests are reported regularly, so too are tests of new and used caravans. However, it is the magazines' data pages that are a particularly helpful point of reference.

In the towcar listings, information is usually given on vehicles' kerbweights; some tables also add information on caravan noseweight limitations and others calculate the maximum weight of a fully laden caravan that each listed vehicle can tow.

In addition there are free supplements dealing with car/caravan matching and these usually accompany Spring issues of magazines. The supplements are written by caravanning specialists and the advice is especially helpful. Contrary to expectations, car manufacturers are not always forthcoming when questions are posed regarding their vehicles' towing potential.

Advice is also available from technical specialists employed by the caravan clubs and this is one of the many benefits available to members.

The Caravan Clubs

Even though their origins and objectives might be slightly different, the two major clubs are an exceptional source of help. Both *The Camping and Caravanning Club* and *The Caravan Club* have an enormous membership and their respective employees have extensive knowledge on towing matters. Moreover, they are able to draw on first hand experiences reported by their many members.

Both clubs also have guidance leaflets on towcars and caravans and both run very popular courses on towing skills. These courses are conducted away from the public highway and offer plenty of opportunity to acquire manoeuvrability skills in controlled situations.

Technical leaflets on other caravan matters are also free to members of both clubs and information appears in their monthly magazines. For example, *The Caravan Club* has around fifty detailed and substantive information leaflets with titles like: *Choice of Towcar, Choice of Trailer Caravan, Choice of Towing Bracket, Automatic Transmission for Towing, Rear View Mirrors* etc.

Caravan Owners' Clubs

If you purchase an older caravan, it is not unusual to find that the original handbook is missing. In some instances, a manufacturer may have ceased trading, or perhaps has been taken over by a larger Company. This can mean you lack important information for your particular model, like the tyre pressures or details about weights. Both are critical contributors to safe towing.

This is where owners' clubs for particular marques are invaluable. Here is an opportunity to make contact with others who tow an identical model and to gain the help you need. The addresses of the Hon. Secretaries of Owners' Clubs are published periodically in the main consumer magazines.

Towcar of the Year Award

Since its inception in 1978, the annual Towcar of the Year Award run by *The Caravan Club* has put hundreds of new cars through rigorous tests in order to evaluate their suitability for towing. As the contest has evolved, so has its scope. Nowadays the contenders are put into one of four price categories and more recently, special class awards are given for all-terrain cars and multi-person vehicles (MPVs) as well. Notwithstanding these divisions, all vehicles are ultimately compared across all classes in order to produce an outright winner.

The contest is conducted at a test track over two days. Weighing is carried out and ballast added to either car or caravan as deemed necessary. This achieves accurate nose weights on the test caravans and overall parity in the evaluation.

Features like ride quality, handling characteristics, hill starts, braking, traction, acceleration, suspension and general performance are assessed independently by a team of experienced judges. However, the evaluation isn't strictly limited to an assessment of a car's towing qualities on a demanding track. Recently a series of tests have evaluated elements like ground clearance, rear overhang from the back axle to the towball and the provision of stowing space for caravanning gear. The test team checks storage in each car using items which include an awning and water containers.

In recent years, entries have included around forty or fifty vehicles, all of which must be new models from the preceeding 12 months. As the information is accumulatively drawn together over successive years, valuable data is thus compiled. The box below shows overall winners since the contest was first carried out, and because the event takes place in September, results are usually published in the December issues of caravan magazines.

Towcar of the Year Winners

1978	Rover 3500
1979	Renault 20TS
1980	Peugeot 505
1981	Toyota Crown Super
1982	BMW 528i
1983	Volkswagen Santana
1984	Citroen BX 16TRS
1985	Volvo 360 GLE
1986	Ford Sierra XR 4x4
1987	Renault 21GTS
1988	Vauxhall Senator 3.0i CD
1989	Vauxhall Cavalier SRi 2.0i
1990	Vauxhall Cavalier 4x4 2.0i
1991	Rover 416 Gti 16v
1992	Volvo 940 SE Turbo
1993	Vauxhall Calibra Turbo 4 x 4
1994	Citroen Xantia 1.9 TD VSX
1995	Renault Laguna RT 2.0
1996	Vauxhall Vectra 2.0l 16v GLS
1997	Peugeot 406 GLX DT 2.1
1998	Citroen Xantia V6 Exclusive
1999	Audi A6 Avant 2.5 TDi
2000	Seat Toledo V5

Noseweight is meticulously checked in the Towcar of the Year Award competition, and ballast is added in order to achieve a coupling head weight that is 7% of the actual laden weight of the caravan.

Weight factors

Irrespective of the power of a car's engine, towing a caravan that is heavier than the vehicle is dangerous. The phrase about the 'tail wagging the dog' assumes a special meaning in the context of caravanning.

Weight matters are important and a potential for confusion is the recent change in terminologies. Before looking more closely at weight relationships, check the terms in the box on the next page.

Drawing on the terms relating to weights, it is recommended that the total weight of a caravan, with everything on board (actual laden weight or ALW) is no greater than 85% of the kerbside weight of the towcar. This is checked using the following equation:

ALW of caravan ÷ kerb weight of tow car x 100 = % weight of caravan to car

A good towcar should provide stowage space for items like an awning and water containers.

This is a recommendation, but caravanners with extensive towing experience may tow a heavier caravan thus achieving a higher weight relationship, as long as the caravan does not exceed the kerb weight of the car.

Note: *Car manufacturers sometimes specify the weight of a trailer that one of their models could tow on the basis of the power of its engine. Occasionally this disregards the weight advice given. Even if the engine has the pulling power, you should not be misled into thinking that it is acceptable for a trailed caravan's weight to exceed the car's kerbside weight.*

The weight issue is very important and in several parts of the country the police are now making road-side spot checks of trailed outfits and it is often found that many caravans are grossly over-laden. It is particularly important to monitor the actual weight of your caravan by taking it – with its full travelling load on board – to a weighbridge. Addresses may be found in the *Yellow Pages* and information is also available from a *Local Authority Trading Standards* or *Weights and Measures Department.*

Load distribution

In addition to the overall weight loading of your caravan, items carried should also be stowed and secured appropriately. The illustrations opposite show the guideline you should follow, keeping note of the noseweight achieved as well.

Weight (Mass) Terminology

THE TOWING VEHICLE

KERB WEIGHT: Defined by the vehicle manufacturer and which normally:
- excludes the weight of passengers;
- excludes any load apart from essential tools e.g. a wheel brace and jack;
- excludes the weight of towing add-ons like a bracket, 12V sockets, extension mirrors;
- includes a full tank of fuel;
- includes other liquids forming part of the engine system.

MAXIMUM TRAIN WEIGHT: Defined by the vehicle manufacturer as the maximum permissible combined weight of both the laden tow car and the laden caravan. Whilst the weight distribution between car and caravan is important, the maximum train weight must not be exceeded.

TOWING LIMIT: Sometimes specified by a car manufacturer and usually referring to the maximum weight a car can tow based on its restart ability on a 1:8 (12.5%) uphill gradient.

THE CARAVAN

(Terms introduced in conjunction with the European standards for caravans EN 1645 Pt. 2. *New terms apply from September 1998, ie 1999 models*)

MAXIMUM TECHNICALLY PERMISSIBLE LADEN MASS (MTPLM), formerly Maximum Allowable Mass or Maximum Technical Permissible Weight: Stated by the manufacturer, taking account of elements like tyre ratings, suspension weight limits, material rigidity etc.

MASS IN RUNNING ORDER (MRO), formerly ex works weight: Weight of the caravan with factory-supplied equipment as defined by the manufacturer.

USER PAYLOAD, formerly Caravan Allowable Payload: The weight limit is established by subtracting the MRO from the MTPLM. The User Payload comprises the following three elements:

i) *Personal effects payload:* items you take including clothing, food, drink, cutlery, crockery, cooking utensils, bedding, hobby equipment. The formula for the expected minimum provision is:

*(10 x number of berths) + (10 x length of body in metres excluding draw bar) + 30
= minimum allowance for personal effect payload (kg)*

ii) *Essential habitation equipment:* any items, including fluids, deemed by the manufacturer as essential for the safe and proper function of equipment for habitation.

iii) *Optional equipment:* the weight of optional items like cycle rack, spare wheel, and an extra bunk must now be itemised by the caravan manufacturer. The weight of items subsequently installed by the owner e.g. solar panels, will also fall into this category.

Heavy items should be as near as possible to the axle – which often means carrying well-secured items on the floor.

Note: *It is wrong to balance a heavy nose by loading something heavy in the extreme rear of the 'van. Compensation might be achieved by doing this, but on the road the so-called 'dumb-bell effect' means that any tendency for snaking is then dangerously accentuated. Fore and aft balance must be achieved by adjusting the loads carried near the axle.*

Noseweight

Noseweight limits are determined by the car manufacturer, taking elements like the suspension and the integrity of tow bracket mounting points into account as well. To achieve good stability, a substantial noseweight is needed, even when the caravan assumes the recommended level or slightly nose down stance. A strongly nose-down stance should be avoided since this affects steering. The traction on a front wheel driven car is affected too, as well as the angle of headlamp beams. To overcome this, it is sometimes necessary to fit spring assisters to the towcar.

To achieve the optimum stability of the outfit, noseweight is generally recommended to be 7% of the actual laden weight of the caravan. When the weight of a laden caravan is multiplied by 7%, you typically achieve a noseweight around 50-90kg. However, some cars limit the noseweight to 50kg and this will severely limit the weight of caravan that can be towed. Others can take extremely high noseweights e.g. Citroen XM (110 kg), Range Rover/Discovery post-1995

When coupled up and with the correct noseweight, a car and caravan should achieve a level or slightly nose-down stance.

■ If the caravan is strongly nose down, the car's suspension needs stiffening.

■ If the caravan is nose up, loading is incorrect or perhaps the tow ball needs a drop plate.

(150kg) – but these examples are unusual.

It should also be pointed out that caravans have occasionally been manufactured where the ex-works noseweights are excessive – even before gas cylinders have been added. Oddly enough, some models have achieved minimal noseweight and their owners have found it especially difficult to achieve the necessary forward weight. Readers' letters published in magazines highlight some of the more unusual problems experienced.

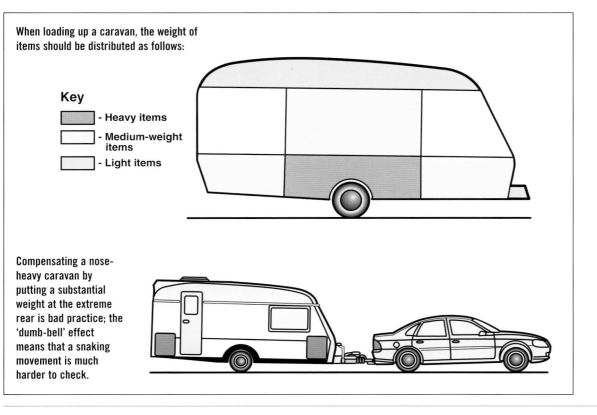

When loading up a caravan, the weight of items should be distributed as follows:

Key

■ - Heavy items

□ - Medium-weight items

▨ - Light items

Compensating a nose-heavy caravan by putting a substantial weight at the extreme rear is bad practice; the 'dumb-bell' effect means that a snaking movement is much harder to check.

The noseweight of a caravan can be checked using a purpose-made gauge as shown below. An example is available from W4 Accessories. Alternatively you can insert a strong batten vertically under the coupling head and then rest this on the platform of a set of bathroom scales to get a weight reading.

When carrying out the operation, make sure the caravan is on level ground with the jockey wheel down and the corner steadies lifted. You then raise the 'van using the jockey wheel in order to insert the batten or the gauge under the coupling head. Then you simply lower the caravan using the jockey wheel so that the entire noseweight is born by the measuring system.

Types of car

Notwithstanding the points already mentioned, there are still some further technical details about potential towcars to take into account.

Low torque preference

It is self-evident that a powerful engine is important, but the point at which an engine achieves its greatest power varies from model to model. The term 'torque' refers to the turning force of an engine and some cars achieve peak torque i.e. pulling power, when the engine is running at slow revs whereas others are most powerful when the engine is achieving very high revs. For instance a sports car, a 'hot hatchback', and a GTi Saloon normally achieve greatest power and best acceleration when the engine is running at high revs.

This isn't much help to a caravanner since the law imposes stricter speed limits on a vehicle towing a trailer compared with one that is driven solo. Moreover, when cruising near the towing speed limit, you want to be in top gear, which of course will determine the speed of the engine.

In a 'sport performance' car, engaging top gear at relatively slow speeds will mean the engine's revs are low – which is not the point at which the vehicle's sparkling performance is achieved. As the analogy rightly indicates, race horses might be able to reach high speeds but they are not usually good at pulling heavy carts.

So the best type of towing vehicle is seldom a model designed to achieve high speed performance. In technical terms, you need a car whose engine achieves good 'low-end torque' – that is one which achieves its best pulling power when the engine is running slowly. The graphs from car manufacturers which match torque against speed will reveal whether an engine is likely to display this characteristic.

Model type

Today there are fewer cars which follow the more traditional style in which a large boot extends at the rear. In this arrangement, it means a tow ball is situated a long way behind the rear axle. The resulting down force from a coupled caravan is not helpful for the rear springs, particularly if the boot is also fully loaded. Herein is a benefit of a hatchback design where the towball is much closer to the rear axle.

A similar benefit might be claimed for multipurpose vehicles and more people are using MPVs as towcars. But then there is the new breed of 'all terrain vehicles'.

In most cases, off-road vehicles are built on a sturdy chassis which is a robust sub frame rather than a series of pressed steel box sections. Some refer to this as a 'true chassis'. However, its sheer rigidity is sometimes claimed to impose additional stress on a caravan – sufficient for some caravan

manufacturers to invalidate the Warranty where this type of vehicle is used for towing.

The concern is based on the idea that a more conventional vehicle permits greater flexion, thereby easing the ride characteristics for the trailed vehicle. It is for this reason that some owners of all terrain vehicles fit a towball which incorporates a cushioning system. When pulling a caravan over a heavily rutted campsite field, this certainly could reduce the shocks that might be imposed on the structure of the caravan. One supplier of these couplings is Dixon-Bate Ltd whose address appears in the Appendix.

Driven wheels

Since noseweight has a tendency to push down the rear of a car and to lift the front, many caravanners prefer a rear wheel driven car. In fact experienced caravanners are often critical that so many winners of the Towcar of the Year Award are front-wheel-driven vehicles, but there is a reason for this.

Rear-wheel-drive is becoming more and more unusual. For instance, in the 1998 Awards, there were 41 competitors and only one vehicle entered was rear-wheel-driven. It was equally significant that 12 of the entries comprised 4WD vehicles.

Quite apart from the merits of 4WD transmission for off-road vehicles, many 4WD saloons achieve notable cornering and overall traction performance on the roads as well. There is no doubt that this configuration – though not essential – is helpful when towing, and both Ford and Vauxhall 4WD models have been overall winners in the Towcar of the Year competition in the past.

Automatic versus manual transmissions

Traditionally the caravanner has preferred a tow car with a manual gear change. This is partly because vehicles with automatic transmission used to experience serious problems when the transmission oil overheated. Overheating can occur when towing in hot, hilly areas and in traffic jams. Nowadays a standard oil cooler overcomes this and if the problem persists, specialists like Kenlowe supply auxiliary gearbox coolers.

Notwithstanding this, the prejudice continues. There is no doubt that manual transmissions have much in their favour. On the other hand, *The Caravan Club* leaflet entitled *Automatic Transmission for Towing* is a long and detailed document that presents the value of automatic systems in a cogent and convincing manner.

Not only is the 'creep' facility of an automatic so good in a traffic jam – with the attendant relief on the leg normally used for the clutch, there are other advantages too. As the leaflet points out:

'Hitch a caravan behind a car and the case for an automatic gearbox to protect an engine, transmission and body shell from the type of

shocks caused by clutch engagement become almost unanswerable. Solo and (particularly) towing, progress is very much smoother, including when reversing'.

Without doubt, the old resistance against using an automatic for towing is scarcely tenable in respect of modern vehicles.

Fuel

In this country, the use of liquefied petroleum gas in vehicles has never achieved the popularity it has in Holland. The debate here is concerned with the petrol versus diesel arguments. On one hand, diesel engines normally have good low-end torque which is fine for towing; on the other hand, petrol engines are often more economical and generally provide better acceleration if you want to overtake when climbing a hill.

There are many arguments but one thing that cannot be ignored is the punitive imposition of tax on fuels. If your caravanning is done principally in Britain, the cost of diesel fuel is not particularly attractive, but if you tour extensively in France, the picture changes dramatically.

From a technical viewpoint, there certainly isn't a heavy balance in favour of one fuel over the other. Rather more concerning is the loss of leaded petrol to owners with older tow cars. It is currently too early to judge the long term effectiveness of lead-replacement additives. These are formulated to reduce the potential damage to exhaust valve seats which is the key problem caused when using lead-free petrol. As regards their efficiency, only time will tell.

Note: *Modern engines are built with hardened steel valve seats so the use of unleaded petrol presents no problem.*

Suspension

Some vehicles are noted for soft suspension whereas others deflect less easily. Generalisations are difficult here and the best advice is to check what manufacturers recommend about suspension strengthening strategies. There are plenty of add-ons available from independent specialists but not all devices meet the approval of car manufacturers. Once again, the *Clubs* usually have information on particular models and their suspension requirements.

Types of caravan

Single versus twin axle

Finally the towing issue is partly determined by the caravan, too. Some achieve better balance than others and test reports in caravan magazines are helpful here. In truth, nearly all modern caravans tow well.

However, when it comes to straight line tracking, there is no doubt that a well balanced twin axle caravan is more likely to hold a straight course than a single axle 'van. The friction imposed by the four wheels helps to resist sideways deflections from passing vehicles. This is one of the advantages.

Of course the case is not clear-cut. A twin axle configuration is inevitably heavier and costly, too. Moreover the benefit endowed by tyre friction on the road is conversely a problem when trying to manoeuvre the caravan on site or at home. The 'scrubbing' of the tyres makes manual handling difficult and most owners of twin axle caravans recognise the importance of being accomplished at reversing their 'vans using the towcar.

To overcome this there are tricks like parking the wheels on thick plastic sheets and wetting these to permit a better degree of side slip when manoeuvring the caravan manually. However, one manufacturer has overcome the problem. Lunar has fitted an optional axle elevation system for several years on their Delta models and the current Knott arrangement is a great facilitator when pushing a caravan into a difficult corner. So ultimately, it is the purchaser who needs to make the decision.

Twin axle Lunar caravans can be fitted with a Knott elevating system so that manoeuvrability on site or at home is much easier.

The Knott elevation system employs hydraulic lifting gear.

Towcar preparation

A number of tasks have to be carried out before a vehicle can be used for towing. Some are successfully carried out by DIY owners; other jobs, however, are best left to the qualified specialists.

Before a car can be used to tow a caravan, a bracket of suitable design is needed. A socket or sockets will also have to be fitted, together with ancillary electrical components. These additions enable a caravan's road lights and other low voltage accessories to function using a supply from the towing vehicle. Furthermore, some vehicles will tow more efficiently if the rear suspension is upgraded and various types of spring assister are available.

Fitting these items is often carried out by owners who have practical skills and technical knowledge. For example, the installation of a towing bracket – sometimes called a 'tow bar' – is one task that many DIY caravanners accomplish successfully.

specialists. The quality of these products, like the price, varies considerably. Long established manufacturers such as Brink and Witter are examples of specialists whose brackets are well respected within the industry.

Then there are bespoke specialists like Watling Engineers who will design and build a bracket for almost any kind of vehicle. Models as diverse as the 1927 Bentley 3-litre Tourer, the 1952 Humber Snipe, the Pontiac Transam or even the Honda Gold Wing motorcycle are examples quoted in the prodigious list. Watling Engineers is a useful contact for owners of restored historic caravans who want to tow behind a 'classic car' of similar vintage.

Towing brackets

A number of specialists are engaged in the manufacture of towing brackets and it is worth spending time comparing the different products.

Manufacturers

Most car manufacturers offer towing brackets for vehicles in their ranges. This is scarcely surprising, since nearly all cars can tow a trailer of some kind or another. Notable exceptions, however, are the Ford Ka and the MGF; the manufacturers did not declare suitability for towing when the vehicles underwent EC Type Approval testing.

In addition to the vehicle manufacturer, there are also a number of independent towing bracket

Tow balls

When choosing a towing bracket, it should also be recognised that there are three types of tow ball:

1. Removable tow balls.
2. Separate units attached to the bracket using bolts.
3. Swan-neck tow balls.

One is a separate unit attached to the bracket using bolts; another type forms an integral part of the structure and terminates with a tubular neck, appropriately called a 'swan neck' design; and different yet again are removable tow balls. These are often favoured for cosmetic reasons – so that the line of the vehicle is preserved when driving solo. For example, removable tow balls from specialists like BMW are engineered to a high standard; even when

Kits from independent manufacturers like Witter are well-respected.

The swan neck tow ball is favoured in some European countries.

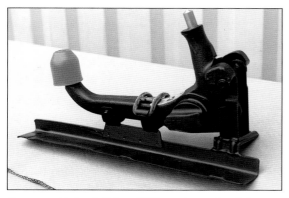

The removable tow ball from BMW mounts on a bracket hidden in the boot.

The attachment mechanisms of some removable balls are less compact than others.

This tow ball doesn't provide sufficient clearance to accommodate an AKS2000 stabiliser.

fitted, the disconnecting mechanism is especially tidy in appearance.

Some removable units are less attractive and inevitably this is reflected in the price of the product.

The British-style bracket usually features a separate 50mm tow ball which is attached to the bracket's face plate using high tensile bolts. The design, also popular in France, is sometimes referred to as a 'flanged ball' and in most instances its attachment is by two 16mm bolts at 90mm (3.5in) centres. Occasionally however, you might find four bolt variations. Particular attention has to be paid to ensure that the bolts are tightened fully as described in the box below.

Note: *It is important to be aware of different dimensions in the stem of bolt-on flange balls. For example, if you decide to fit an AL-KO Kober AKS coupling head stabiliser, a different bolt-on ball is usually needed. To accommodate the stabiliser's movement, the projection of the tow ball rearwards needs to be greater than normal because the coupling head is much bulkier than a standard coupling. This means that when it articulates around the ball, it is more likely to foul sections near the base flange and the attachment bolts.*

Bolt-on tow balls

■ The standard M16 (16mm) high tensile bolts used to attach a flange-type tow ball must be tightened to the correct torque setting. A torque setting of 195Nm (143lb.ft) is typical, but check the actual figure for your bracket with the manufacturer.
■ Torque settings are usually calculated on the assumption that the threads are clean, free of rust particles but NOT greased. Do not apply lubricant to the threads.
■ If self-locking nuts are fitted instead of standard ones, the torque setting is 215Nm (158lb.ft).
■ All metal locking nuts like the Stover pattern can be used up to three times. However, Nylock self-locking nuts should only be used once.
■ Where spring washers are fitted to a standard nut, these should be replaced every time the fixing is loosened off.

Finally, there is the swan neck design, preferred by many Continental caravanners. The ball and integral stem usually forms part of the bracket assembly itself which has structural merit; but there are disadvantages with this design. For example a swan neck tow ball is less suitable if you want to fit an accessory item or a mounting plate for the electrical sockets. There are stem clamps to provide mounting points for stabilisers like the Scott or Bulldog models, but these are seldom as secure as a plate that can be attached behind a bolt-on tow ball.

Adding accessories

An advantage of the bolt-on tow ball is that you can attach additional components like a bumper guard, stabiliser coupling, drop plate, cycle rack or a mounting plate for 12N and 12S sockets. However, there is a strict limit to the number of accessory items that can be carried between the ball and the

A bolt-on tow ball is advantageous if you want to fit an accessory like a bumper stop.

15

Drop plates

Even though tow brackets are manufactured to produce a standard towing height, if you have a bolt-on tow ball, a drop plate is easy to fit. But you may only use a drop plate on a 94/20/EC approved bracket if the product gained type approval with the plate installed.

Directive 94/20/EC specifies that the centre of a tow ball should be between 350mm and 420mm (13.8–16.6in) to the ground when the vehicle is laden to maximum weight.

Problems arise, however, with some older caravans which have an unusually low coupling. Equally, if a car is only partially laden, it might be helpful if the tow ball was slightly lower. In either case, a drop plate which lowers the ball height is permitted on vehicles registered *before 1st August 1998* in order to achieve an outfit where the caravan front is very slightly 'nose-down'. However, a drop plate must *never* be used to *raise* the height of a tow ball.

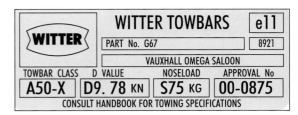

WITTER TOWBARS		e11
PART No. G67		8921
VAUXHALL OMEGA SALOON		

TOWBAR CLASS	D VALUE	NOSELOAD	APPROVAL No
A50-X	D9. 78 KN	S75 KG	00-0875

CONSULT HANDBOOK FOR TOWING SPECIFICATIONS

Under the latest legislation, all brackets passing type-approval tests are required to display an approval plate.

mounting face plate on the bracket. Bear in mind that:

• it is the responsibility of the caravanner to check with the tow bracket manufacturer whether additional accessory items can be added;
• some major manufacturers have suggested that as long as the additional item doesn't move the towball more than 15mm (⅝in) away from the mounting face plate, the arrangement is acceptable;
• when an accessory is added, it is usually recommended that at least three clear threads are visible at the end of the nut – that's a minimum protrusion of about 6mm (¼in). If necessary, a longer bolt of the required tensile strength should be fitted.

Legislation

For many years, bracket manufacturers designed their products on the basis of knowledge that had been built up over a long period of time. Sometimes the components were fitted to attachment points recommended by the vehicle manufacturer; sometimes the designer used other mounting locations considered to offer suitable integrity.

In the last decade, some cars have been fitted with threaded captive nuts at the time of manufacture. Additionally there might be dimple points in steel panels to indicate drilling points. These locations match the design of the manufacturer's purpose-made bracket and an installation is simplified considerably as a result. However, this practice only tends to be a feature on more expensive vehicles.

When considering the subject of installation, a bracket designer is confronted with the fact that modern vehicles:

i) are much lighter than older models, and
ii) are built with accident crumple zones.

This means there are only a few points of suitable integrity for the attachment of a tow bar. In recognition of this, a car owner should never attempt to make up his or her own bracket.

Furthermore, there is now legislation which requires adherence to strict standards. For instance, a new towing bracket design has to pass

Legal points

■ **European Standards for towing brackets have replaced the former British Standards in respect of passenger cars registered in the UK after 1st August, 1998, but note that the former British Standard BS AU 114b is still applicable for vehicles registered *before* this date.**

■ **The European Directive, 94/20/EC – now with legal status in the United Kingdom through an amendment to the *Road Vehicle (Construction & Use) Regulations 1986* – has brought significant changes to the design of towing brackets to be fitted to newer vehicles. The directive applies to all light passenger vehicles which have a *European Whole Vehicle Type Approval (EWVTA) Certificate of Conformity* and which have been registered in the United Kingdom on and after 1st August, 1998.**

■ **At the time of publication, commercial vehicles such as light commercial vans – including motorcaravans built on these base units – fall outside the legislation.**

■ **The Directive requires that only Type Approved towing brackets can be fitted to post 1st August 1998 vehicles registered in the UK. Fitting a non-Type Approved bracket can lead to prosecution, an invalidation of a vehicle warranty, and a likely invalidation of the vehicle's insurance cover.**

■ **Since one of the objectives of the new Directive is to encourage free trade, a vehicle manufacturer can no longer insist that you fit *only* the bracket listed under their accessory items. Provided the alternative product is of 'equivalent quality', you should not – in theory – be in conflict with the vehicle's Warranty. It is the interpretation of 'equivalent quality' which is the problem area and some vehicle manufacturers are checking the wording of their Warranties with particular vigilance so that there's no chance of ambiguity.**

On some vehicles there are captive nuts already *in situ* to accept a towing bracket.

16

The clip held on the left is the new type that CAN be clipped directly to a security eye. The conventional type on the right is NOT strong enough for direct clipping.

Type Approval tests if it is to be fitted to vehicles registered on and after 1st August, 1998. This applies to 'S' registered cars and later – although motorcaravans and light commercial vehicles which might be used for towing are currently exempt. Further details are provided below.

To verify the status of a Type Approved tow bracket, a Euronorm Type Plate or label has to be affixed to the unit. An example of a typical plate is shown on page 16 and the implications for bracket design are:

1. Type Approved tow brackets must be attached to all the recommended fixing points identified by the vehicle manufacturer.
2. Type Approved tow brackets must not obscure a vehicle number plate when not being used.
3. To achieve Type Approval, towing brackets have to pass a Euronorm Standard.

Breakaway cables

Braked caravans weighing over 750kg and less than 3500kg have to be fitted with a sacrificial breakaway cable. In the event of a caravan accidentally becoming unhitched from its towing vehicle, the purpose of the cable is to instantly engage the caravan's brakes and then to snap. Whereas the link with the tow car is then severed, the caravan would be left with its brakes fully engaged.

To achieve this intention, the correct coupling of a breakaway cable is crucial. Note the following points and the Tip panel.

• Traditionally it has been recommended that a breakaway cable should NOT be clipped directly to a security eye on a towing bracket. That's because movement during towing sometimes causes a clip to settle in an upright position on the eye and a modest tug forces the spring section to distort and open. Should that happen, the breakaway cable wouldn't achieve its intended job in the event of the caravan breaking loose. Accordingly caravanners have been instructed to thread the breakaway clip THROUGH the eye and then to clip it back onto its cable.
• The idea is fine except that the diameter of many security eyes is too small for the clip to pass through. To resolve this, AL-KO and BPW chassis introduced a new clip (in 2004) which uses a spring "gate" system of the type found on rock climbing security devices.

It is unfortunate that many towing brackets are not manufactured with a security eye for a breakaway cable.

The cost of this improved breakaway cable is around five pounds and the re-designed clips CAN be clipped directly to a security eye. However, at the time of writing, very few of these improved products have come into general use.
• In addition, most towing brackets fitted on cars don't have a security eye at all. Others are located badly and an eye should be no further from the centre of the tow ball than 100mm (4in). This is particularly prevalent on brackets made with removable balls.
• Some owners fit a "pigtail" accessory sold by caravan dealers but its position doesn't always fall within the recommended (100mm max.) proximity to the ball itself.
• In consequence, some caravanners loop the cable around the neck of a towball and clip it back on to itself. This should never be done more than a single turn. A Code of Practice published in 1998 (BS AU 267) acknowledged that this strategy is acceptable but clearly isn't the preferred method of attachment. Towing specialists also assert that this practice should never be adopted on brackets with detachable tow balls.
• There are several DO's and DON'Ts concerning breakaway cables now published in an NCC Advice Sheet referred to in the Technical Tip panel.

Technical Tip

A number of caravans have recently been badly damaged by burnt-out brakes; the drums have sometimes became so hot that they have been irreparably damaged. Research conducted by AL-KO Kober with Police assistance found that the incidents were particularly prevalent with these car/caravan combinations:

a) where a caravan is fitted with a gas strut-assisted hand brake lever as described on Page 44.

b) where a breakaway cable has insufficient slack when coupled to the tow car.

c) where a powerful 4x4 off-road vehicle is being used.

Even a modest tug on this type of hand lever causes it to engage a caravan's brakes fully; that is very helpful when you're parked but NOT when you're towing. The research also found that 4x4 types of towing vehicles are sometimes so powerful that drivers have not always realised that the caravan's brakes have started to bind. Equally significant has been the fact that on several vehicles of this type, the attachment point for the breakaway cable is positioned a long way forward of the towball. This causes the connected cable to be too tight and when a corner is turned it tightens and activates the brake lever. If there's an assisting gas strut fitted, the lever immediately flies up to fully engage the caravan's brakes.

The National Caravan Council has since published a free Advice Sheet which lists the right and wrong ways to connect a breakaway cable. The sheet is distributed through dealers and is also displayed on the NCC website: www.thecaravan.net

An electric drill will probably be needed when installing a towing bracket.

Always offer-up the bracket loosely assembled – then tighten all the fixings progressively.

Testing

Today, prototype brackets are rigorously tested before a new design is manufactured. However, the integrity of a bracket is of little merit if the key points of attachment on a vehicle are showing signs of rust. Sound fitting points are crucial.

During testing, a prototype bracket is usually fitted on a rig and submitted to a two million cycle fatigue test. This ensures the bracket design is sound, but it pays no regard to the attachment itself. Car manufacturers, however, are now expecting a test to be conducted with a bracket fitted to a bare body shell to confirm that the whole installation is sound. This type of test adds considerably to the cost and if you buy a vehicle manufacturer's 'own model', this will undoubtedly be reflected in the price.

Safety matters have gained more attention in recent years and car manufacturers are also more aware now of the needs of the towing public. So they include their own towing brackets as accessory items and urge owners to choose them. However, brackets from many independent manufacturers are especially well-made too, and may be considerably less expensive.

When you prepare a vehicle for towing, purchase a reputable product from a well-established manufacturer – and if you decide to fit it yourself, be certain to follow the instructions with meticulous care.

Every design of car is different and there's no such thing as a universal towing bracket. Accordingly, the fitting tips and photographs overleaf highlight typical fitting tasks that relate to installations in general.

If you have to tighten a bolt-on ball without a torque wrench, get it checked at a garage before coupling up your caravan.

Fitting advice

Tools usually needed:

- Open-ended ring spanners and sockets
- Electric drill
- Selection of drill bits
- Enlarging drill or rotary file
- Means of elevating the car in safety
- Torque wrench

Note: *Special tools are sometimes needed to remove a rear skirt and bumper.*

General points

- Few brackets are finished with more than an undercoat of paint. It is wise, therefore, to add further top coats; you could use cellulose paint or Hammerite, both of which are available in spray cans.
- When working under your car, observe all safety precautions. Either drive on to a raised platform of planks or use robust ramps. Never work under a car that is only supported by a jack.
- On many modern vehicles, the first job is to remove the rear bumper and sometimes a small section has to be cut away. If the fixings are rusted in place, loosening them off can often be harder than fitting the towing bracket itself. Sometimes special tools are needed.

In many installations the rear bumper has to be removed first; it may also need a cut-out.

- It is advisable to offer up an assembled bracket with its bolts left loose. This ensures the fixings locate in the prepared holes in the towcar. Once in place, the assembly can be tightened up later – but be meticulous so that fixings are not overlooked.
- Since vehicle bodies may have small dimensional variations, bracket manufacturers sometimes provide spacers; however, small discrepancies are often absorbed when the fixing bolts are tightened.
- If you are fitting a bolt-on tow ball and do not have access to a suitable torque wrench, have the tightness of the fixings checked at a garage or caravan service centre *before* using the vehicle for towing.
- Look out for threaded nuts held captive in the bodywork of the vehicle. Quite often these will be hidden below an application of underseal.
- If you have to drill attachment holes, look for dimples in the steel panels which are provided for guidance. Otherwise use a centre punch to produce a small indentation in the panel so that the drill doesn't slide off-course. Start with a narrow drill bit for accuracy e.g. 3mm (⅛in) and enlarge the hole later.
- Some holes may need to be enlarged so that a tubular steel bush can be inserted into a box section in the vehicle, thus preventing it from collapsing when the bolts are tightened. A conical drill is useful for enlarging holes and these are available from a specialist tool shop.
- If you have any doubts about the installation, have it checked by a specialist before use.

Electrical modifications

It is a legal requirement that a caravan's road lights operate in conjunction with the lights on the tow car. Furthermore, when towing, there's also a need to keep a caravan battery charged and to ensure that the refrigerator remains in operation. To achieve these objectives, a towing vehicle has to be appropriately wired to provide the power.

Until recently, this was a job that owners with a rudimentary understanding of auto electrics would tackle themselves – and on some vehicles, the job is

Electrical kits for vehicles fitted with bulb failure and other electronic devices include special components and connectors.

Wiring a socket demands patience and manual dexterity rather than electrical knowledge.

still relatively straightforward. However, the electrical systems on more and more high specification vehicles are becoming extremely sophisticated. For instance, integrated circuits and advanced electronic components are used in the following items:

- control units for maximising engine performance,
- ABS systems to control braking on slippery surfaces, and
- devices which warn the driver of failures in the exterior driving lamps.

These developments are fine, but they have made the task of preparing a car for towing considerably more involved. For example at one time you could merely attach extension wires from each of the light clusters at the rear of the car and feed them through the boot into a black 12N socket.

This is still possible, of course, if you tow with an older car, but an increasing number of vehicles now have bulb failure warning devices and these are upset if you merely connect extension cables to serve the caravan's road lights. Recognising that procedures are less straightforward, many caravanners wisely entrust this part of the installation to an automotive electrician or specialist towbar fitter.

However, if you are eager to delve further into modern vehicle electrics, with particular reference to towing, a valuable source of information is *The Practical Guide to Towbar Electrics* published by Ryder Towing Equipment, whose address appears in the Appendix.

Equally, there are still a number of preliminary

Be careful when working under the dashboard; emergency air bags have sometimes been triggered accidentally.

Some caravanners may prefer to use a European 13-pin coupling in future. The allocation of pins under ISO 11446 is as follows:

Pins 1 to 7 – allocated exactly as Pins 1 to 7 on the 12N system.

Thereafter, the allocation is:

Pin 8 – **Reversing light (Yellow)**
Pin 9 – **Continuous power supply (Green)**
Pin 10 – **Ignition controlled power supply (Red)**
Pin 11 – **Earth return for Pin 10 (Black)**
Pin 12 – **No allocation**
Pin 13 – **Earth return for Pin 9 (White).**

Note: *Pins 11 and 13 must be kept separate and should not be coupled together in the caravan.*

jobs that a competent DIY enthusiast might wish to carry out. For instance it is relatively easy to fit the black 12N and the white 12S sockets to a plate on the rear of the vehicle. If these are purchased as part of a fitting kit, they may even be pre-wired. On the other hand, if the components are purchased separately, connecting each coloured wire to the respective socket terminal isn't difficult if you follow the diagrams on pages 21 and 22. Patience and manual dexterity are needed here rather than electrical knowledge.

Once the sockets are mounted, the two cables can be routed through to the boot or loading bay making sure that if you drill a hole in the vehicle's body, it should be treated with a rust preventative and fitted with a rubber grommet to prevent the cable chafing.

Going one step further, you might feel confident to couple up to a permanent live supply from the vehicle battery to feed the caravan's interior lights. Similarly, you might want to couple up the supply to the refrigerator as described later. In this regard, points made in *Chapter 7, Low Voltage Supply* and *Chapter 11, Refrigerators* provide further guidance.

However, when it comes to coupling into a vehicle's road light circuits, or fitting a heavy duty flasher unit, this can be surprisingly difficult. For instance, in one well-known model, it is necessary to remove the steering wheel merely to connect the pre-installed towing direction indicator in the dashboard cluster. Furthermore, when working behind an instrument fascia, be aware of the risk of a false detonation of a safety airbag.

Some cars are certainly more difficult to wire-up than others. Various aspects of the work are described here to provide a clear insight into the scope of the installation, and there are ways of easing problems like fitting the mandatory warning to

confirm your trailer direction indicators are working. Instead of fitting a dashboard warning light, you are permitted to fit a buzzer in the boot instead and kits are available for this purpose.

Socket connections

Coupling the road lights on a towing vehicle with the road lights on a caravan is achieved using a seven pin plug and socket. The connection components are referred to as the 12N plug and the 12N socket, where 'N' stands for 'normal'. In Germany, however, a 13-pin system has been introduced instead and imported vehicles may be fitted with this different socket. The coupling complies with an international standard for trailer electrics although owners in the UK often replace this item with the 12N and 12S sockets more familiar here. Alternatively an adaptor lead can be fitted – though this is an expensive accessory.

Irrespective of the system preferred, a full complement of road lights is required on caravans, although you are not legally required to have a rear fog lamp on trailed vehicles constructed before October 1979. Equally, reversing lights on caravans are not fitted on many models and are not a legal requirement.

Pre-1979 caravans

Prior to October 1979, caravans were fitted with only one plug. This supplied the caravan road lights and Pin 2 was used as a feed for a caravan's interior lights; pin allocation was as follows:

Pin 1 *(sometimes marked L)* – Yellow wire: left indicator.
Pin 2 *(sometimes marked 54G)* – Blue wire: caravan interior lights
Pin 3 *(sometimes marked 31)* – White wire: earth i.e. negative return
Pin 4 *(sometimes marked R)* – Green wire: right indicator
Pin 5 *(sometimes marked 58R)* – Brown wire: right hand tail light
Pin 6 *(sometimes marked 54)* – Red wire: stop lights
Pin 7 *(sometimes marked 58L)* – Black wire: left hand tail lights and number plate illumination.

The ruling on fog lamps made it necessary to change this allocation, but so too, did the fact that caravans were being built with many more 12V interior appliances. The supply feeding a refrigerator, for example, needs to have a higher rating than that provided by wire used in a black 12N multicore cable.

Post-1979 caravans
(up to 31st August 1998)

Caravans built after 1st October 1979 were wired up so that Pin 2 on their 12N plug – previously used for interior lighting – would now be used to provide the electrical feed for a caravan fog lamp. In addition, a 12S, (supplementary) plug and socket system was introduced, leaving the 12N system to deal exclusively with road lights.

Some foreign vehicles are supplied with a single 13-pin socket as a standard coupling.

Adaptors are available to convert a 13-pin socket to the preferred UK twin socket system.

Pin allocations
for 12N and
12S sockets
(up to 31st
August 1998)

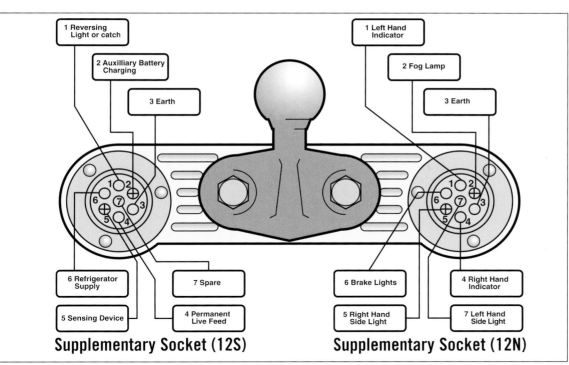

Supplementary Socket (12S)

1 Reversing Light or catch
2 Auxilliary Battery Charging
3 Earth
6 Refrigerator Supply
5 Sensing Device
7 Spare
4 Permanent Live Feed

Supplementary Socket (12N)

1 Left Hand Indicator
2 Fog Lamp
3 Earth
6 Brake Lights
5 Right Hand Side Light
4 Right Hand Indicator
7 Left Hand Side Light

Features of the 12S coupling

• A plastic 12S plug is distinctively coloured in either white or grey; the 12S plastic sockets have a white cover flap – though occasionally you may find a cover flap in grey plastic.

• To prevent wrong connection, the male/female brass tube contacts in the centre of the cluster of a 12S plug are reversed. This means you cannot insert a 12S plug into a 12N socket and vice versa.

• The 12S multicore cable is thicker than its 12N counterpart. This is because wire of higher rating is needed to supply the fridge and charging facility; there is also a need for the shared white earth return wire to be thicker, too.

• The 12S cable is covered in a grey sheath so that it doesn't get confused with the thinner, black sheathed, multicore cable connected to a 12N plug or socket.

From the introduction of the 12S system in 1979 until 1st September 1998, nearly all British caravan manufacturers allocated the pins in accordance with a standard approved by the National Caravan Council. In most cases, only four connections were used, namely Pins 2, 3, 4 and 6.

However, when new European Regulations were anticipated (and implemented in the United Kingdom on 1st September, 1998 as described on page 28) some manufacturers decided to act on these alterations much earlier. For instance the 12S plugs on Bailey caravans were wired differently in 1996 and the 12S plugs on caravans from ABI, Crown and Elddis some time later – as their handbook diagrams revealed.

Notwithstanding these individual changes, in the 1979–1998 period, the majority of caravan 12N and 12S connections were wired as follows:

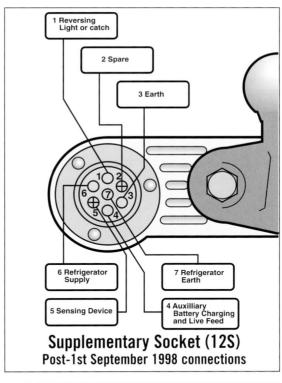

1 Reversing Light or catch
2 Spare
3 Earth
6 Refrigerator Supply
5 Sensing Device
7 Refrigerator Earth
4 Auxilliary Battery Charging and Live Feed

Supplementary Socket (12S)
Post-1st September 1998 connections

12N pin allocation

Pin 1 *(sometimes marked L)* – Yellow wire: left indicator

Pin 2 *(sometimes marked 54G)* – Blue wire: caravan fog light

Pin 3 *(sometimes marked 31)* – White wire: earth i.e. negative return

Pin 4 *(sometimes marked R)* – Green wire: right indicator

Pin 5 *(sometimes marked 58R)* – Brown wire: right hand tail light

21

Pin 6 *(sometimes marked 54)* – Red wire: stop lights

Pin 7 *(sometimes marked 58L)* – Black wire: left hand tail lights and number plate illumination.

The only variation on this allocation is where a switchable 12N socket is fitted.

12S pin allocation (up to 31st August 1998)

Pin 1 – Yellow wire: reversing lights or for a catch on an inertia brake.

Pin 2 – Blue wire: auxiliary battery charging.

Pin 3 – White wire: earth (i.e. negative return)

Pin 4 – Green wire: permanent power supply from the car battery

Pin 5 – Brown wire: a sensing device

Pin 6 – Red wire: refrigerator

Pin 7 – Black wire: no allocation

The diagram on the previous page and the section on page 28 describes 12S pin allocation from 1st September 1998 onwards.

Switchable sockets

Whereas a conventional 12N socket is fitted to the majority of towcars, switching versions are available which disconnect the tow vehicle's rear fog lamp when a caravan is being towed. Some products use a mechanical switch housed in the socket itself like the Hella unit; other systems use an automatic electrical switch like the Ryder single or double fog cut-out relays.

With regard to the mechanical system, when a 12N plug is inserted into a switching socket, the supply to the caravan's rear fog lamp is connected and the feed to the towcar's fog lamp is mechanically disconnected by pushing two contacts apart.

Alternatively, the automatic electrical switch system employs a fog cut-out relay which is fitted in the boot or hatchback area. The sensing device recognises when the caravan fog lamps are in operation and automatically switches off the feed to the vehicle's fog lamps.

A disabling system has several advantages:

• when towing in fog, the car's fog lamp isn't reflected from the front of the caravan;

• less load is placed on the alternator;

• there's less chance of blowing a fuse on the tow car due to the greater load imposed when operating fog lamps on both car and caravan.

Note: *Fitting a fuse with an increased amp rating would solve this when towing but it means the circuit is now 'over-fused' when the car is driven solo.*

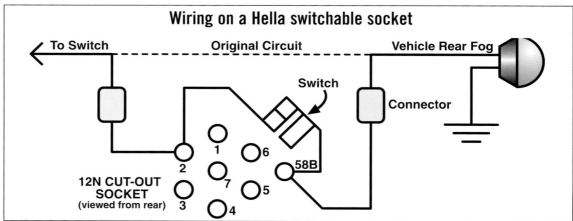

Wiring on a Hella switchable socket

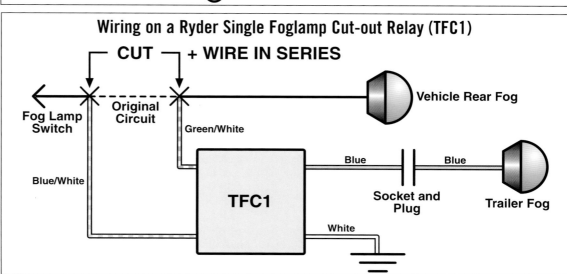

Wiring on a Ryder Single Foglamp Cut-out Relay (TFC1)

A water repellent lubricant like Tri-Flow will not react with the plastic used for the sockets.

When fitting a switchable socket, you have to cut the feed cable supplying the vehicle's fog lamps and carry out a small modification. After the modification has been made, whenever the car's fog lamps are switched into action when driving solo, the current will be taken to the lamps via the 12N socket. This is shown in the diagram on page 22.

It is thus important that a switchable 12N socket is kept free from road dirt and damp. You are therefore recommended to spray the contacts with a water repellent product such as Tri-Flow. Unlike many similar products, this penetrative lubricant doesn't damage the socket plastic. Furthermore if you accidentally knock a 12N switchable socket on an obstruction, check immediately that the operation of the vehicle's rear fog lamp hasn't been affected.

If a switchable 12N socket is preferred, a length of *eight* core cable is needed to connect up to its *eight terminals*. Some automotive suppliers do not stock eight core cable but it is included in a Hella 12N switchable socket kit and is pre-connected to the socket terminals.

If, however, the components are purchased separately, connections are as follows:

1. The end of the severed wire coming from the car's fog lamp switch is connected to the blue wire in the eight core cable with a crimp connector.
2. The other end of the blue wire is wired to Pin 2 in the 12N socket.
3. The bi-coloured red and brown wire in the eight core cable (purple in some UK kits) should be connected to the special eighth pin in the socket – marked 58B.
4. Using a crimp connector, the other end of the bi-coloured wire is coupled to the feed supplying the vehicle's fog lamp(s).

If it is decided to fit the Ryder single lamp or double fog lamp cut-out relays rather than a switchable socket, all the components are positioned in the rear of the car. Again it is necessary to cut the feed or feeds to the vehicle's fog lamps but the connections with the cut-out relays are self explanatory as shown in the diagram on the previous page. However, some Japanese vehicles fit what is known as 'negative switched fog lamps' in which case Ryder can supply an additional switching relay. Whichever unit is needed for your car, the devices are easy to fit.

Fitting 12N sockets

Owners of vehicles that do not have advanced electronic monitoring devices might decide to fit a 12N socket using a kit – some of which include pre-connected sockets. On more sophisticated vehicles, however, it often pays to buy the purpose-designed kit for the particular model being prepared for towing.

Components needed:

- a 12N black socket;
- a length of 12N black sheathed multicore cable with a small grommet;
- a socket mounting plate;
- a protective rubber gaiter to prevent road dirt entering the rear of the socket;
- three bolts to secure the socket to its mounting plate;
- a heavy duty flasher unit, or booster, or a flasher monitoring device;
- a warning lamp or audible warning device to verify direction indicator operation;
- connectors – either Scotchlocks or crimp connectors.
- on some vehicles a memory protection device may be needed temporarily when the battery is disconnected as explained later.

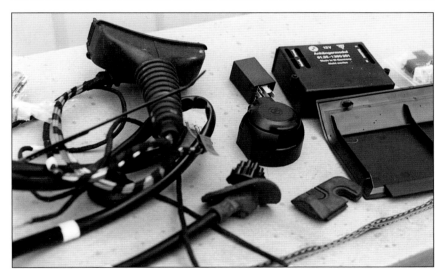

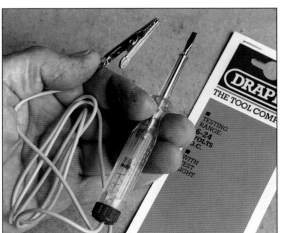

If a wiring kit is purchased from a franchise dealer, all the connections and ancillary components will be purpose-made to suit the particular model.

A 12 volt socket tester is worth having in a caravan tool kit.

23

Some towing brackets only carry a plate to accept a single socket so a modification is needed.

On some vehicles, a removable body panel reveals a location for the towing sockets.

No specialist tools are required, apart from a good wire stripper which will remove insulation without severing any of the copper strands. It is also useful to have a 12V circuit tester that looks like an electrical screwdriver with a trailing wire fitted with a crocodile clip, and a lighting filament in the handle. Even better is a digital multimeter since this can check if there is any serious loss of voltage in the system.

Mounting the sockets

- Choose positions well clear of the ground.
- Swan neck tow balls – and some other products too – often need adaptation; frequently there is only provision for a single socket and the plate needs extending.

Connectors

Snap-lock connectors or 'Scotchlocks' derive a feed from a cable by making a small penetration through its insulation sheath. Although a hinged plastic flap covers the metal tag which penetrates the copper core, there will always be a small cut left in the insulation if the coupling is later removed. This is one reason why some electricians dislike these components.

Crimp connections are more positive but necessitate cutting the original cable in order to fit a double female connector socket and 'bullet connectors' on all the coupling cables.

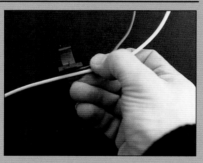

A metal tag in a snap-lock connector incises through the insulation of the wires to be coupled up.

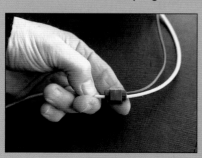

Once the snap-lock tag is squeezed through both wires, a protective flap covers the exposed metal.

Crimp connectors are preferred by many auto electricians but a sound joint is only achieved if a good quality crimping tool is used.

- On some passenger vehicles there's a recessed location covered by a removable plate on the underskirt of the car.

The cable

- Purpose-made seven core cable sheathed with black insulation should be used.
- Alternatively, eight core 12N cable is needed if you decide to fit a switching socket to control foglamps as described earlier.
- *The white earth wire* has a cross sectional area of 2.0mm^2 to yield a continuous current rating of 17.5A. It is made up of 28 filaments.
- *The other coloured wires* have a cross sectional area of 1.0mm^2 to yield a continuous current rating of 8.75A. It is made up of 14 filaments.

Connecting up the socket
(on vehicles not fitted with a bulb failure warning)

1. Prepare the socket.
- When cutting individual coloured wires to length, remember that the black one for the centre pin needs to be slightly shorter than the others.
- Carefully remove the insulation with a wire stripper to preserve the copper filaments. Twist the filaments between your fingers.
- Follow the colour code and pin locations shown in the diagram on page 21.
- Fit the protective rubber gaiter around the back of the socket and fit both socket and gaiter to the mounting plate with the three bolts.

2. Plan the cable routes and earth connection point in the car.
3. Check whether the car needs extra relays to protect its circuits. Look for bulb-failure devices; check fuse rating and wire thicknesses; see if there are inboard computers and multiplex devices to avoid.
4. Drill holes and prepare cable routes. When routing the multicore cable into the back of the car, apply anti-rust paint and fit a rubber grommet in the drilled hole to prevent chafing.
5. Before making connections, the battery will have to be disconnected. However, this can sometimes cause problems with security codes, computer memory, central locking systems and so on. To

avoid this, memory protection devices are now available which can be temporarily fitted prior to disconnection. Typically these devices are plugged into a cigar lighter.

6. Make connections to the car.

• The white cable must be fitted to a good earthing point on the vehicle. Make sure any paint or underseal is removed from the metal connection point.

• The other coloured wires are coupled up to the cables that feed the appropriate lamp clusters in the car.

• Scotchlocks are often used to make the coupling but auto electricians often prefer crimp connectors. Some make soft solder connections.

• Lamp clusters from both sides will need access in order to make connections for the direction indicators and the side lights.

7. Test the system.

Lighting checks

A 12V test light can be used on each pin in turn to confirm correct operation. More convenient is a trailer lighting board which can be plugged in and laid by the driver's door. Some fitters even make up their own board with lamps to check connections on the 12S socket as well.

Vehicles with electronic light check systems

Problems are more acute in vehicles with bulb failure monitors which give a dashboard warning if lamps fail. In this instance you cannot merely make

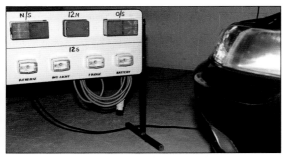

The 12V tester recommended is useful for checking each connection in the 12N and 12S sockets.

Specialist fitters often have a full test board made up for confirming the operation of the towing sockets.

Relays

Relays are used in both cars and caravans. At its simplest, a relay is merely a switch, except that it isn't operated manually. The switching action is activated by an electric current. This has a number of advantages over a conventional switch.

First a relay can create a switching action automatically when fed with a triggering current. This means that the user doesn't have to remember to operate a manual switch, so a relay can stop current going to a caravan refrigerator from a car battery as soon as the engine is switched off. The driver doesn't need to remember to disconnect the supply.

It is also important to recognise that when a relay is used, a large current feeding an appliance can be switched on or off by using a very small current to activate the switching system.

Most relays are made with a mechanical make and break system. A current fed to a coil creates an electro-magnet which in turn pulls a spring-loaded make/break lever – which then works just like a manual switch. This type of relay is used a great deal in cars – and in most of the latest caravans too.

Self-switching relays, now very popular with towbar fitters fitting 12S systems, incorporate electronic sensing circuits to activate the current to the relay coils. The sensing circuits monitor the voltage coming to the relay through the supply line from the battery and only switch the relays on when the alternator is providing its full charge.

an additional connection to the feed wires to each of the vehicle lights in the way described above.

There are two completely separate strategies that can be followed.

1. Some auto electricians locate the bulb sensing device and then make couplings for the caravan's

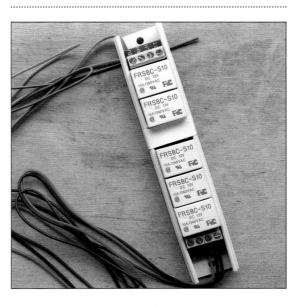

The switching relays and monitoring relays from Ryder Towing are very popular. This one switches power directly from the car's battery to all the caravan's road lights.

This Ryder component is a self-switching combination relay for the caravan fridge and battery.

road lights on the input side of the central sensing unit. Some franchised dealers will follow this strategy, but then they are likely to be fitting the tailor-made electrical kit made for the particular model. On sophisticated vehicles this is a wise strategy. The kits may be expensive but the full assembly of items is made to plug into all the existing connection points on the vehicle. So coupling into a 'black box' item like a bulb sensing device is straightforward.

2. A wholly different strategy is to use components specially designed and manufactured by companies such as Ryder Towing Equipment. Many of these employ relays, the features of which are described in the box on the previous page.

In the Ryder system, it is recognised that you often cannot take an extension feed to power a caravan rear light from the supply being sent to the equivalent light in the tow car. However, you can take a very small current from a car's rear light to trigger a special relay, i.e. one with a very low coil current. So if, for example, you were to take a supply to the caravan's side lamps direct from the tow car battery – using a fuse for safety, all you would need is a relay to switch the supply into operation. The small current needed to activate the relay could be drawn from the car's sidelight supply. This is the principle behind many of the Ryder systems. It is well-proven and more and more towing bracket fitters are using Ryder

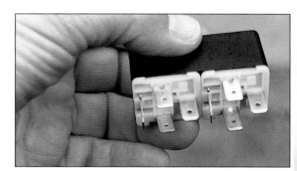

Under the NCC wiring system, two relays are often fitted in the vehicle engine compartment to provide fridge and battery charging facilities.

components to carry out the tasks involved in wiring up a towcar.

Heavy duty flasher unit

Adding a caravan's direction indicators into a vehicle's electrical system sometimes demands the fitting of a heavy duty flasher unit. This is a replacement for the original component and Hella's catalogue lists types to suit most vehicles.

Included on a heavy duty relay is a connecting tag to operate an additional warning light to confirm that the caravan's direction indicators are operating correctly.

Alternatively you can fit a warning buzzer and the Ryder list includes several monitoring devices which fulfil the legal requirement.

Fitting a 12S socket

A 12S (supplementary) socket performs four functions. First it offers a connection for reversing lights for which there is no vacant pin in the 12N socket. In practice, few caravans are fitted with reversing lights.

The remaining features concern supplementary facilities in the caravan:

1. A connection which provides 12V power to operate the fridge when the engine is running.
2. A charging facility for keeping the caravan battery topped-up using the tow car's alternator.
3. A permanent live feed for other accessories.

Bear in mind that although the allocation of the pins has remained the same for many years, from 1st September 1998, some connections have been changed. More information on the re-assignation of pins is discussed later.

One of the easiest ways to install a system is to purchase a kit such as the Hella 12S package. Alternatively the components can be purchased separately.

Components needed for towing (for caravans up to 31st August 1998)

- A 12S white-capped socket.
- A length of 12S grey sheathed multicore cable with a small grommet.

When installing a towing bracket, it is sometimes necessary to fit a heavy-duty replacement flasher unit.

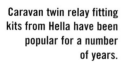

Caravan twin relay fitting kits from Hella have been popular for a number of years.

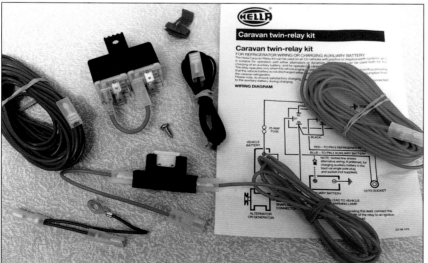

- A socket mounting plate.
- A protective rubber gaiter to prevent road dirt entering the rear of the socket.
- Three bolts to secure the socket to its mounting plate.
- Relay provision. In a Hella kit, two relays are supplied for the fridge and charging functions respectively. Alternatively the Trend product is a single combination relay. Since 1998, however, combination relays that are self-switching are often used and reference is made later to the example from Ryder Towing.
- An in-line fuse holder and a 15A fuse.
- Connectors – either Scotchlocks or crimp connectors.
- A length of automotive wire 1.5mm², preferably with green insulation to match the wire in the 12S multicore cable, to run from the vehicle's battery, through the car interior and into the boot or loading bay to couple up with the 12S multicore cable coming from the socket.
- Two lengths of automotive wire which is at least 2mm² (17.5A current rating) to run from the engine compartment through to the boot to couple up with the 12S cable. One length will be for the refrigerator supply and would ideally have red insulation to match the colour scheme in the multicore cable. The other for battery charging would ideally have blue insulation to couple with the blue wire in the multicore 12S cable.

Note: *Wire of this rating meets the Electrolux recommendation, but the thicker it is the less resistance and the greater the flow of current. For this reason the Hella kits contain 36-strand auto wire which is 2.5mm² in cross sectional area to offer a continuous current rating of 21A – well within the Electrolux recommendation. To avoid voltage drop, Ryder is likely to use even thicker gauge wire in the future.*

As regards mounting the socket, the procedures outlined in respect of fitting a 12N socket are the same. However, the multicore cable is different.

The cable

- Even though several pins are unallocated in a 12S socket, you should use seven core cable sheathed with grey insulation. This should be slightly larger in girth than the 12N cable to suit the demands of the appliances. For example, whereas a caravan side light bulb might be rated at 5W, a caravan fridge is around 95W.
- *The white earth wire* has a cross sectional area of 2.5mm² to yield a continuous current rating of 21.5A. It is made up of 36 filaments.
- *The coloured wires* have a cross sectional area of 1.5mm² to yield a continuous current rating of 13.0A. These wires are made up of 21 filaments.

Connections in a 12S socket (for caravans up to 31st August 1998)

- Advice included for the 12N socket should be noted again, particularly the point about producing a

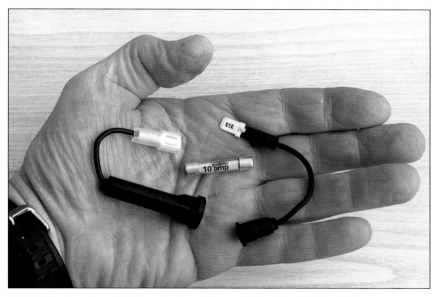

A 15A in-line fuse is needed when drawing a 12v supply from the vehicle's battery.

good earth (neutral) connection for the white return wire.
- The cable going in to pin 4, is the green wire to provide a permanent power supply from the car battery. It should be coupled to the positive pillar on the towing vehicle's battery with an in-line fuse holder fitted as close to the battery as possible. A 15A fuse is needed. The cable should be discreetly hidden as it is routed through to the boot or hatchback area. Here it will be connected up to the green wire in the multicore cable using a crimp connector.
- Both the blue wire for auxiliary charging and the red wire for operating the refrigerator on 12V should only be live when the car engine is running. The reason for this is as follows:

1. A refrigerator takes a considerable amount of current and would discharge a car battery very quickly. Therefore a system is needed whereby the fridge can only operate when the engine is running i.e. when the car's alternator is replenishing the battery. This is achieved by fitting an electrically operated switch called a 'relay'. Some relays are connected up so that they take a 'triggering feed' from the alternator. This alternator connection switches the relay as soon as the engine starts whereupon the current can then flow from the battery through to the fridge.

2. The supply from an alternator to charge a caravan battery should similarly only be available when the car engine is running. The reason for this is that if you were to connect up the caravan battery directly to the vehicle's battery, the caravan battery would not only be a receiver of charge current; it could also become a provider. So when operating the starter on the car, some current would be 'stolen' from the caravan battery. Not only would this help to discharge it; premature damage is possible because a leisure battery is not designed to produce the sudden burst of power that a starter motor needs.

Safety

When wiring a permanent live feed for pin 4 (green) on the 12S socket, do not be tempted to connect up to a vehicle clock feed or the feed to the boot light. Although these are permanently live, they are usually served by wire in the car loom which is not of a high enough rating to operate additional items such as a caravan TV or water pump.

Whilst the appliances might work, in spite of an inevitable voltage drop, the thin wire in the car could overheat due to the additional load. So always take the supply direct from the vehicle's battery with a fuse in the line.

You will notice that the multicore wires in a 12S cable do not match the rating recommended for wires needed to connect the car battery to the rear of the socket. In effect, the multicore 12S cable represents a 'weak link' in the run of wires that supply the refrigerator and the caravan auxiliary battery. This is recognised by Electrolux designers, who specify that the total length of multicore cable in the car and on the caravan draw-bar should not exceed 2.5m. To limit voltage drop, the shorter the run the better.

One way to produce a supply of current that only flows to pins 2 and 6 when the engine is running, is to fit the relays supplied in a Hella kit. The procedure is described later and these relays are usually fitted in the engine compartment. Alternatively a single combination relay can be fitted in the boot and products are available from Trend, PCT, Maypole and other specialists. Additionally the self-switching combination relay from Ryder Towing Equipment is also popular now and this is also described here in more detail.

If the Hella system is used, the relays need to be switched from the alternator whose operation signifies that the engine has started. The relays should not be triggered by an ignition-controlled accessory since this usually means the starter motor will steal power from the caravan battery when being cranked. The exception to this is that you can connect to an ignition controlled accessory which the car designer has arranged to become temporarily disabled when the starter is turning over. You should discuss this with a main dealer.

The ideal connection is undoubtedly the ignition light circuit from the alternator. To achieve this, Terminal 86 on a Hella relay should be connected to terminal WL or IND on the alternator. This means it is wired to the ignition light circuit and a typical Bosch, Lucas or Delco alternator has a warning light terminal.

Unfortunately, however, this connection cannot be made on some French, Japanese and Italian vehicles. It is also difficult on vehicles like BMW and Volkswagen models where the alternator connections are encased in a shielding material.

One way to overcome the problem of finding an alternator connection is to fit the Ryder TF1169 trigger device. This adopts a different strategy and is connected to a single feed on the vehicle battery and is specially designed to recognise the point at which a charge is coming from the alternator. In effect, this provides the signal that the engine is now running and the trigger device then switches the relays on, thereby permitting current to start flowing to both pins 2 and 6 in the 12S socket.

However, there are a few instances when this kind of trigger device might need 'fine tuning' e.g. if the battery is in a very poor state. Full details about its operation are given in *The Practical Guide to Towbar Electrics* published by Ryder Towing Equipment.

Connections in a 12S socket
(for post-1st September 1998 caravans)

When the European Standard EN1648-1 was introduced in the United Kingdom on 1st September 1998, the changes only affected the 12S socket and caravan plug.

The intention was to reduce the number of live current-carrying cables and it changed these from four to three. Some specialists claim this reduction in the number of connections was prompted by the belief that current-carrying cable can create a magnetic field which could affect some of the electronic control devices being fitted in the latest cars. The term associated with this is electro-magnetic compatibility or EMC. Others, however, suggest there is no EMC risk involving these cables

When a Hella twin relay kit is purchased, the connections are clearly shown on the wiring leaflet.

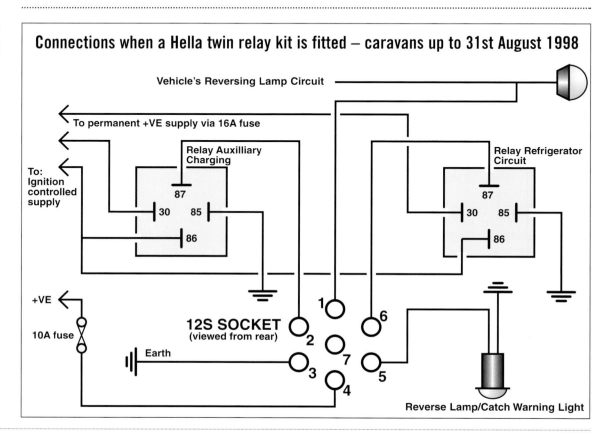

Connections when a Hella twin relay kit is fitted – caravans up to 31st August 1998

Vehicle's Reversing Lamp Circuit

To permanent +VE supply via 16A fuse

To: Ignition controlled supply

Relay Auxilliary Charging

87
30 85
86

Relay Refrigerator Circuit

87
30 85
86

+VE
10A fuse
Earth

12S SOCKET
(viewed from rear)

1
2
3
4
6
7
5

Reverse Lamp/Catch Warning Light

– but the change occurred nonetheless.

On caravans wired to the new standard the following changes have been made:

■ **Pin 7.** (black cable) in the 12S connection. The pin in the centre of the cluster is now wired as an earth (i.e. neutral) cable specifically to serve the fridge.

Comment: *This means that if you purchase a 1999 or later caravan, you must make sure that pin 7 in the 12S socket is connected to a sound earthing point in the tow car. Failure to do this means that the refrigerator is unlikely to operate in the 12V setting.*

Meanwhile, pin 3 continues to be used as a further earth connection, albeit for the battery charging function and supply function of pin 4.

■ **Pin 2.** This is no longer allocated, so the pin originally wired specifically for charging your caravan battery on the earlier system goes nowhere in a new caravan.

Comment: *Even if you've got the 12S socket wired up for battery charging on your car, it won't be going anywhere in the caravan. Moreover, it hasn't provided a charge in caravans made by Bailey, Elddis, ABI or Crown for rather longer as explained earlier in this chapter. Nevertheless, there is no need to disconnect a pin 2 connection if fitted; it would prove useful if your car is later purchased by someone owning an older caravan.*

■ **Pin 4.** This connection now serves a double function. When the towcar engine is *not* running, it is a live feed that serves the caravan's appliances – with the exception of the fridge. But when the engine *is* running, a relay in the caravan now diverts the supply exclusively to the battery to provide a charge. **To serve this double function, cable connection to the vehicle's battery must be of 2.5mm² rating.**

Comment: *Since this is carried out automatically, caravan battery charging will still take place, even if the towcar is wired to the previous standard where a relay-operated feed is connected to pin 2. In reality,* the charge will come via the vehicle's battery and pin 4. As far as wiring the tow car is concerned, when towing 1999 and later caravans, there is only a need to fit one relay in the engine compartment – to control refrigerator operation. On the other hand it is likely that twin or combination relays will continue to be fitted for many years so that all cars can still tow old and new caravans.

As regards the wiring in new caravans fitted with this new supply system, this is covered in Chapter 7, *The 12 Volt supply system.*

Implications for owners

During the period of transition from one system to another, some problems occur when matching cars and caravans of different ages. Here are the possible combinations and the implications:

1. If you own an older car and older caravan there are unlikely to be problems from car-caravan wiring compatibility. The older 12S wiring arrangement is fine.
2. If a new caravan is coupled to an older car which was wired to the previous standard – the caravan internal circuits should work automatically. On the other hand, an earth wire taken from the car body must be fitted to pin 7 on the 12S socket. Failure to do this means that the refrigerator is unlikely to work on 12V.
3. A match of new car and new caravan should present no problems – in theory; but members of the caravan clubs have reported that some tow bar fitters have not realised there has been a change and are wiring up new cars to the old standard in which pin 7 is left unused.
4. If you buy a new car to pull your older caravan, there are two strategies:

a) Some technical specialists advise you to get the caravan wiring altered to embody the

---

Checking a 12S socket to suit caravans up to 31st August 1998

Using the tester described earlier:

1. Hold open the cover on the 12S socket.

2. Clip the small bulldog clip on the neutral ('earth') pin 3 terminal.

3. Touch the tip of the tester on pin 4. The light in the handle should *immediately illuminate* – even if the engine isn't running.

4. Touch the tip of the tester on pin 2. It should *not illuminate* because there shouldn't be any current flowing. Equally it should not illuminate when turning the ignition key to position 1, 2 or 3. Now start the engine and re-test. The light in the handle should *now illuminate*, proving that the relay has been correctly wired up (see the point below if it lights prematurely). NOTE: *For caravans made after 1st September 1998 this pin is NOT allocated – see socket wiring diagram on page 21.*

5. Repeat the process described in 4 but testing pin 6. Again the test light should only illuminate *when the engine is running.*

■ Some installers connect a relay to any accessory which becomes live as soon as the ignition is switched on – rather than the alternator itself. This is not good practice since it means the current triggers the relay as soon as the ignition is switched on – and before the car is started. It therefore means the starter motor will steal from the caravan battery during cranking.

■ Recognising that pin 4 is permanently live, it is important to prevent this shorting-out through water ingress. Use a moisture repellent like Tri-Flow.

internal circuit changes discussed in Chapter 7, *The 12 Volt supply system*.
b) Other specialists suggest there's unlikely to be problems if you wire up a new car to the former 12S standard as long as it includes the extra earth for the fridge using a black cable wired through pin 7. Recognising that different views are held within the towing industry it is therefore advisable to seek advice from a franchise dealer for the vehicle.

Spring assisters

Another matter to consider is the towcar suspension. Depending on a caravan's laden weight, the National Caravan Council (NCC) advises that noseweight falls somewhere between 50-90kgs (110-198lbs). Drawing on experience, *The Caravan Club* recommends a noseweight around 7% of the actual laden weight of the caravan – which typically falls within the NCC guideline.

Either way, this imposes a significant load on a vehicle's rear suspension and if the boot or hatchback is full as well, the springs may be under a far greater loading than normal.

Removing heavy items from the boot and carrying them in the caravan may help, but this could result in overloading and/or instability. The loading potential of a caravan is often fairly modest.

In practice, many vehicles manage without alterations to the springs.

Some cars, like models from Citroen, have load-sensitive suspension systems with ride height compensation. But there are also vehicles which suffer badly and too much tail end sag could be dangerous.

One problem with the rear sagging is that headlight beams are correspondingly deflected up into the air – at great inconvenience to oncoming drivers. Front wheel drive vehicles can also lose

This weighing device developed by AL-KO Kober is used to check nose weights where the utmost accuracy is needed.

The Caravan Club has found that a noseweight which is 7% of the full laden weight of the caravan is usually best for stable towing.

traction and wheel spin on acceleration will often be experienced. Equally there can be problems with braking and tyre adhesion when cornering. Without doubt, this is the time to consider firming-up or replacing the springs.

Owners' Manuals: The first step is to check the towing advice section in the vehicle manual. A second step might be to discuss this with a franchise dealer.

Shock absorbers: When looking for an answer, some owners wrongly attribute the problem to the vehicle's shock absorbers. However, a shock absorber is simply a damping device to prevent the vehicle bouncing along on its springs; most shock absorbers contribute little, if anything, to the firmness of the suspension system. It is the springing system which needs reinforcement.

Suspension diversity: One problem with producing 'universal' suspension aids is the fact that vehicles have a variety of systems including coil spring, leaf spring, torsion bar, hydro-elastic and hydraulic systems. This is why a discussion with a franchise dealer is recommended.

Spring assisters: A number of products are designed to strengthen a vehicle's springs. However, some mechanics claim that the attachment of rubber supports on coil springs introduces stress points which can hasten a fracture. This is why you should check their acceptability with a main dealer. On the other

hand, there's no doubt that many caravanners find products from specialists like Grayston or Aeon successful in achieving the objective.

Spring replacement: On an older vehicle, whose springs may have deteriorated, fitting new replacements might be the immediate answer. Upgrading the springs is another option but whilst this might be fine when towing, ride quality is likely to be too hard when driving solo. Sometimes progressive rate coil springs are available which overcome this element. These have a lighter gauge section that deflects when the load is modest, after which more robust parts subsequently take effect when the load is more substantial.

Additional coil springs: Another strategy is to add additional springs. Products from the Dutch manufacturer MAD are well known – as are the products from Monroe. In the case of Monroe's units, these include variable rate coil springs which offer progressive resistance as the load increases; these are mounted on the outside of a telescopic shock absorber thereby producing a 'two-in-one' configuration. The Monroe Load Leveller, as it is called, is made in versions to fit a large number of vehicles.

Air spring addition: Alternatively Monroe Ride Levellers are shock absorber units which incorporate an inflation facility to increase ground clearance. The units can thus be adjusted to suit solo driving or towing. A pressure gauge indicates the level selected and the units are joined by plastic tubing to an inflation point. This is positioned so that a standard air line or foot pump can be connected to provide inflation. A de-luxe version of the Ride Leveller system includes a compact on-board 12V compressor with a dashboard control switch.

Bump stop springing: A completely different way to overcome the problem is to replace standard

bump stops with larger units that offer a concertina action. When the tow car is loaded, these make contact with the steel stop plate but assume the role of additional springs on account of their construction.

All-in-all there are a number of solutions, and the caravan clubs hold a large fund of information drawn from their members regarding their tow cars and preparatory tasks that need carrying out as a pre-requisite to towing. Normally, however, detailed advice is only available to club members.

Adding supplementary coil springs from MAD is one way to reinforce a tow car's rear suspension.

A Monroe Ride-Leveller shock absorber is inflated to suit the particular weight of the towed caravan.

Coil spring assisters from Grayston have been used successfully by many caravanners.

4

Contents

Caravan chassis and running gear

For many owners, these are the least interesting parts of a caravan. On the other hand, safe and certain towing is dependent on a well-designed chassis matched with a good suspension and efficient brakes.

Chassis design has changed significantly in the last twenty five years. In the 1970s, caravan chassis were undoubtedly robust; but by modern standards they were also comparatively heavy. Structural members were welded together and the steel sections were usually painted rather than galvanised.

Around 1980, chassis design and construction changed in a very short space of time. This was partly intended to reduce the weight of caravans – prompted in turn by the fact that car manufacturers were producing lighter vehicles with better performance and improved fuel efficiency.

So with the help of computer-aided design systems, caravan chassis specialists created lighter structures without compromising strength. The era of the lightweight caravan chassis had arrived.

Pre-1980 chassis and running gear

A number of older caravans still provide sterling service, and it would be wrong not to include brief reference to their chassis and running gear. This can be helpful to a 'first timer' contemplating the purchase of an elderly model.

The B&B (Bird & Billington) chassis used prior to 1983 was a popular design.

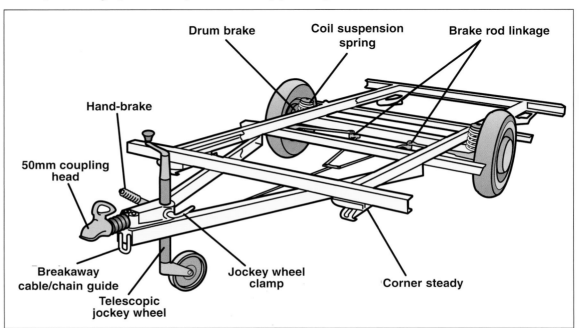

Drum brake · Coil suspension spring · Brake rod linkage · Hand-brake · 50mm coupling head · Breakaway cable/chain guide · Telescopic jockey wheel · Jockey wheel clamp · Corner steady

Background

In the 1960s and 1970s, nearly all caravan manufacturers ordered chassis from specialists such as Ambergate, B&B (Bird & Billington) and Peak. One manufacturer whose strategy was different was CI Caravans (Sprite Group) of Newmarket. This Company built their own chassis, although the brakes and suspension – referred to as *running gear* – were supplied by B&B, Harrison or Axles Ltd.

Practices changed around 1982 when most caravan manufacturers started to use a new 'lightweight chassis' designed and built by AL-KO Kober. Once again, CI Caravans, famous for the Sprite models, chose not to follow the majority and continued building their heavier traditional chassis. The policy was unchanged until 1990, after which many of the Company's 1991 models were subsequently built on a lightweight chassis with undergear supplied principally by F.T.F. and sometimes by Knott (UK) Ltd.

Running gear

As regards running gear on 'old-type' chassis, the suspension used coil springs and telescopic shock absorbers. Brake assemblies were often made by Lockheed Girling and there were a number of models using the same drums and brake shoes that were fitted to Morris Minor and Austin A40 cars. This often proves helpful when looking for spares.

One problem often experienced is a failure of the shock absorbers due to fluid loss. Anyone buying an older caravan should check for signs of seepage; replacement 'shockers' can be fitted, but the work is not easy.

Over-run braking

The over-run brake mechanism and coupling head assembly is different from more modern units as well. Coupling heads are normally of cast construction – whereas most recent models are made from pressed steel. However, the most significant difference is a brake disabling lever that

Before reversing, a lever was used to disable the brakes on older types of over-run system such as this B&B Beta IV unit.

has to be manually engaged before a reversing manoeuvre can be carried out. Without doubt, the need for a passenger to alight in order to operate a lever prior to every reversing manoeuvre is extremely inconvenient. Moreover, it is now illegal to fit such a system on a modern caravan.

Chassis maintenance

The section on page 37, entitled *Working safely under a caravan*, should be read before contemplating chassis maintenance.

Usually the steel members need to be painted periodically to prevent rusting. In particular, forward-facing cross members need regular inspection since these receive the brunt of stone chip damage from the towing vehicle.

As with most jobs, preparation is important and surface rust should be removed using a wire brush. A rotary brush driven by an electric drill is better than a hand brush, *but it is essential to wear safety goggles*. Filaments of wire often become detached and fly in any direction.

Once surface rust has been removed, there are several pre-painting treatments available. Some leave a coating of phosphate as a base for

Over-run braking – how it works

When horse-drawn carts were driven down steep hills, the load would roll forwards, giving the poor old horse an undignified push in the rear. Were it not for the invention of the over-run braking system, a caravan would do exactly the same thing to a tow car. This would *also* happen every time you applied your car's brakes. So how does it work?

By mounting the caravan's coupling head on a sliding steel bar, an automatic brake operating mechanism can be activated. Here's the sequence of events:

1. Tow car brakes are applied; the caravan rolls forward unchecked.
2. The coupling head's mounting tube or rod remains fixed and as the caravan comes forward, the rear-most part of the rod presses against a short lever.
3. Lever movement actuates the brake rod which then pulls the cables that finally apply the brakes.
4. On a well-adjusted system, the caravan's brakes will respond almost immediately, thereby working in conjunction with the car.

The only problem with this device is that you get exactly the same effect of pressure against the rear of a towing vehicle when starting to reverse an outfit. On older caravans you therefore have to operate a lever to disable the over-run system prior to reversing. On newer caravans, a mechanism in the brake drum disables the brakes automatically as soon as a reversing manoeuvre is detected.

33

subsequent applications of undercoat and cellulose topcoat. Another popular treatment is a special protective metal paint called Hammerite. Available in both smooth and 'hammered' finishes, this can be painted directly on to bare – or even rusty – metal in one thick coating. Check the instructions carefully; remember to buy Hammerite thinners/brush cleaner, and note that the product dries quickly.

Spare parts

Spares for pre-1980 chassis and running gear are becoming increasingly scarce. Some items were held by AL-KO Kober but stock is now supplied by Johnnie Longden Ltd whose address is in the Appendix. In some instances parts need to be sourced through a caravan breakers.

Aluminium chassis

Different yet again is the aluminium chassis. For instance some of the caravans from Lunar, Swift and Cotswold (now part of Swift) were built on an aluminium structure matched with either AL-KO or Knott axles, overruns and brake linkages. These came from several chassis specialists; from around 1983, Lunar's Clubman and Delta models were built on a product made by TW Chassis Ltd of Lostock Hall, Preston, and a number of Cotswold and Swift models have been built on a Syspal chassis manufactured in Broseley, Shropshire.

However, it was Lunar that became most closely associated with the aluminium chassis and weight-saving was one potential benefit. Unfortunately, timber floor supports were normally used to contribute to under-floor bracing and this tended to counter the weight-saving intention.

Undoubtedly the use of aluminium sections has advantages, but two problems should be noted:
1. When towing in winter, road salt can damage an aluminium structure more than galvanised steel. In salty conditions, the surface soon becomes pitted and coated with oxide – so hosing off the chassis members is a necessary chore.
2. Problems occur in respect of damage to an aluminium section if it comes into contact with steel. The mismatch of material leads to an electrolytic action; so any junction needs a spacer such as a heavy duty neoprene gasket which is explained in the box on the left.

Today, aluminium chassis are no longer used. In 199 Lunar switched to lightweight galvanised steel chassis for virtually every model and products from AL-KO Kober and Knott are now exclusively used instead.

Lightweight steel chassis

The change to lightweight, computer-designed chassis occurred in the early part of the 1980s when AL-KO, a German Company, took over the B&B operation based in Leamington Spa. However, the changes were more far-reaching than just the chassis structure itself.

Background

The new approach to design and construction involved a radical change in the suspension as well

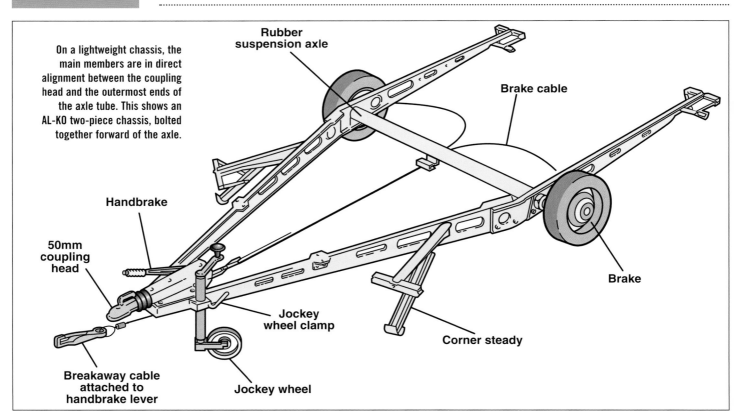

On a lightweight chassis, the main members are in direct alignment between the coupling head and the outermost ends of the axle tube. This shows an AL-KO two-piece chassis, bolted together forward of the axle.

Rubber suspension axle

Brake cable

Handbrake

50mm coupling head

Jockey wheel clamp

Corner steady

Brake

Breakaway cable attached to handbrake lever

Jockey wheel

Caravan chassis and running gear

as the chassis. It also coincided with new thinking on the construction of caravan floors; bonded ply composite panels were being developed.

Prior to this, a caravan builder would start with a completed chassis fitted with running gear, to which was added wooden joists and a thin plywood floor. Today, most manufacturers start with a prefabricated floor panel comprising a bonded sandwich of plywood and block foam insulant. This is inverted and the chassis members and axle are then assembled and bolted in place. There is no welding involved.

Strength

Even though far less material is used in a lightweight chassis, strength is achieved through the interplay of three principal components:

- the chassis members,
- the axle tube,
- the composite floor panel.

The layout of the chassis members is important. In contrast with the earlier heavy structures, there are no cross members. Moreover, the main longitudinal chassis members run in a straight line from the coupling head at the front to the outermost ends of the axle tube. This means the pulling action of the towcar is in alignment with points slightly inboard of the caravan wheels. This geometry is an important feature.

Other strength-giving elements which also save weight include fold backs on the edges of the longitudinal chassis members.

Axle position

The all-important matter of nose-weight is partly determined by a caravan's axle position; so this is computer-calculated, taking into account the intended layout of the finished caravan. For instance if a caravan manufacturer is designing a model with an 'end kitchen', this will be taken into account when calculating the precise location of the axle. Kitchen appliances are among the heaviest items in a caravan and play an important part in respect of stability, too.

On a modern lightweight chassis there are no cross members, but the axle tube is one of the contributors to rigidity. This is the AL-KO Delta axle discussed on page 40.

Introduced in 1999, the AL-KO Kober Vario chassis can be used for caravans of different dimensions.

Chassis assembly

When the AL-KO Kober chassis first appeared in Britain, it was constructed with bolt-together sections that had to be assembled at the caravan factory. However, some manufacturers, e.g. ABI, specified continuous main members made without any joins. Subsequently, the use of one-piece chassis members was sometimes adopted.

Finally in early 1999, AL-KO Kober introduced the sectional 'Vario Chassis' that can be assembled using several alternative coupling positions, thereby providing a more universal application. Hence by working to AL-KO Kober's build plan, the components supplied can be assembled to suit a number of models in a manufacturer's range.

Design evaluation

In spite of the weight-saving features of modern chassis, some traditionalists still prefer the older form of construction. There are advantages and disadvantages in respect of the lighter units:

Advantages

- Whereas some AL-KO Kober chassis were painted in the early 1980s, most are galvanised.
- The AL-KO Kober galvanised chassis is virtually maintenance-free.
- The weight/strength relationship is most favourable.

Disadvantages

- You could position a jack under almost any main member on an old-style chassis. On a lightweight chassis, jacking can *only* be carried out by:
  a) using a factory-designed side jack fitted into lifting brackets on the chassis;
  b) positioning a portable jack under the outer end of the axle tube;
  c) jacking directly under the steel plates that secure the axle tube to the main side members.

- It is not permitted to drill a lightweight chassis built in the 1990s, see the Technical Tip box on the right.

Technical Tip

On lightweight chassis built in the 1980s, the manufacturer recognised that some owners would wish to fit a single-leaf type of stabiliser like the Scott or Bulldog models. It was then deemed acceptable to attach its mounting bracket on the chassis member provided the two fixing holes were drilled in horizontal alignment. When this is done, the holes have to be formed in the mid point of the member measured vertically. However, two holes drilled one above the other have never been permitted since this could lead to chassis failure.

Whilst drilling an early chassis in exceptional circumstances might be approved by AL-KO, the manufacturer does not recommend it, so stabilisers now use clamp-on brackets instead.

With later chassis, requirements are even more stringent.

No drilling of *any* kind is permitted on a 1990s AL-KO Kober chassis and disregarding this will invalidate the chassis warranty. Moreover, in Germany and Holland, drilling a chassis is deemed illegal unless the altered design is submitted for special Type Approval.

Galvanising protection

When first galvanised, steel chassis members sometimes suffer from a surface discoloration referred to as 'wet storage stain'. Galvanised components need time to cure completely, during which time the coating changes from a shiny finish to a dull grey. If used prematurely on a salted road during winter, a new chassis should be washed-off after use in order to prevent 'wet storage stain' forming on the surface. In practice this doesn't cause the chassis to deteriorate, but it *does* give an unsightly appearance to chassis members.

The stain can also occur after a prolonged lay-up period – especially if air circulation around the chassis members has been restricted. Caravan skirts and front 'spoilers', for example, can hinder air movement. If this occurs, unsightly deposits can be removed with a stiff nylon brush.

In time, however, the zinc coating on a new chassis reacts with the atmosphere, and becomes a dark grey colour. This shows that the zinc treatment has developed its full protective potential and further incidence of wet storage stain is unlikely.

The protective benefit of galvanising is notable. Indeed it should never be painted because this tends to allow moisture to become trapped between the galvanised surface and the subsequent layer of paint.

Maintenance and repair

A galvanised chassis is virtually maintenance-free. At most, an owner merely needs to brush away road dirt. However, if a chassis gets dented or distorted, repairs should be carried out by a specialist. In the case of a modern sectional chassis, the specialist is sometimes able to unbolt and replace a damaged component and check alignment. Without question, this is *not* a do-it-yourself repair.

On the other hand, if surface abrasion exposes part of the steel underneath, you can treat this with a cold galvanising compound. Typical products comprise granules of zinc suspended in a liquid binder. These are usually brush-applied after which the binder evaporates, leaving the zinc behind. Products are sold in auto accessory shops and even Builders' Merchants – cold galvanising compounds are often used for treating wrought iron fences.

Corner steadies

The much abused 'corner steady' has a tough life. This is *not* a jack and if you try to lift a caravan using corner steadies you will not only distort the mechanism; you are likely to damage the chassis and might also split the floor panel as well.

Some corner steadies often take an age to lower and the quick-operating types are comparatively costly. As a rule, these are only fitted to more expensive models.

Most caravanners take a small block to position under each steady although load distribution is also possible using 'Big Foot' plates from Cosmic Accessories. These are permanently attached to standard steadies.

Maintenance

Even when used correctly, the spindle threads can soon get rusty. The mechanisms must therefore be lightly greased on a regular basis and the steadies raised and lowered as often as possible – especially during a long period of outdoor storage. Be careful not to *over-grease* the spindle because this attracts grit. A multi-purpose grease made to DIN 51825 standard is recommended by AL-KO Kober.

Accessories

Various corner steady locking systems are available but few would deter a competent thief.

Fast acting corner steadies from AL-KO Kober can be fitted as replacement items.

The 'Big Foot' from Cosmic Accessories can be attached permanently to many types of corner steady legs.

Lead-in tubes are often being fitted to help when locating a corner steady brace in the dark.

There are also add-on tubes to steer an operating brace directly on to the head of the spindle when it's dark. Some caravanners even take rechargeable drills fitted with a special socket to speed-up operation.

Finally there is the Caralevel system which comprises 12V motorised steadies whose operation is monitored by a central control unit. The Caralevel rig – often demonstrated at caravan exhibitions – gives a convincing demonstration of the way each motor is brought into sequential operation thereby facilitating levelling as well. The Caralevel can be fitted professionally or purchased for DIY installation.

Note: *When a device such as a Caralevel is fitted, points made in the Technical Tip box on page 35 must be recognised. No drilling of any kind is approved on a post-1990 AL-KO chassis.*

Working safely under a caravan

Whether repainting an older chassis, adjusting brakes or working on any other job that necessitates access under a caravan, it is *absolutely essential* that the elevation support systems are completely fail-safe.

One approach is to drive a caravan on to a pair of scaffold planks. Having raised both sides equally, two or three further planks can subsequently be added, thus raising the height progressively. The corner steadies should then be lowered and the wheels chocked. Provided the ground is firm, this controlled elevation to a modest level has much to commend it.

An alternative is to use a jack, chocks and axle stands. Start by elevating one side of the caravan with a jack – make certain that the hand-brake is on, corner steadies are *raised*, the wheel on the far side is firmly chocked and a steady balance is provided by the jockey wheel. A stand can then be inserted under the axle, inboard from the road wheel. The procedure is then repeated on the other side. Once the caravan is elevated, corner steadies can then be lowered, using wood blocks where necessary and both wheels chocked. Note the following:

• Under no circumstances use the corner steadies to elevate a caravan.

• Some plastic wheel chocks can slip badly on certain surfaces – such as smooth tarmac. Use robust chocks, bearing in mind that heavy timber chocks shaped to the wheel curvature might be worth making.
• Axle stands vary in quality. Some DIY stands have a very small base and offer inadequate stability to support a caravan.
• Soft and/or sloping ground can render an arrangement unsafe.
• Never rely on a jack alone when working under a caravan.

Jacks

For work at home or for emergency roadside repairs, the AL-KO Kober scissor jack was purpose-made with a support to match the profile of a modern axle tube. This is no longer available and the AL-KO side-lift jack has taken its place.

Hydraulic bottle jacks sold in auto stores would be useful if they included a similar support that would cradle the hexagonal axle tube, but this is seldom the case. Moreover, if you have a puncture, there might also be insufficient ground clearance to position a bottle jack.

The AL-KO Kober compact scissor jack was made to fit the shape of the chassis tube.

The best type of jack for a modern caravan is a side-fitted unit.

The yellow plastic caravan lift fitted by Elddis is ideal for quick wheel changes by the roadside.

The Rolljack is a 'drive-on' unit that lifts the axle automatically as you gently drive the caravan forward.

Side-lift jacks

When using this type of jack, you are strongly recommended to keep your caravan attached to your towcar. This is especially important during a roadside wheel change. You should also engage the caravan's handbrake lever and chock the opposite wheel.

A better system fitted to more expensive caravans is a side-lift jack. Attachment holes were punched into the side members of AL-KO Kober chassis built from 1992 onwards. However, the caravan floor had to have strengthening pieces fitted at the time of manufacture. This was no longer a requirement when the MkII AL-KO Kober version was introduced.

The MkII side-lift jack can now be fitted to most later caravans. Its different attachment bracket gives direct vertical lift through the chassis alone. Never transfer a MkI side-jack to another caravan; you could split the floor.

For road-side caravan elevation, Elddis introduced a support that is fixed to the axle tube (as shown above) and this effects elevation as you reverse the 'van. It's cam-like shape causes the caravan to lift as the unit rotates. A similar system called the Rolljack, marketed by Air Muscle, is suitable for any single axle caravan.

Note: *When using self-elevating jacks, it is crucial that the caravan isn't pulled beyond the high point. Severe underside damage could occur if it falls abruptly.*

Coupling heads and over-run assemblies

The opening section on pre-1980 chassis explained that modern coupling heads are usually made from pressed steel, whereas older units were made from a heavy casting. There are exceptions, of course, and some cast units are still manufactured.

Modern coupling heads

A feature of modern coupling heads (rather imprecisely referred to as 'hitches') is the fact that they usually offer 'one-hand' operation. Whether it's a release button system or a unit whose handle has a release position, the design enables you to attach or release the coupling head single-handed.

Cast coupling heads were commonplace on older caravans – though a few couplings today are of cast construction.

Many caravans are fitted with a pressed steel coupling head which features a red/green button to confirm when the unit is correctly coupled.

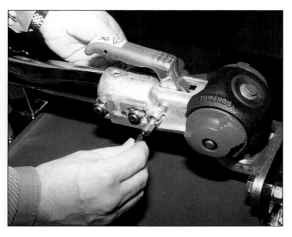

Some coupling heads include a brass insert containing a barrel lock which is fitted as a security measure.

Note: *You might damage a coupling mechanism if you take all the nose-weight by lifting on a handle in its unreleased position.*

Two particularly notable safety features found on more recent products such as the AL-KO AK 300 are:
• a tow ball and mechanism wear indicator,
• a positive coupling indicator button with red (danger) and green (coupled) markings to verify the coupling head has engaged on the ball.

Some products also incorporate a brass insert that is fitted into the body of the coupling and then locked. This security device prevents the locking cam inside the enclosure from being moved.

Modern over-run assemblies

The function of an over-run system was explained in the box on page 33. The design of this all-important brake activating system has improved in the last two decades and legislation has played a part, too. For instance in EEC countries, caravans manufactured from October 1982 onwards are not permitted to have an over-run system which employs a spring mechanism for smoothing the operation. The ruling requires that a hydraulic damper is used.

Maintenance

The lubrication of all moving parts on an over-run assembly is important and the accompanying diagram shows greasing points. Whereas the uppermost pair of grease nipples are easy to identify, a third grease nipple usually fitted underneath can be difficult to locate. In fact it often gets missed altogether – partly because road dirt and remnants of grease obscure its location. The recommendation of AL-KO Kober is to use a multi-purpose grease which meets DIN 51825 standards.

As a further measure, it is appropriate to protect the over-run unit and coupling head with a waterproof cover whenever a caravan is laid-up for an extended period. However, try to attach the cover in such a way that air can circulate around the whole assembly.

Axles and suspension

Several types of suspension system have been fitted to caravans. These have included leaf springs, torsion bar suspension and coil springs. Earlier

The lower grease nipple is well-hidden and can all-too-easily get overlooked during a service.

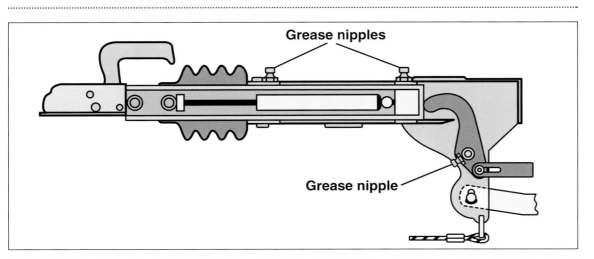

Grease nipples

Grease nipple

An over-run assembly must be serviced regularly and three grease nipples are fitted on most units.

Three lengths of rubber are inserted into an AL-KO Kober caravan axle tube at the time of manufacturer and this forms the rubber-in-compression suspension.

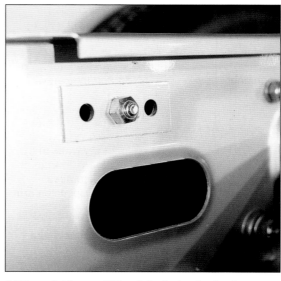

A fitting point for an additional shock absorber has been included on an AL-KO Kober chassis since the early 1990s.

reference has been made to pre-1980 chassis where coil spring systems and hydraulic dampers were used.

Nowadays the suspension system employs lengths of rubber which are forced into compression as a caravan rides the bumps. The diagram below shows that within both ends of a six-sided tubular axle, three lengths of compressible rubber are seated within an inner tube which has tri-lobal flutings.

Provided the rubber suspension isn't over-stressed, it will afford excellent service. Moreover, since it is self-damping, shock absorbers are not normally needed. However, they have sometimes been fitted to heavy caravans and are also necessary on the AL-KO Kober Delta axle which has a conspicuous arrow-like appearance as shown in the photograph on page 35.

In view of these self-damping characteristics, it is a paradox that shock absorbers are commonly fitted to many post-1993 caravans built on AL-KO Kober's Euro-Axle system. Installation points are also provided on models that haven't had them fitted and AL-KO supplies 'Octagon Shock Absorbers' which can be easily attached. The reason for this trend is that shock absorbers are standard in Germany and many British caravanners have wanted to follow suit. Nevertheless, AL-KO Kober's UK technical staff make the position clear; the performance characteristics of the rubber suspension mean that 'shockers' are not normally necessary.

The AL-KO Kober Octagon telescopic shock absorbers are easy to fit and many owners install them without difficulty.

AL-KO Kober 'Delta Axle'

A special feature of a modern hexagonal axle is that its tube structure contributes strength to the chassis as well. However, there are variations in its basic design. For example, the AL-KO Kober 'Delta Axle' with its prominent arrow-head shape has been used for some time on the Continent. Now it is available in the United Kingdom and has been fitted to several British-built caravans such as the ABI Award range. Research has shown that the Delta-shaped axle achieves better stability than is

The rubber in a caravan suspension deforms in varying degrees as the suspension arm rises and falls.

Rebound or Free position
(25% below horizontal)

Normal laden position
(5% below horizontal)

Maximum bump
(15% above horizontal)

obtainable on conventional designs, particularly when a car and caravan are negotiating a sharp bend. In this situation, the caravan wheel on the outside of the corner increases its toe-in and negative camber angle. This creates an improved alignment between the vehicle and the caravan (see photograph on page 35).

AL-KO Kober 'Euro-Axle'

The 'Euro-Axle' was first used for caravans in the 1994 model year and remains current. In truth, the term is imprecise because it also embraces alterations to wheel bearings, the suspension arm and stub axles – as discussed later.

With regard to the axle tube itself, this is now galvanised rather than painted and a metal data label affixed to the tubing bears the letter 'E' in a circle within the entry box headed CAPACITY. The same rubber suspension system is retained.

Maintenance

A notable benefit of a compressed rubber suspension is that no routine maintenance is required. However, you can extend the life of a suspension system by taking precautions whenever the caravan is being unused for a long period.

Since rubber always returns to its original shape after a load has been removed, the manufacturer recommends that whenever a caravan is stored for long spells, it should be supported on axle stands. In consequence, its weight is no longer borne by the suspension. Some caravanners pursue a similar strategy for extending the life of the tyres by fitting products such as 'Winter Wheels'. However, these supports only take the weight from the tyres; they do not take the load from the suspension.

Wheel bearings

Another development of significance to owners concerns wheel bearings. For many years, the wheels on caravans – like those on cars – revolved freely on tapered roller bearings. In fact this type of bearing was commonplace until the early 1990s.

The inner and outer bearing units are seated in the brake drum which in turn is held to the stub axle by a castellated nut. This descriptive term refers to the fact that its notched shape is reminiscent of a castle tower. Indeed it is these notches that provide a point of retention for the split pin that ensures the nut will not shake loose. The accompanying photograph (top) shows the attachment.

Provided the retaining nut is tightened to permit free rotation without play and as long as new split pins are fitted every time a bearing is reinstated, the system is hard to fault. Periodically the bearings should be greased using multi purpose grease meeting DIN 51825 specifications, noting that it is important not to over-pack the grease cap. These procedures follow established automotive practice.

Notwithstanding the success of the system, sealed-for-life bearings were introduced around

Tapered roller bearings used to be fitted to caravans; but these were superseded when sealed bearings were introduced in the early 1990s.

The sealed bearings now fitted into the brake drum of modern caravans can only be replaced by returning the drum to the chassis manufacturer.

Modern sealed bearing units are superbly engineered and are expected to last for around 100,000km (62,500 miles).

Nowadays a brake drum is held in place by a 'one-shot' nut and this has to be tightened using a calibrated torque wrench.

1992. Caravans built on Knott running gear ran on sealed bearings first; subsequently the use of sealed bearings formed part of the AL-KO Kober's Euro Axle components used on many 1994 models.

With a lifetime guarantee, these superbly engineered bearings are unlikely to give problems. Unfortunately, however, if a replacement is needed, it is a factory-only job and the drum has to be sent back to the manufacturer, but there is a further problem.

41

Rather than having a castellated retention nut with a split pin, the drum is now held in place by a 'one shot' nut that grips the stub axle threads tightly. This starts with a mildly oval shape but once used, it cannot be used a second time.

During nut replacement a mineral grease (AL-KO Part No 800.052) is used on the stub axle threads. Then a red marking paint (AL-KO Part No 800.015) is used on the nut which confirms it has not been pre-used.

Perhaps the biggest disappointment is the fact that few DIY owners will now be able to remove a drum to inspect the brake assembly, clean away dust, or fit replacement shoes. Not only is considerable force needed to remove a 'one-shot' nut, but re-tightening the new replacement item to an exact setting is critical. A calibrated torque wrench is an essential tool and a suitable product like a Norbar wrench costs around £300. This is a bitter blow to competent and experienced self-help enthusiasts who have hitherto kept their brake assemblies in good order using a standard tool kit.

Brakes

Part of this section concerns maintenance of braking systems but there are also a number of general points that deserve attention.

General features

Virtually all caravans employ a drum brake system. Other brakes have been tried, however, and the German chassis makers, Peitz, introduced a disc brake in the 1980s. Cotswold was the first British

On nearly all caravans, the brake lever must be raised to a vertical position to achieve full braking security.

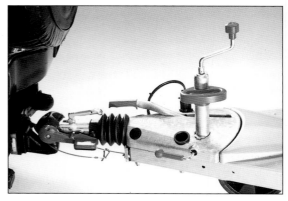

The Euro Over-run Automatic Self-adjusting handbrake was introduced in the UK by AL-KO Kober in 1999.

caravan manufacturer to fit these units and the 1986 Celeste could be ordered with Peitz disc brakes fitted as an optional extra. More recently,

The brake assemblies built with tapered roller bearings are often serviced by DIY owners because no special tools are needed.

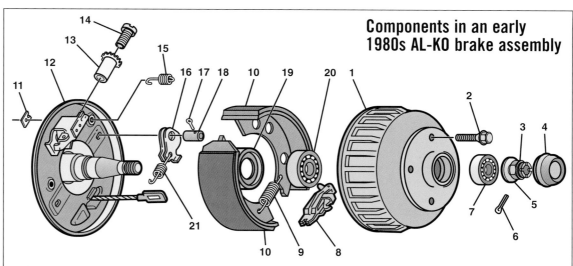

Components in an early 1980s AL-KO brake assembly

1 Brake drum	8 Expanding clutch
2 Wheel bolt	9 Brake shoe tension springs
3 Castellated nut	10 Brake shoes
4 Grease cap	11 Cover plates
5 Lock washer	12 Backplate
6 Split pin	13 Starwheel adjusting nut
7 Outer tapered roller bearing	14 Adjusting screw

15 Shoe mounting pressure springs
16 Spring loaded reversing lever
17 Floating pivot pin
18 Split pin
19 Oil seal
20 Inner bearing
21 Tension spring for reversing lever

The green bung covers the brake adjustment point. A lost bung should be replaced in order to protect the mechanism.

When a caravan is reversed, this cam rotates and allows the trailing shoe to pull away from the friction surface on the drum.

Difficulty in reversing

1. If the brakes are set too tightly, difficulty will be found when reversing the caravan because this can prevent the reverse mechanism from operating properly.
2. The minimum permitted thickness of an AL-KO brake shoe is 2mm. Linings which wear below this critical thickness can also interfere with the correct operation of the reversing mechanism.

disc systems have been shown at major exhibitions on BPW chassis. Hydraulically-operated disc brakes, however, are comparatively costly – hence the preference for drum systems.

Points about the operation of drum brakes include the following:
• During towing, a caravan's brakes operate automatically via the over-run system – described earlier in this chapter on page 33.
• The auto-reverse braking system causes the brake shoes to release automatically whenever a caravan moves backwards.
• As explained in the box on the right, a hand-brake on post-1980 caravans is not correctly engaged until it reaches a vertical position. This takes considerable effort to achieve.
• When storing a caravan for a long period, it is best to park on level ground, chock the wheels and leave the brake in the off position.
• Modern brakes use asbestos-free linings and AL-KO Kober has fitted these since April 1989.

Auto reverse systems

The invention of an over-run brake which releases automatically when an outfit is reversed has been a great asset for caravan and trailer owners. Several products achieving this objective have been developed and a few older caravans were fitted with the AP Lockheed system. This features trailing brake shoes which are mounted loosely within a carrying cradle. Whenever the wheel rotates backwards, these shoes slide along the cradle, and move away from the friction surface of the drum. However, the Lockheed system is not currently used on new models.

Nowadays nearly all caravans are fitted with either AL-KO Kober or Knott auto-reverse brakes; whilst the objective is the same, the operating mechanism is different.

Shoe withdrawal

Reverse operation in these units is dependent on a specially shaped spring-loaded cam or 'reversing lever' which touches one end of the trailing brake shoe. This is shown in the photograph and also in the exploded diagram on page 42. As soon as the expanding shoes touch the drum, the fact that the wheel is rotating in a *reverse* direction causes the spring-loaded cam to pivot. On account of its eccentric shape, as soon as the cam pivots, the trailing shoe releases pressure from the friction surface of the drum. The wheels then turn easily.

Shoe reinstatement

As soon as a caravan is subsequently towed in a *forward* direction, a spring on the cam now pulls it back to its normal position. Once the cam is back in its usual place, the trailing brake shoes will now bear against the drum in the usual way whenever the brakes are applied.

Auto-reverse braking and handbrake engagement

When a caravan is moved backwards, its brakes are automatically released. This is fine when you're reversing your caravan – the auto-reverse system on post-1980 caravans is a great asset – but there is a problem if an unhitched caravan is parked on a backward facing slope.

In this situation, the handbrake must be correctly applied. If there's the *slightest* backward movement, the auto-reverse mechanism comes into play and the brakes are automatically released. On a hill, a caravan could unexpectedly roll away.

To counter this, a modern caravan has a coil spring, housed in a metal tube and forming part of the brake rod arrangement. This is referred to as the 'energy store' and is located just behind the lower extremity of the handbrake lever. To engage a brake fully, you need to ensure this spring is fully compressed – *hence the need to haul the handbrake lever into a vertical position.* This gives you a 'second chance'.

If the caravan moves backwards and the brakes release, the spring in the energy store is then suddenly released, thus re-applying the handbrake. This provision can prevent a parked caravan from rolling backwards down a hill, but of course it's essential to reset the handbrake lever to the vertical once again. Better still – chock the wheels.

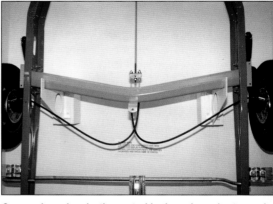

On a modern chassis, the central brake rod couples to a pair of cables at the axle tube. Note the Delta axle here.

Gas strut handbrake

Acknowledging that a handbrake demands a reasonable amount of strength to engage correctly, AL-KO Kober manufactures a gas piston version which is standard on many Continental caravans. To fit a gas strut assembly as a replacement, the entire over-run has to be replaced and the brake rod changed.

The great benefit is the fact that a gas piston forces the handbrake firmly into a fully engaged position as soon as the brake release button is depressed. It takes a certain amount of pressure to return the lever to its normal unbraked position later, but the technique of doing this is mastered after a little practice. Without doubt, the product is a great help to anyone uncertain about securing a caravan parked on sloping ground. However, the new Euro over-run automatic brake is even better.

Euro over-run brake

In 1999, AL-KO Kober exhibited the Euro Over-run Automatic Self-Adjusting Handbrake. The mechanism identifies forward or backward wheel movement and reacts automatically, applying increased pressure to hold a parked caravan. In the United Kingdom, models in the Vanmaster range were the first to have this product fitted.

The Euro over-run brake represents a big step forward.

Brake rods and cables

Whereas earlier caravans had brakes operated exclusively by rods, current practice is to use cables for coupling into the brake drums. These are called Bowden cables.

The cables couple to the rod in the vicinity of the

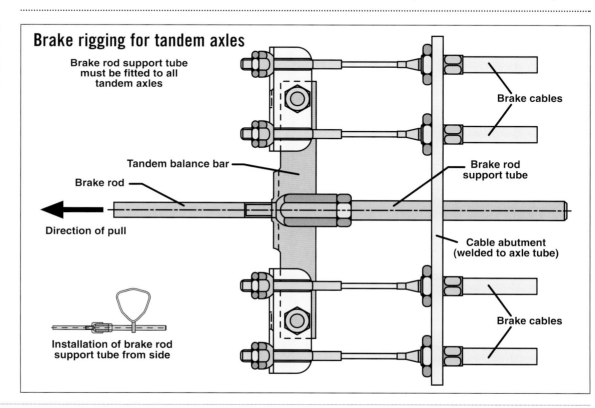

Brake rigging for tandem axles

Brake rod support tube must be fitted to all tandem axles

Brake cables

Tandem balance bar

Brake rod support tube

Brake rod

Direction of pull

Cable abutment (welded to axle tube)

Installation of brake rod support tube from side

Brake cables

axle tube and connection is achieved using a floating plate referred to as a 'balance bar'.
It is the balance bar which plays a part in confirming that the amount of braking going to each wheel is balanced. If the brakes are correctly set at the drums, the balance bar should lie in parallel alignment with the axle tube.

In addition the outer sheath of the Bowden cable is fixed to a plate welded to the axle tube.

Rod support

It is important that the central brake rod is fully supported and chassis manufacturers recommend that either metal brackets or flexible support straps are fitted at intervals no greater than 1.3m (51in) over its entire length. If support is lacking, when driving along a bumpy road, an excessive rise and fall of the brake rod can pull on the cable and intermittently activate the brakes – causing unwanted wear.

Regrettably, a number of manufacturers fail to provide the amount of support specified. Fortunately support straps are often available from service centres and a practical owner can carry out the necessary remedial work, but owners of twin axle caravans should also note the next point.

Balance bar support

On a single axle caravan, the balance bar is comparatively light. However, on a twin axle caravan, the assembly is much heavier and on a

bumpy road surface this can bounce up and down causing unwanted intermittent braking. To prevent this occurring, there should be an additional brake rod support tube that extends rearwards from the balance bar. This should fit within an enlarged hole in the centre of the cable fixing plate welded on to the axle tube. The component is shown in the diagram on the previous page.

Unfortunately this all-important support tube has not been fitted on some twin axle caravans. It is a component that is easily added, however, and AL-KO Kober can supply the part.

Cable renewal

Normally a Bowden cable lasts for many years although damage can occur if it gets caught on a high obstruction. Provided safe access can be arranged under a caravan, it is not a difficult item to replace. The photograph above shows the balance

When the brakes are correctly set at the drums, the balance bar should lie parallel to the axle tube.

Disconnecting a Bowden cable at the brake drum

1. A support throat helps to attach the brake cable at the rear of the bracing plate.

2. When replacing a cable, the top section of the support throat is lifted away.

3. The cable is now clearly visible at the backing plate.

4. The attachment nipple on the end of the cable has now been disconnected from the brake assembly.

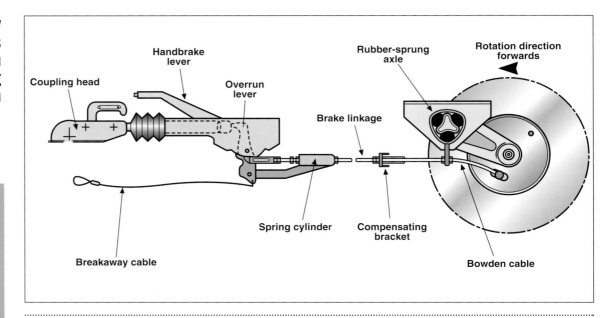

Coupling head

Handbrake
lever

Overrun
lever

Rubber-sprung
axle

Rotation direction
forwards

Brake linkage

Spring cylinder

Compensating
bracket

Breakaway cable

Bowden cable

Brake check

One of the signs that
the brakes need
adjusting or the
shoes need
replacing is an
excessive movement
of the handbrake
lever.
■ Where AL-KO
undergear is fitted, it
is recommended
that when a caravan
is parked on level
ground, the brakes
should start to
engage on the
second or third click
of the hand lever.
■ If Knott brakes
are fitted,
engagement should
commence on the
second click.
New brake shoes
must be fitted when
the lining is less
than 2mm in any
part of its length.

Before adjusting the
brakes, the coupling head
must be pulled fully
forward.

bar attachment; the sequence on the previous page
shows the connection at the drum.

Brake adjustment

In one key respect, brake adjustment is the same
for both rod only and rod/cable systems, i.e. that
work *must* commence at the drums. Some owners
erroneously think that they can take up play by
adjusting the rod just behind the handbrake. This
is not the case. Work at the forward end of the
entire system is the *last* part to be adjusted.

Procedures and setting distances may vary
between different products and the description here
relates to post-1980 AL-KO Kober systems Check
running gear guidance for other models, particularly
with regard to clearances.

a) Preparatory tasks

Safe access will be needed underneath the
caravan; check the guidance given earlier.
• Park the caravan on firm, level ground.
• Make sure it cannot move. Chocks are needed
because the brakes will not be operable during the
adjustment.
• With a sustained pull, draw the coupling head
forward to its full extent.

• Release the handbrake *completely.* If a badly-
fitted fairing hinders its range of movement,
you may need to elongate the opening.
• Jack up one side of the 'van and support the
axle tube on a robust axle stand.
• Lower all the corner steadies to provide further
support.
• When the security of the caravan has been
confirmed, have an inspection lamp or torch to
hand. Markings can be hard to see. The job is also
more comfortable if you've got an old piece of
carpet to lie on.

b) Drum adjustment

• Remove the plastic bungs from the access holes
in the backing plate.
• Look through the outer hole to confirm that the
linings are not badly worn. You will need a torch
and only a rough assessment is possible.
• Select a screwdriver whose blade is small
enough to pass through the inner hole to engage
with the star wheel.

Technical Tip

When checking
braking, a caravan
wheel must *not* be
turned in the
reverse direction,
i.e. as if the 'van
were being
backed. If you
make this mistake,
the auto-release
mechanism automatically releases the pressure
applied to the shoes – just as it does when you're
reversing a caravan – and the wheel will then
rotate freely. So checking brake resistance must
always be done by rotating a wheel in the direction
it would turn when the 'van is moving forward.

Brake adjustment on most modern brakes is done by rotating a star wheel.

An arrow stamped in an AL-KO Kober backing plate indicates which way a star wheel adjuster must be turned to tighten the brakes.

• Rotate the adjuster until brake resistance is felt when the wheel is turned in a forward direction, i.e. as if the caravan were being towed *forwards*. See the Technical Tip box on page 46.
• An arrow stamped on many backing plates indicates which way to turn the adjuster to increase braking. Otherwise the direction is established by trial and error.
• Once firm resistance is felt, back off the adjuster. Slacken off the mechanism just enough to allow the wheel to turn freely in a forward direction.
• The process is now repeated on the other brake drum – or the remaining three drums if working on a twin axle model.

Note: *On some Knott brakes the practice of fitting a square-ended adjuster (called a 'set nut') has been employed on recent units, e.g. 1995 Elddis models. A similar system was used on the older Lockheed brakes. Whereas a screwdriver is needed to turn a star wheel, the Knott and Lockheed systems need a brake spanner.*

Recent developments on BPW chassis show that brakes are being fitted that need spanner adjustment.

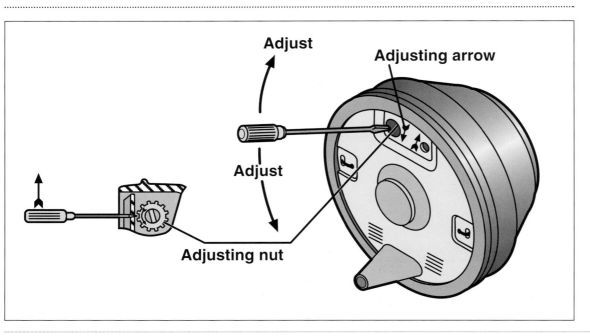

Adjusting an AL-KO Kober brake using a screwdriver

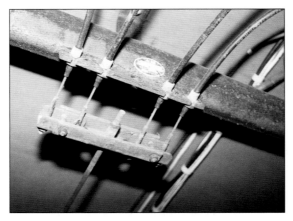

Before checking brake adjustment, this balance bar on a twin axle caravan needs to be dismantled. Note that a rod support tube has not been fitted on this 1990 caravan.

When correctly adjusted, a brake's cables should start to operate the shoes when pulled between 5 and 8mm.

c) Brake cable and balance bar check

• Now turn attention to the plate welded to the axle tube which secures the sheath of each brake cable. If brake adjustment has been done correctly, the cable inner, when pulled, should extend between 5 and 8mm. To check this properly, disconnect the locking nuts that secure the brake cable inner to the balance bar. Now pull on the cable and check the amount of movement.

• Reconnect the cables and adjust the locking nuts so that the balance bar lies parallel to the axle tube. On twin axle caravans there's a tandem balance bar and full alignment must be achieved.

d) Installation check

• It is important that the brake rod is parallel to the caravan floor when viewed from the side.

• It *must* be supported at least every 1.3m (51in) over its entire length.

• With twin axle AL-KO Kober models – which have a double balance bar – there *must* be a support tube bolted to the rearward face of the bar. This should pass through the abutment plate welded to the axle, to stop the unit sagging as shown on page 44.

e) Forward end adjustment

• The brake rod may need fine adjustment to ensure that at the front, the overrun lever *just* touches the rear of the towing shaft.

• Adjustment may be needed at the leading end of the spring cylinder, described earlier as the 'energy store'. AL-KO Kober specifies a clearance of 1mm at the forward end of this cylinder and the gap can be set by adjusting the locknuts.

f) Final checking

• Check the brakes engage at the appropriate point on the handbrake ratchet as described in the box on page 46. If they engage prematurely, the auto-reverse mechanism is unlikely to operate correctly and the brakes might lock when backing the 'van.

It is difficult to confirm the brakes operate efficiently when an over-run mechanism is depressed by the coupling head. Engineers at the Welland Service Centre near Peterborough solved this by constructing a controlled compression tool made up with an old jockey wheel mechanism and a dummy tow ball. This device will compress the shaft in a controlled manner to enable wheels to be rotated and brake checks carried out.

When correctly adjusted, the over-run lever should just make contact with the over-run shaft.

There should be a clearance gap of 1mm between the lever and the 'energy store' tube.

Caravan chassis and
running gear

When correctly adjusted, AL-KO Kober brakes should start to engage on the second or third click on the hand lever ratchet.

The service engineers at Welland devised a test rig which confirms correct operation of the over-run braking system.

Checking brake assemblies

a) Pre-sealed bearing models

Before sealed bearing units were fitted in the early 1990s, you could remove a brake drum quite easily to clean the assembly and to check or change the brake shoes. Some owners do this themselves and if you have a pre-1994 AL-KO Kober Euro-Axle or a pre-1993 Knott system, the job is not difficult.

Start by jacking up the caravan, setting it on axle stands and removing a wheel, taking full note of the safety points given in the earlier section, *Working safely under a caravan* on page 37. Then:

1. Remove the grease cap.
2. Withdraw the split pin from the large castellated nut on the end of the stub axle.
3. Undo the nut with a socket spanner, removing it together with the large washer.

Note: *On the 2050 and 2051 AL-KO brake systems, no washer is fitted under the castellated nut. On the 1635, 1636 and 1637 systems the dished washer must be fitted with the concave side outermost.*

4. Tap away the brake drum and lift it from the stub axle.

Note: *Use a leather hammer where possible to prevent drum damage. In exceptional cases, a puller might need to be hired to remove a drum.*

5. The outer bearing is easily removed from its seating. It will often be dislodged with the first sign of drum movement.
6. Check condition of shoes and remove any excess dust. A product like Tetroson brake and clutch cleaner can be used.

Note: *On earlier brake shoes with brackets (prior to April 1989), the friction material contained asbestos. Under no circumstances should the dust be blown away. Remove it carefully with a rag, making sure that it is not inhaled. It is advisable to wear a protective mask.*

Re-assembly reverses the operation:

1. Tighten the nut with a torque wrench to between 30-35Nm (22-26 lbs/ft);
2. Back off the nut 180° (half a turn);
3. Re-tighten nut 90° (quarter of a turn);
4. Fit a new split pin folding over each leg in opposite directions;
5. Ensure the grease cap is not more than half full of multi-purpose grease meeting DIN 51825 specifications;
6. Grease should also be applied in the hub between the bearings.

If you don't own a torque wrench, a way of confirming that the centre nut is sufficiently tight is to carry out the following check:

1. Ensure the caravan is stable on its axle stands.
2. Replace the wheel.
3. Tighten the nuts (or bolts) as much as you are able on the stands.

Identification of AL-KO Brake Systems

All AL-KO brake systems are identified by four-digit numbers which should be quoted when ordering parts. These are located on the outside of the backplate. Prior to 1994 (black-painted backplates), the number is situated towards the centre. In 1994, the introduction of the Euro System (gold coloured backplates), the number is situated on the outside edge. These systems are:

> 1635, 1636 and 1637 Systems – lightweight axles up to 900kg and most tandem axles sets.

> 2035, 2050 and 2051 Systems – medium range axles up to 1300kg and some large tandem axles (e.g. ABI Superstar).

> 2360 and 2361 Systems – heavy range axles up to 1850kg but tandem sets on trailers only, not on caravans.

If the four-digit number cannot be read due to age or corrosion, then the trick to identification is to measure the brake drum and shoes. For example, measure the diameter of the brake drum in centimetres (i.e. 16cm) and the width of the brakes in millimetres (i.e. 37mm). This indicates a 1637 System. This rule applies for all AL-KO Brake systems.

Note: *On 1635, 1636 and 1637 systems, the brake shoes are handed left and right. All other AL-KO systems use matching pairs.*

Checking brake assemblies on a system fitted with taper roller bearings

1. Remove the grease cap.

2. Withdraw the split pin from the large nut on the end of the stub axle. Undo the nut with a socket spanner, removing it together with the large washer.

3. Tap away the brake drum and lift it from the stub axle.

4. In some instances a brake drum has to be removed with a puller.

5. The outer bearing is easily removed from its seating.

6. Check condition of shoes and remove any excess dust. A product like Tetroson brake and clutch cleaner can be used.

Technical tip

The flanged hub nut that secures a drum fitted with sealed bearings is described as a 'one-shot nut'. This is manufactured with a slightly oval centre to grip the threads – which means that once it has been undone, it has to be thrown away and replaced with a new one. Types to suit AL-KO Kober and Knott brakes are stocked at most dealers.

4. Grasp the tyre firmly on either side and move the wheel about to ensure there is no looseness.
5. Any play that might not be evident when you check on the brake drum is more pronounced when the wheel is judiciously shaken.

Note: *Do not shake the wheel so vigorously that the caravan is under risk of falling from the axle stands. Remember that the wheel fixings have not been properly tightened for road use.*

b) Sealed bearing models

In essence, the job of removing a brake drum on a caravan fitted with sealed bearings is not difficult. The problem is the fact that you must have the following items:

a) A calibrated torque wrench that can set the fixing nut to a setting of 290Nm (plus or minus 10Nm) This is equivalent to 214lbs/ft (plus or minus 7.5lbs/ft). The setting is 280Nm on a Knott axle (204lbs/ft).

Note: *The torque wrench often purchased from AL-KO Kober to check the tightness of wheel nuts (or bolts) will not operate in this range. A Norbar wrench suitable for the job and available from AL-KO Kober costs around £300.*

b) A 32mm socket is needed to fit the nut.
c) Replacement 'one-shot' nuts are needed.

Here lies the problem as far as the DIY service engineer is concerned. You cannot do the job with normal hand tools and the essential torque wrench would have to be purchased or hired.

Provided you have the tools for the job, jack up the caravan, setting it on axle stands and removing a wheel, taking full note of the safety points given in the earlier section on page 37, *Working safely under a caravan.*

Then, follow this procedure:

1. Remove the dust cap (note that this isn't any longer called a 'grease cap'.)
2. The dust cap on a sealed bearing system should be dry inside. If grease is visible it should only be the tiniest smear caused by unavoidable seepage.
3. A 32mm socket with a long lever is needed to undo the flanged hub nut; it will be *very* tight.

Note: *There's no split pin or castellated nut on the Euro-Axle system.*

4. Tap the drum away from the stub axle.

Note: *On very large single axle caravans a heavy duty 2361 brake system is used. Because of the* *weight of the drum, a special removal and refitting tool is needed (AL-KO Part No. 605.267) to prevent the bearing from being damaged.*

Re-assembly points

1. When the new nut is fitted, a small amount of mineral grease should be applied to the stub axle threads (AL-KO Part No 800.052).
2. It is essential that the nut is tightened to the *torque* specified. A calibrated torque wrench is needed as described above, and the nut should be tightened to a setting of 290Nm (plus or minus 10Nm) on an AL-KO Kober system: 280Nm on a Knott system.
3. Any surplus mineral grease must now be removed.
4. The nut should be marked with a special red paint available from AL-KO Kober to signify it has been replaced and correctly torqued up (Part No 800.015).
5. The dust cap should be tapped back into place – completely dry, of course.

Other Euro Axle features

In addition to sealed bearings and one-shot nuts, several other features were introduced when the AL-KO Kober Euro-Axle was first fitted to 1994 caravans. In summary these include:

• A stub axle which is bolted to the suspension arm rather than welded. This means the final position of the wheel on the road – called 'toe-in' – can be adjusted at the factory to fine tolerances using sophisticated machinery. The setting-up work is strictly a factory operation and the attachment bolt is security marked.
• The backing plate of the brake is zinc treated rather than painted. It is also bolted to the suspension arm, thereby offering greater choice for the brake cable's point of entry.
• Sealed-for-life bearings are factory-fitted in the brake drum. A bearing is expected to last for around 100,000km (approx. 62,500 miles) and is pre-greased and double-sealed. In the unlikely event of bearing failure, the drum has to be sent to the factory; a service centre would not have the equipment to fit a replacement bearing.
• To accept the sealed bearings, the stub axle is now larger in diameter.

Replacing brake shoes

Before brake shoes are removed, it is always wise to take note of the assembly before starting the job. For example, on the older Lockheed brake it is advisable to make a sketch of the fitting position of the brake-shoe springs. The array of holes and slots in the shoes can lead to confusion when you later re-assemble the units.

On brake systems fitted to more recent caravans, the shoes are held to the backing plate with small coil springs and a location tab that seats on the outside of the backing plate. These are often rusty, so have some replacements ready.

Before fitting the new shoes, remember to back

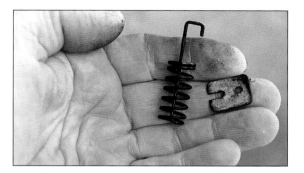

On most modern caravans, brake shoes are held to the backing plate with a small spring and tab.

The shoe is located carefully in the brake activating lever.

off the adjuster fully before endeavouring to refit the drum. Check the accompanying Tip box regarding brake grease. When the drum is finally replaced, operate the hand lever several times to allow the shoes to settle.

Once the assembly is reinstated, adjust the brakes following the procedures described earlier.

Wheels

Wheels should be fitted whose permitted load is appropriate for a caravan's maximum technically permissible laden mass (MTPLM) – previously called maximum allowable weight. Since a caravan's weight is shared by two wheels (four in the case of a twin axle model), the MTPLM should be divided by two before making a check with the maximum load rating stamped on the wheel. The division would be by four in the case of a twin axle model.

Wheel fixings

As regards the means of attachment, the fixings that hold a wheel in place are either nuts or bolts. The latter are now standard, presumably on the basis of production cost. But irrespective of the *type* of fixing employed, it is very important that its shoulder profile matches the seat formed in the wheel. This is important. The recess for the fixing, referred to as a 'seat', is not standard and there are a number of variations. It is critical that the surfaces mate exactly.

Moreover when a fixing is tightened on a steel wheel, it will start to deform the seating and the metal has a natural springiness which helps to grip on to the shoulder of the fixing. Provided the fixing isn't over-tightened – which would lead to damage – this grip helps to hold the wheel securely.

51

The shoulder profile on a wheel fixing must exactly match the seat in the wheel.

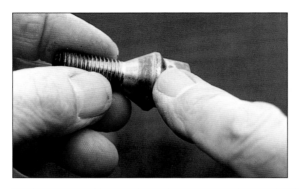

Graduated settings on a torque wrench are checked as the adjusting knob on the end of the lever is rotated.

Threads on fixings

Nowadays, caravan wheels are usually held in place by a threaded bolt and it is advisable to brush the threads periodically to remove dust. The same is recommended for the threads on studs. However, the application of a film of grease is not recommended because a torque setting to denote the tightness needed for a fixing is usually quoted on the presumption that its threads are dry.

Furthermore, grease on the threads might contribute to premature loosening and subsequent wheel loss.

The same reactive effect cannot be achieved by an alloy wheel which is more rigid than steel. This is why the wheel fixings have to be tighter. Incidentally if you decide to have alloy wheels fitted, enquire if different fixings will be needed to match the seats. There have been instances where this has been overlooked.

Wheel trims

Since the shoulders on the fixings need to mate in close register with the wheel seats, it is bad practice to introduce *anything* between these two surfaces. In clear disregard of this requirement, some caravan manufacturers recently introduced bridging brackets that are fastened under two wheel bolts. The brackets include a threaded central hole for securing plastic wheel embellishers. The system is not satisfactory. Nor, for that matter are many wheel embellishers. Most end their life on roadside verges and their unexpected break for freedom is a danger to pedestrians, cyclists and other vehicles. A well-designed wheel will be attractive enough not to need a clip-on plastic cover, but embellishers are commonplace and it is wise to secure them by adding plastic tape ties available from DIY and auto stores.

The Safety Band system from Tyron prevents a punctured tyre from falling into the well of the wheel and pulling away from the rims.

Wheel and tyre matching

Bear in mind that there's a relationship between a wheel pattern and the type of tyre fitted. For example, a tubeless tyre must be matched with a wheel having a 'safety rim'; this is specifically designed to achieve the air-tight junction required. So you must insist when buying a spare wheel that it is identical in every respect to the types already on your caravan.

On many caravans over fifteen years old, the wheels do not have safety rims and cannot be used with a tubeless tyre. However, it is often permissible to fit a tubeless tyre together with an inner tube. The suitability of the matching arrangement should be checked with a tyre dealer.

Safety bands

Most wheels are made with a deep well and this can become a problem if you have a serious puncture. The edges of the tyre can slide into the well, which means they lose contact with the rim of the wheel. The result is that the wheel rim itself then rolls on the road surface, whereupon the caravan can slide about through lack of friction.

To overcome the problem, many people have a well-fitting collar fitted and the Tyron Safety Band is one of the best-known examples. In the event of a sudden puncture, this prevents a tyre dropping into the well and pulling away from the rim. In consequence, tyre rubber remains in contact with the road instead of the metal of the wheel rim. A degree of road holding is thus maintained while the outfit is slowed down.

Wheel braces

For years, the brace provided with a caravan (or a car) was hopelessly inadequate for removing a wheel by the roadside. In 1988 things improved when to achieve National Caravan Council Approval, one of the checking criteria was that manufacturers should include a satisfactory wheel brace.

In practice the word 'satisfactory' is vague and you often find that a tyre fitter has over-tightened the fixings. Accordingly it is wise to purchase a telescopic wheel wrench which is sold with sockets to suit four different sizes of fixings. The sockets thus suit both the car as well as the caravan and an 'extending bar' wrench affords excellent leverage for fixing removal. However, a calibrated torque wrench is always needed

Changing a wheel

1. Lower the jockey wheel, apply the caravan brake firmly, then chock the wheel on the opposite side; slightly loosen the wheel fixings.

2. Ensure all the corner steadies are raised.

3. Locate the jack; a scissor type is compact enough to slide underneath.

4. The caravan is raised and an axle stand inserted. Then the caravan is lowered so the axle rests in the cradle of the stand. Finally, lower the corner steadies to provide stability.

5. The fixings are now fully loosened and withdrawn; the wheel is removed.

Wheel brace

A telescopic wheel wrench is sold with sockets to suit four different sizes of fixings, and is suitable for use on a car or caravan.

Roadside wheel changing is very different from wheel changing in the safety of a service centre.

The photographs above show procedure, on the presumption that an axle stand is available to achieve better stability than you can achieve with a jack alone. By the roadside, you would need to use the levelling blocks normally carried in your caravan instead. Equally there might be roadside debris to help with chocking. Every possible precaution *must* be taken to keep the 'van stable and to ensure that you are safe from passing vehicles. Hence it is very important that you only jack up a caravan by the roadside when it remains hitched to the towcar. Shock waves from passing vehicles can rock a caravan off its jack. The whole wheel-change operation should be completed as hastily as possible. Under no circumstances crawl under the 'van.

Having completed the tasks shown in the sequence illustrations, wheel replacement involves the following:

■ Make sure the brake drum presents a clean, flat surface.
■ Centre the wheel by doing up the fixings by hand.
■ Tighten further using a brace, but watch jack stability as you do it.
■ Raise corner steadies; remove axle stands.
■ Lower the caravan to the road surface; remove jack.
■ Tighten the fixings further in the order north, south, east, west – or by the clock face – 12, 6, 3, 9 o'clock positions.
■ Finally set the tightness with a torque wrench.

In a remote roadside breakdown when a torque wrench is unavailable, use the brace, bearing in mind that you should exert effort, but that the operation should not be seen as a tough test. If using a telescopic wrench in particular, it is certainly possible for some athletic men or women to over-tighten the fixings and to cause wheel damage.

Having made an assessment of tightness, proceed immediately to a garage to have the torque checked. Experts then advise that this setting is re-checked again after either thirty miles or thirty minutes driving.

Fitting an AL-KO Kober spare wheel carrier

1. The caravan must be safely elevated. This is critical.

2. Components are assembled using normal spanners.

3. Before installation, make sure the telescopic tubes are well greased.

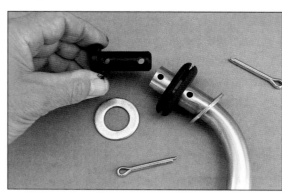

4. Dummy run – the chassis attachment components are checked.

5. A rubber grommet is inserted into the pre-punched hole in the chassis.

6. The fixed end of the carrier is offered-up and fastened into place.

AL-KO Kober spare wheel carrier

The small nuts on the spare wheel carrier will be tight to do up and will feel as if they are cross-threaded. This is not the case. The threads are intentionally deformed to achieve a tighter grip. This prevents them from shaking loose while travelling.

when replacing a wheel to ensure the fixings have been tightened correctly.

Tightness of fixings

Also safety-relevant is the issue of wheel fixing tightness. There have been a number of instances where wheels have become detached from caravans and a similar problem is also well-known by drivers of goods vehicles. As a rule this seems to happen more often to a near-side wheel, i.e. one which revolves in the same direction as the loosening direction of a wheel nut.

Research has not produced conclusive evidence why this happens but the need to have the fixings tightened to the appropriate torque setting is indisputable.

- If the fixing is not tight enough, it can shake loose and the wheel can come off.
- If the fixing is too tight, the seating on the wheel can get damaged and this can again lead to the loss of a wheel.
- The correct tightness is most important and this can only be checked by using a torque wrench whose calibration is verified regularly.

Check the settings recommended for *your caravan* in its handbook. Typical settings are detailed in the box opposite.

Spare wheel

This is an essential item which is not provided with many caravans at the time of purchase. The

7. The spare is held to the double rails using a large spigot.

8. The carrier is rested on the ground and checked.

Damaged and faulty wheels

■ A sudden loss of air from a tyre can occur if a rim is damaged – rims are often distorted after collisions with kerbs.
■ The fixing holes on wheels also get enlarged if a caravan is frequently over-laden.
■ Sometimes faults develop in wheels as a result of poor manufacture.

On the last point, one type of Delachaux wheels fitted to Castleton and Vanroyce caravans in the early 1990s developed faults. All wheels manufactured in 1990, 1991 and Jan/Feb of 1992, and bearing the code 4½Jx13FH/4+27C/CD 034 were subject to a recall. These units have been found to develop a small pin hole that leads to a fatigue crack – which can subsequently lead to unexpected tyre deflation.

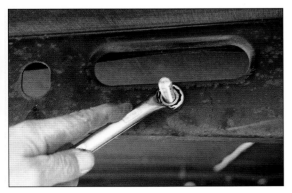

9. A locking bolt for the main securing nut is fitted to the chassis.

10. The carrier is now raised and the plastic securing wheel is fitted in place.

importance of obtaining a matching spare has already been emphasised and the suggestion that a suitable alternative can be found at a car breakers is ill-founded.

Methods of carrying a spare vary. Some manufacturers e.g. Lunar, have made stowage provision in the front locker, although nose weight needs checking carefully if this location is adopted. Avondale has developed an under-floor wheel pan which is accessed from inside the 'van. Vanmaster has included a sliding drawer system accessed from outside. One well-known manufacturer took the ill-advised decision to mount the spare on the rear wall of the caravan which can lead to instability problems. The majority of caravans, however, are fitted with an under-floor carrier.

Wheel carriers have been developed by AL-KO Kober and BCA Leisure. In addition, Safe and Secure Products market the Dart carrier.

In general a carrier uses a telescopic arrangement so that it can be slid out from underneath the caravan. This is fine – *as long as* the tubes are kept well greased. If overlooked, the tubes soon seize up completely.

Carriers can be fitted to many caravans built on a modern lightweight chassis and the photographs above show a DIY installation.

Typical torque settings

Steel wheels

Nuts on AL-KO Kober products – 8.0kg/m (60lb/ft)
Nuts on Ambergate and CI products – 9.0kg/m (65lb/ft)
Bolts on AL-KO Kober products – 9.0kg/m (65lb/ft)

Alloy wheels

Bolts – 10.0kg/m (70lb/ft)

Tightening order

Having confirmed that the bearing surface on a brake drum is clean, the wheel should then be offered-up and the fixings tightened progressively in a set order as follows:

Wheels with four fixings
Use the visual picture of North, South, East, West; if you prefer the clock face, this is 12, 6, 3 and 9.

Wheels with five fixings
Tighten each opposite nut in succession.

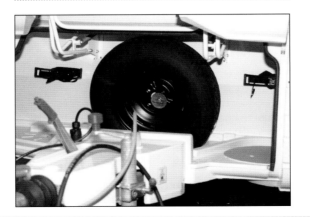

Locating a spare wheel in a forward locker is very convenient, but it must not cause excessive nose weight.

Tyres

Caravan tyres are safety-critical items and are manufactured to exacting European standards. The user will also be prosecuted if the tyres are faulty as explained in the box on the left.

Tyre life

Bearing in mind that in the case of most caravans, the entire weight has to be born on *two* wheels, the assertion is often made that life is much easier for tyres fitted to cars. Also caravans tend to remain stationary for longer periods and this places demands on the tyres. So caravan tyres nearly always need replacing due to the walls deteriorating; the tread, in contrast, can look scarcely worn.

Consequently, the serviceability of caravan tyres should not be judged solely on tread depth. Specialists state that you should never use tyres on a caravan which are more than seven years old. They point out that tyres more than five years old are due for replacement; their deterioration by then will be significant, irrespective of tread depth.

Tyre care

Deterioration occurs when a caravan is stationary for prolonged periods, and it undoubtedly helps to relieve the tyres by supporting the 'van on axle stands. If these provide full support, removal of the caravan's wheels for storage in a place away from sunlight is particularly helpful. Provided the strategy doesn't infringe the conditions of an insurance policy, this precautionary measure will afford a degree of security as well.

Alternatively, it helps if the caravan is periodically moved a short distance – either forwards or backwards. This ensures that different parts of the tyre wall are distended during the period of storage.

Keep a constant check on tyres too, looking at both the side walls as well as the tread. An inspection lamp will be helpful when checking the inner face. Cuts, bulges and penetrating flints can lead to a sudden loss of air, and a driver is legally obliged to ensure the tyres are sound. However, remember that age-related failure is often sudden and there might not be warning signs of a pending problem.

Pressure check

Handbooks will indicate the pressures needed for the tyres installed and these should be checked frequently. A reliable dial-type gauge is recommended.

Remember that tyre pressures should be checked when the tyre is cold. The pressure will rise when the vehicle is used and this is taken into account when a 'cold pressure' reading is specified by a manufacturer. Do *not* make adjustments for hot conditions or sustained fast towing situations.

Commercial tyres

Caravans are either fitted with car or commercial tyres. However, recently, manufacturers have been more inclined to fit the latter type; their higher permitted pressures offer the potential to carry larger loads.

A problem associated with this is a tendency to recommend the same inflation pressure for all the caravans in a particular range and this has been the subject of investigation by The Caravan Club. When a caravan with a substantial MTPLM (maximum technically permissible laden mass, formerly referred to as the maximum authorised weight), is towed with its tyres inflated to a high pressure, the combination might be fine. But if the same tyre at the same pressure is specified for a model with a *much lower* MTPLM, there's a risk of the caravan suffering from an excessively bumpy ride.

As a result of problems reported by members, The Caravan Club sought the support of the National Caravan Council after which caravan manufacturers were urged to be more model-specific when quoting tyre pressures. This appeal was made in 1996 so handbook information should now be better in this respect.

Load and speed limits

Tyres are built to cope with different load limits and different maximum speeds. On modern tyres, a load index figure appears in the coding moulded on the wall and reference to a load index table reveals the maximum load-carrying performance applicable when the vehicle is driven at the maximum speed rating. The diagram opposite shows what the moulded rubber markings on the side wall signify.

Having identified the load limit figure, read the kg limit from the Load Index table opposite and then double it for a single axle caravan (multiply by four for a twin axle 'van). Then compare this with the manufacturer's quoted maximum technically permissible laden mass (previously referred to as Maximum Authorised Weight) to ensure the carrying capacity of the tyre exceeds that of the caravan's MTPLM (formerly MAW). Bear in mind that tyres are only one element contributing to a caravan's quoted MTPLM. Chassis and suspension design are other elements.

In certain circumstances, for maximum towing speeds not exceeding 62mph (100km/h), e.g. in the UK where the statutory speed limit is 60mph, bonus loads may be applied to tyres. However, in the interest of maximising safety margins, it is recommended that bonus loads are not taken into consideration for tyre selection purposes.

As regards speed ratings, alphabetical designations have been used for a number of years to indicate the maximum speed at which a tyre can carry the load calculated from the Load Index table. Speed ratings in the range applicable to caravans are listed below with the most commonly used ratings shown in italic:

J = 62mph (100km/h)
K = 68mph (110km/h)
L = 75mph (120km/h)

M = 81mph (130km/h)
N = 88mph (140km/h)
P = 94mph (150km/h)
Q = 100mph (160km/h)
R = 105mph (170km/h)
S = 113mph (180km/h)
T = 118mph (190km/h)

Since the maximum towing speed limit in Britain is 60mph on motorways, it might seem logical to purchase a 'J' rated tyre. However, if you take your caravan to France, it is illegal to have a rating lower than the maximum permitted speed (81mph on many of the motorways) even if you have no intention of towing at anywhere near that speed. So if you intend towing abroad, a tyre with a speed rating of 'M' or higher is needed.

Buying replacement tyres

When buying new tyres, make sure they are:
• the correct size
• the correct type
• of the appropriate speed rating
• of the appropriate load rating.

Even though commercial tyres offer higher load-carrying possibilities, switching from car-type tyres has a number of implications. The potential for increased tyre pressures might present problems.

Load Index Table

Load Index	Kg	Load Index	Kg	Load Index	Kg	Load Index	Kg
60	250	71	345	82	475	93	650
61	257	72	355	83	487	94	670
62	265	73	365	84	500	95	690
63	272	74	375	85	515	96	710
64	280	75	387	86	530	97	730
65	290	76	400	87	545	98	750
66	300	77	412	88	560	99	775
67	307	78	425	89	580	100	800
68	315	79	437	90	600	101	825
69	325	80	450	91	615	102	850
70	335	81	462	92	630	103	875

Equally, switching to a larger sized tyre in the hope of increasing the loading limit is unwise since there might be insufficient room under the wheel arch. For example, there must be at least 30mm (1¾₆in) of free space at all extremes of wheel movement – and this could be unachievable if a larger tyre is fitted. In other words before making a change to the type of tyre fitted, seek the advice of the caravan clubs, a tyre specialist or the British Rubber Manufacturers' Association.

Technical Tip

The recommended pressures for caravan tyres vary quite considerably. For instance, models running on car tyres might have a typical pressure quoted in the handbook of around 33psi (e.g. the 1998 Avondale Leda Chiltern) whereas models running on commercial tyres might require a pressure of 52psi (e.g. the 1998 Avondale Leda Pentland). So reference to the handbook is important and if this has 'gone missing' when a caravan is purchased second-hand, the Caravan Clubs can often advise members about correct tyre pressures.

BRMA CAR TYRE SIDEWALL DRAWING

Car tyre markings
(Reproduced with permission of the British Rubber Manufacturers' Association).

SIZE DESIGNATION
NOMINAL SECTION WIDTH (mm) ASPECT RATIO RIM DIAMETER (INCHES)

SERVICE DESCRIPTION
LOAD INDEX SPEED SYMBOL

165/70R13 79T

RADIAL

MADE IN GREAT BRITAIN

REINFORCED

* LOAD AND PRESSURE REQUIREMENT

MAX. LOAD 437 kg (963 lbs) MAX. PRESSURE 300 kPa (44 psi)

REINFORCED WHERE APPLICABLE

COMMERCIAL NAME OR IDENTITY

"TRADE NAME" "KP 200"

DENOTES TYPE OF CONSTRUCTION

ASPECT RATIO IS THE TYRE SECTION HEIGHT EXPRESSED AS A PERCENTAGE OF THE SECTION WIDTH

COUNTRY OF MANUFACTURE

TREADWEAR 160 TRACTION A TEMPERATURE B

MANUFACTURERS NAME OR BRAND NAME

PLIES SIDEWALL 2 RAYON 2 STEEL PLIES TREAD 2 RAYON

DATA CODE

(E11) 021234

DOT ABC DEF 343

* UNIFORM TYRE QUALITY GRADING REQUIRED BY USA CUSTOMER INFORMATION REGULATIONS

* NORTH AMERICAN DEPARTMENT OF TRANSPORTATION COMPLIANCE SYMBOL

TUBELESS

TYRE CONSTRUCTION DETAILS

M&S

LOCATION OF TREAD WEAR INDICATORS (MARKINGS VARY WITH MANUFACTURER)

TWI

* TYRE CONSTRUCTION DETAILS

TUBELESS OR TUBE TYPE (NB. IF NEITHER IS SHOWN A TUBE MUST BE FITTED)

ECE TYPE APPROVAL MARK AND NUMBER. THE ALTERNATIVE EEC APPROVAL MARK IS [e11]

TYRES SPECIFICALLY DESIGNED FOR MUD AND SNOW (WINTER)

* NORTH AMERICAN TYRE IDENTIFICATION NUMBER

*Not applicable in the UK and Europe

Exterior body maintenance

Cleaning techniques, window replacement, dealing with delamination and locating leaks are subjects discussed in this chapter. Before jobs like this can be tackled, however, it is important to understand how a caravan is constructed.

When lighter chassis were developed around 1980, their radical new designs went hand-in-hand with changes in body construction. In fact the interplay between a chassis and its accompanying composite floor panel makes a critical contribution to the total structure.

Previously, the heavy type of chassis used for a caravan was a self-sufficient foundation; the ply and timber joists that sat on top were merely a rudimentary form of staging. Now there is interdependency so that both floor and chassis work together to provide rigidity. Strength is thus achieved in a different way, and yet the total weight of the two elements is considerably less than it has previously been.

Constructional features

The floor section, side walls, front walls, rear walls and roof are all built differently – a fact which has implications for both maintenance and repair work.

Floor panels

On the older type of chassis, longitudinal timber joists support a panel of treated plywood – typically 13mm (½in) ply. The advantage of this is there's little to give trouble. However, this construction is quite heavy and lacks thermal insulation – which means you get cold feet when caravanning in winter. Some DIY owners improve this shortcoming by glueing block polystyrene between the joists. A product like Jablite, used in the building industry for floor insulation and available from builders' merchants, is a popular product for this upgrading work.

In contrast, the floor panel fitted to a lighter chassis is completely different in construction. It has no supporting joists and strength is achieved by using a prefabricated composite panel instead. This comprises a three-layer 'sandwich' in which two layers of thin, treated plywood (typically 5mm ³⁄₁₆in) are bonded to an insulating material in the middle. The core often consists of styrofoam insulation with timber battens around the perimeter and strengthening wooden cross-members as well. When the styrofoam and the reinforcing timbers are bonded to the plywood with special adhesive, the resulting composite board has remarkable strength.

The advantages are that the floor is light, strong, and well insulated. A disadvantage, however, is that strength is seriously impaired if the bond between the ply and the core material starts to fail. Dealing with 'delamination', as this condition is known, receives attention later in the chapter.

Side walls

The traditional way to build a caravan is to start by constructing a skeleton framework using timber struts. This is clad on the outside with aluminium sheet, and finished on the inside with faced hardboard or thin pre-decorated plywood. An insulation material is fitted in the void between the inner and outer skins. However, if a fibre-glass 'quilt' or 'Rockwool' insulant is used, it tends to slump in the void, leaving cold spots. More rigid products like block polystyrene are preferred.

Some manufacturers still adopt this form of construction, particularly low volume specialists who build high quality models e.g. Carlight Caravans. However, the majority of manufacturers now use prefabricated bonded panels for the side walls and these are formed in an industrial press just like the bonded floor sections.

The difference from floor panels, however, relates to the materials used for the 'sandwich'. The interior surface is 3mm decorative ply, the core is often polystyrene, and the outer surface is usually sheet aluminium. Wooden battens will be

58

Some high quality caravans like the Carlight are still constructed traditionally using a skeleton framework constructed in wood.

(Photograph courtesy of Carlight Caravans)

To achieve accuracy in construction, the traditionally built wall framework of a Buccaneer caravan was assembled in a jig.

(Photograph courtesy of Andrew Jenkinson)

Most caravan side walls are now made using prefabricated composite bonded sections.

used within the sandwich as well, especially around apertures like windows or locker openings, to provide a strengthening surround. The wood provides a solid framework which is necessary when fitting hinges, catches and so on.

Some manufacturers bond small galvanised sheets at key points in the sandwich to provide fixing points for furniture; others insert additional timbers. These are important because rivets and self-tapping screws would not achieve a secure hold in the thin decorative ply that faces the interior part of the side walls. Similarly, timber strengthening battens are built into the core to reinforce the overall rigidity of the panel.

Front and rear walls

Although the front and rear walls are sometimes built with the same type of bonded board used for the side walls, most are constructed using a ply and softwood framework. This provides a base on which to mount moulded panels, which in turn gives a particular model a distinctive appearance. The shapely front and rear sections are an undoubted improvement over the featureless side walls.

Two types of material are used for these front and rear panels as discussed later.

Roofs

In most caravans, the roof is constructed with a framework of wooden strutting and shaped plywood formers. The structure is often assembled in a jig before being offered up. Thin decorative 3mm ply may be used to line the ceiling although faced

Exterior body maintenance

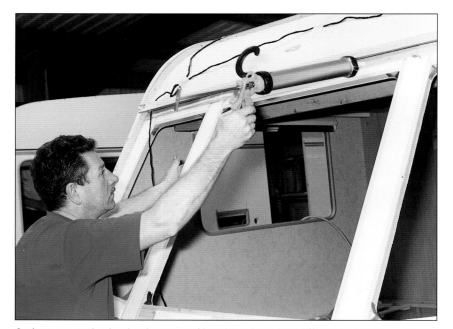

Sealants are used to bond and waterproof junction points where different body sections are joined together.

A roof structure is made using a timber framework that will often be assembled in a jig.
(Photograph courtesy of Andrew Jenkinson)

Roofs are usually filled with a fibre-glass wool insulant and then capped with either aluminium sheet or a GRP moulding.

hardboard is sometimes preferred because its flexibility will negotiate curved sections more readily.

On the outside, sheet aluminium is the most common cladding material although some manufacturers fit one-piece glass reinforced plastic (GRP) roof panels instead, e.g. Avondale.

Some caravan roofs are built with flat sections whereas others adopt the inverted 'boat' style where a ridge runs longitudinally along the centre. This helps to shed water more effectively on account of the pitch.

The traditional 'lantern-style' roof in which a raised section is bordered by small roof-light windows, is now only used in Carlight caravans. In fact the Company holds this as a registered design.

Doors and windows

Few owners realise that the door on their caravan is unlikely to have been made by the caravan manufacturer. Most doors are provided by specialists who supply the caravan industry with units to suit their particular models.

Windows, similarly, are items that are 'bought-in'. At one time a window comprised an aluminium frame and a piece of glass. In 1978, however, it became illegal to fit 'non-safety' glass. Moulded acrylic windows which fulfilled this requirement seemed an obvious answer – and eliminated the need for an aluminium frame fitted with rubber weather strips. 'Plastic' windows were instantly adopted and have been used ever since.

At first, moulded acrylic windows were single section panels and these were fitted to many models built in the early 1980s. However, double-glazed versions were a more logical choice in view of the greater level of insulation being achieved by using bonded wall panels. So in spite of their considerable cost, double-glazed units became the standard fitment.

Materials

Not only is it helpful if you know how your caravan is constructed, it is also useful to differentiate between the materials used. This is important if damage occurs and a repair is needed.

Sheet aluminium

When sandwich construction first arrived, it was found that timber battens within the core of a wall panel could be seen on the side elevations if you looked closely at a caravan. To hide this, manufacturers used aluminium sheet that had a surface texture. Rippled, pimpled and stucco surface finishes are common examples and if an outside wall gets dented, you cannot replicate the appearance if a body repair filler is used.

Some years later, fabrication techniques improved and some manufacturers e.g. Avondale and Compass, reverted to plain aluminium again.

Many others have since followed and textured surfaces seem to be going out of fashion.

Glass reinforced plastic sheet (GRP)

When the technique of manufacturing thin glass reinforced plastic (GRP) sheet was mastered, this provided an alternative to aluminium cladding. The material is thin and so flexible that it is supplied on a roll. When the Abbey Domino was launched in 1995 with its GRP impact-resistant sidewalls, a new chapter in construction was opened.

Other models like the Abbey Chess and Solitaire have followed, but the use of aluminium sheet still predominates in caravan construction. It is worth noting that the GRP alternative is more widely used by manufacturers of coachbuilt motorcaravans such as Auto-Sleepers, Bessacarr and Swift.

One disadvantage with sheet GRP is that it lacks the high gloss finish of painted aluminium. On the other hand, dented aluminium usually involves major repair work because large areas have to be overlaid with a completely new sheet. In contrast, damaged GRP can often be repaired using conventional car bodywork fillers. This is an important benefit and it will be surprising if this cladding material does not gain greater acceptance in the future.

Moulded glass reinforced plastic

Glass reinforced plastic, or 'fibre glass' as it is affectionately known, is a long established material used in the construction of cars, boats, light aircraft – and caravans. Note that in this application, we are referring to *moulded* GRP sections as opposed to the thin, flat, flexible GRP sheet mentioned above.

When a contoured panel is built by an experienced laminator using a well-finished mould,

The side walls of the Abbey Domino are clad in GRP impact-resistant sheet.

the final product will not only look smart; it will also give exceptional service. Most better-quality caravans have moulded panels on both the front and rear. Some caravans, like recent Bessacarr models, often have GRP side skirts and chassis cover-fairings, too.

The main feature is ease of repair. Many specialists can undertake GRP repair work and DIY owners often achieve smart results as well. This is discussed later in the chapter.

Acrylic-capped ABS

Acrylonitrile-butadiene-styrene is a tongue twister by anyone's standards; so this type of plastic is more commonly referred to as 'ABS'. Versions of ABS often have a matt finish and are used for items like wheel arch embellishers. A similar material is used for vehicle bumpers, wing mirrors

The one-piece rear panel on this model is made from GRP, which has the advantage of being easily repairable.

The rear of this caravan is built using a bonded panel for the upper part and a GRP moulding for the lower section.

Identifying ABS and GRP

These distinctive types of plastic used for body panels are easy to identify. The rear surface of ABS and acrylic-capped ABS panels is very smooth. In contrast, the rear of a GRP panel has a roughened surface. On closer inspection you can often see the strands of glass used as the reinforcing binder in the lamination. The inside surfaces of items like locker doors, side skirts and front fairings are therefore the 'give-away' feature.

There is just one exception. On the gas locker doors of Vanroyce caravans, two GRP mouldings are bonded back-to-back in order to provide an enhanced appearance on the inside of the doors as well. Close inspection, however, together with the greater rigidity of the product, reveals that two GRP mouldings have been used.

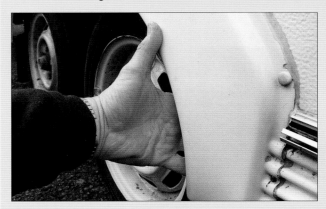

The inner surface of this wheel arch cover is smooth, confirming that it is made from ABS plastic.

The roughened surface on the inside face of this locker door indicates that the component is moulded using GRP.

and a host of other automotive accessories.

By capping the material with a coating of acrylic, the surface finish is much shinier and this is more suitable for caravan front and rear panels. Equally, the material is also used for bathroom cabinets, washbasins and even moulded shower cubicles.

On caravans built a decade or more ago, it is sometimes found that rainwater has penetrated the exterior body panels, and capping and blisters have formed. Subsequently there may be localised areas where the shiny coating chips away. This defacement is one of the shortcomings and it appears that there is no permanent cure.

Repairing cracks in acrylic-capped ABS is another matter of concern. For a number of years, it has been believed that when an acrylic-capped ABS front panel of a caravan receives damage, the entire section will have to be replaced. This can come as a great shock to an owner who has merely split a small part of the front underskirt on a high kerb. Car owners have similar shocks when they find how much it costs to replace a damaged ABS bumper; and so do motorcyclists whose race-replica bikes sustain a small crack in a fairing.

In response to this, chemists have been working on plastic repair kits and these have recently become available. It is too early to say how successful a repair will be on the thin acrylic-capped panels used on caravans. One service centre, West Riding Leisure of Huddersfield, developed expertise in ABS repair work some time

ago, but most caravan service centres still prefer to replace an entire panel. It is certainly true that to date, few service engineers have had an opportunity to receive training in ABS repair procedures.

Sealants and mastics

The ability of a caravan to resist weather damage is largely dependent on the sealants used in its construction. An ever-present problem is the fact that different materials expand and contract at different rates in different temperatures. Thermal stresses are a potential threat.

Then there are mechanical stresses – a caravan is subjected to relentless movements when towed along bumpy roads. So the sealants selected to bridge the junctions between adjoining materials have to permit flexion without loss of adhesion or self-destruction. It's a tall order.

Products are classified into a number of types depending on their chemical formulation and the method of use. Types include:

- Non-drying bedding sealants supplied in cartridge form for injection from a dispenser gun, e.g. Hodgson Phoenix Seamseal.
- Butyl rubber sealant in tape form, supplied with a backing strip for easier handling, e.g. Caraseal 303.
- Silicone-based sealant supplied in cartridge form for sealing joints around caravan wash basins and shower cubicles, e.g. Caraseal SC1.

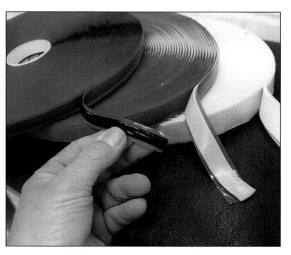

The butyl sealants in ribbon form from Carafax create an instantaneous grip at the junction where components are joined.

- Polyurethane-based adhesives which create a strong, waterproof elastic bond as well as acting as sealants – usually supplied in cartridge form, e.g. Sikaflex 221.

A problem to bear in mind is that the higher the strength of a product in terms of its bonding capacity, the lower the likelihood of it having flexibility. Conversely high flexibility is usually off-set by a lower level of bonding strength.

Notwithstanding this point, a product like Sikaflex 221 is used extensively throughout the automotive, boat and caravan industries because of its ability to resist differential movements, even when coupling two completely dissimilar materials. The latest car windscreens which lack a rubber surround, for example, are often glued into the opening of the metal shell using Sikaflex.

Where problems of leaking occur in caravan structures, these can be attributed to:

- bad design in the body construction;
- unsatisfactory surface preparation;
- bad workmanship when the sealant is applied
- wrong choice of sealant;
- the product drying out, becoming brittle and losing elasticity.

There is no doubt that leaks can be a problem in some caravans and the subject of sealants is of particular importance.

Routine cleaning

Inevitably a caravan gets dirty and if parked under a tree for a prolonged period it will be coated with algae and a fair share of bird droppings. Under some species of tree e.g. limes, the surface will also become coated with a sticky film.

When being towed, mud, grease and tar stains will spoil its appearance, too. Routine cleaning is a necessary chore.

Washing

Most owners resort to a bucket-and-sponge approach which is fine – but tedious. A high pressure hose fitted with an extension lance and a cleaning chemical dispenser makes much lighter work of the operation. But there are precautions to note.

The power of water should be carefully monitored since plastic decals can get damaged and – in extreme circumstances – a window can get broken. Remember, too, that the paint layer on some aluminium panels is surprisingly thin.

Also at risk are the sealants which provide a bedding for trim strips and other wall-mounted components. When ageing sealant loses its flexibility, the power of a water jet can blast pieces away. This is when the leaks are likely to start.

Provided you recognise these points, high pressure hoses are a great asset. Specialists who use these machines regularly advise you to:

- spray the cleaning chemical from the bottom and work upwards;
- use increased power for stubborn stains – but only where it is safe to do so;
- exercise caution around vents, windows, locker lids and the door;
- finally apply the cleaning chemical to the roof;
- rinse the entire surface with fresh water.

When parked for long spells under trees, a caravan soon accumulates stains, bird lime and algae deposits.

It is important not to get too close to trim strips or handles when using a pressure hose at a high setting.

Cleaning items

When adopting other cleaning techniques and applying polish, the following items are strongly recommended:

A hard compound rigid sponge is good for cleaning interior faced ply surfaces. These are often used by interior decorators.

A hard bristled brush is useful for cleaning wheels and around the coupling.

A long handled cranked brush sold for painting the back of radiators is ideal for agitating liquid cleaning chemicals when applied around fittings.

Open-weave cloth made from 100% cotton stock. For polishing, avoid material that contains lint; items of clothing like old T-shirts are not recommended for this reason.

When tackling a major clean, start with the really dirty jobs and then move to the finishing operations. For instance, in a full schedule, the recommended order is:

1. Clean the wheels and tyres.
2. Clean the door and locker shuts.
3. Remove individual tar spots.
4. Remove stubborn stains and black streaks.
5. Apply shampoo to the body.
6. Polish sections of the body.
7. Polish the glass.
8. Apply cleaner to black plastic items.
9. Apply tyre dressing.

Two specialists who market a number of cleaners particularly suitable for the different materials used in caravan construction are Auto Glym and Mer. Caravans have particular problems of their own and disfiguring black streaks are an example – as the box below explains.

When following the order of cleaning recommended, note that there are plenty of proprietary products for wheel cleaning e.g. Mer Alloy Wheel and General Wheel Cleaner. Equally

When Auto Glym Engine Cleaner is applied to algae-coated and black-streaked trim strips, it should be agitated with a brush before rinsing off.

there are tar removal and tyre refurbishment treatments, but whereas this part of a cleaning operation is done first, application of a tyre dressing should be left until last.

Around the body generally, Auto Glym Caravan Cleaner is very effective for removing algae from trim strips and bird lime marks. Once applied, the cleaning action should be accelerated by using the cranked brush mentioned earlier to agitate the chemical. When the deposits are shifted, rinse off with clean water.

The application of a shampoo conditioner is recommended next, but when it is time to rinse away the suds, avoid using a high pressure hose. This has the effect of 'bouncing off' the conditioning film that most shampoos leave after application. Gentle flooding on aluminium panels will also enable some conditioners to electrostatically bond to the surface, thus affording protection.

Windows should be tackled next and there are many cleaners that are suitable on the glass units fitted to older caravans. Acrylic windows are different. These 'plastic' windows are easily scratched and the first task is to ensure that preceding shampoo and rinse work has removed all the dirt and dust. Then you can apply a product specially formulated for plastic windows such as Auto Glym Fast Glass. This is sprayed on to the window and then promptly spread across the surface with a piece of paper kitchen roll. In equal haste it should be removed with another piece of clean kitchen roll. The cleaning fluid mustn't be allowed to dry – so avoid doing this job in direct sunshine.

As regards polishing work, it is best to leave patterned aluminium, such as a stucco surface finish, with the sheen left by the shampoo. The point is that some paints applied to aluminium can be lifted by polishes. This is not the case on

Stain removal

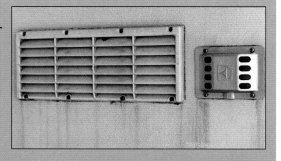

Black carbon stains that form below caravan guttering, ventilators and other wall-mounted fittings can be successfully removed with Auto Glym Caravan Cleaner. The container has a piston dispenser so that stained areas can be sprayed with the chemical. It should then be agitated with a brush or sponge and finally rinsed off with clean water. For even worse streaks use Auto Glym Engine Cleaner. In addition to its function cleaning engines, the product is especially good for removing grease from tyres and cleaning plastic covers, discoloured vents, exhaust marks from the tow car, caravan ovens, barbecue equipment and even stains on the outside of saucepans.

Another cleaning compound specially formulated to deal with carbon stains is Camco Black Streak Remover. This American product is now available in this country and you will find it stocked at leading Caravan Accessory Specialists.

A proprietary vehicle polish is applied to this GRP locker door to achieve a long-lasting shine.

A number of rubber treatments are available for cleaning and re-establishing the flexibility of rubber seals.

Technical tip

There are numerous different materials used externally on caravans and a prodigious array of different cleaning compounds, too. As a general tip, always conduct a preliminary check by applying a product to a small area first – using a trial section which is out of the immediate line of vision. This will confirm beyond doubt that there are no unfavourable reactions with the material being cleaned or revitalised.

moulded GRP or acrylic-capped ABS and a coat of polish will achieve protection that may last for six months or more.

Always take note of product instructions and when applying a polish, be careful to keep it from black plastic components like door handles and rubber seals around the windows. The black sheen on plastic door handles can be revived with a product like Auto Glym Bumper Care or Mer Bumper & External Vinyl Cleaning Gel and this is applied after the polishing is complete. There are also rubber-care products intended for maintaining the cleanliness and flexibility of window seals.

To finish the task, a final application of a tyre treatment like Auto Glym Tyre Conditioner completes the valet. Rubber paints that were once used are less popular nowadays. Tyre conditioner is sprayed on to the rubber and its white streaks initially look unpleasant, but these mustn't be touched and the conditioner is merely left to dry for ten to fifteen minutes. Later, the revived surface makes a tyre look like new again.

Reviving dulled GRP and acrylics

Over a period of years, it is not unusual for moulded GRP and acrylic panels to lose their sheen. A point is reached when polish doesn't revive the appearance and many cutting compounds are far too abrasive.

A product that will revive a dulled finish very successfully is Farécla Caravan Pride Colour Restorer. This was introduced to the caravan market in early 1999 but the product is a long-established favourite in the marine industry, albeit under the name of 'Boat Pride Colour Restorer'.

The product is a standard grade finishing paste and whereas a professional would apply Colour Restorer using a slow-speed buffing machine whose pad had been liberally dampened with

water, the treatment can also be applied by hand. The procedure is:

- Use a damp rag and apply the Colour Restorer in straight backward and forward motions. Change direction quite regularly to ensure you achieve even coverage.
- It is important to keep the cloth damp. A plant spraying atomiser, available from Garden Centres, is very helpful here.
- Before final buffing, wipe away any residue of the compound – again using a damp cloth or damp sponge.
- The final buffing should be done with a clean, dry cloth.

Note that Farécla Caravan Pride Colour Restorer can sometimes be used on painted aluminium surfaces, but this should be checked on a small corner of a panel because the depth of paint is often extremely shallow.

If a GRP surface becomes dulled, it can be revived using an application of Farécla Caravan Pride Colour Restorer.

65

Window repair and replacement

One of the biggest disincentives to purchasing a pre-1978 caravan is the fact that if a window gets broken, it is unlikely to be repairable. Aluminium framed glass windows are no longer manufactured for caravans and the only source of a replacement is a specialist breakers.

Obtaining a more recent plastic window ought to be easier, but this can also be difficult if a caravan manufacturer has ceased trading. Once again, this may mean contact with a breakers, and Frank's of Luton stocks a wide range of second-hand windows.

Alternatively, EECO is a caravan window specialist whose service involves sending a carrier to collect the remnants of a broken window, and then making a replacement in the same colour and to the same pattern. Even at busy times, the new unit can be delivered in two or three weeks.

Apart from breakage, other problems include the formation of condensation between double glazed units and external surface scratching. Finding a permanent cure for the condensation problem is less easy, but before buying a costly replacement it is worth removing the window, withdrawing the tiny sealing plug and leaving the unit in a warm airing cupboard. When the condensate has dried, the plug is reinstated using a plastic-specific model-making adhesive.

In contrast, dealing with scratches is more certain of effecting a permanent cure.

Removing scratches in acrylic windows

Driving too close to hedgerows often leaves scratch marks on acrylic windows – but these can usually be removed. Anyone who has seen demonstrations at exhibitions by staff from Farécla will know that Caravan Pride Scratch Remover restores a high gloss surface to a scratched plastic window. This fine rubbing compound can be applied either with a slow-rotating buffing machine or by hand. Procedures are shown in the photographs below and important tips are given in the box on the facing page.

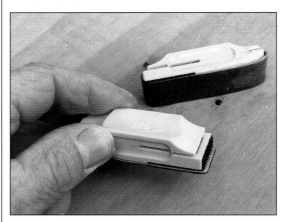

1. Deep scratches are normally removed by starting with 1200 grade wet-and-dry paper mounted on a small block. The water acts as a lubricant.

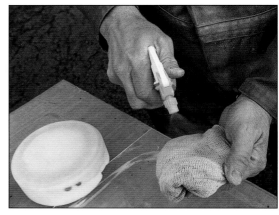

2. Use an open-weave cloth made from 100% cotton stock and ensure it is wet. A garden spray bottle is useful for delivering a fine mist to the rag.

3. Apply Scratch Remover over the entire surface and be meticulous about regularly re-applying a fresh mist of water to the surface from a spray bottle.

4. A machine is quicker but only use a purpose-made polisher. This revolves much more slowly than a drill with a mop attachment.

Handy tip – scratch removal

■ When using wet-and-dry paper on an acrylic window, don't use a circular action until the final polish. Rub in straight lines instead; six to eight in one direction, followed by the same number at right angles. If you see a fresh scratch, this technique allows you to identify which piece of abrasive paper caused the fresh mark. There's no need to work solely across the original scratch mark.

■ If the 1200 grade wet-and-dry paper starts to remove the scratches, continue with 1500 grade which is even finer. If it proves too fine, try a 1000 grade – or even 800 grade.

■ Remember to change the paper frequently or you will inflict new damage on the surface.

■ If a machine is used with a foam mop, water is critical and serves four functions:
  1. It keeps the cleaning compound out of the deep pores of the mop
  2. It keeps the acrylic surface cooler
  3. It acts as a lubricant
  4. It prolongs the life of the mop.

■ Whether the scratch is removed manually or by machine, the work should be completed using a clean rag, buffing up the surface using circular motions.

Removing and replacing an acrylic window

Replacing windows is quite an easy operation on most caravans. It is especially straightforward when the mounting is on a flat surface but more involved if the window is seated in a deep, moulded recess. In the latter case, the aluminium moulding that holds the unit has to be eased away from its seating. Some types of fully-flush window units are more difficult to deal with and you should seek advice on removal procedures from the manufacturer. The photographs below show a typical replacement operation.

1. An end cap often needs to be removed and the window centralising block fitted just below it must be detached. Be careful not to drop any tiny screws.

2. Window stays and fittings will need to be detached by undoing their self-tapping screws. All items will be transferred to the new replacement unit.

3. If the aluminium support strip needs pulling away from the wall to provide withdrawal space, remove the plastic insert and then undo the trim's retaining screws.

4. After easing the aluminium support strip away from the recess on this moulded front, a cracked window was then slid out of its channelling.

67

Moisture test meters
are fitted with a
battery. They usually
have two probes
which are offered up
to the interior ply of
a caravan at key
points – especially
around windows,
near light clusters, in
the vicinity of an
awning rail and so
on. If there is a
problem in the area
being checked, a
small current will
track through the
damp section from
one probe to the
other. The passage
of current activates a
series of graduated
warning lights which
indicate the
seriousness of the
problem.

Problems with damp

Caravans have suffered from leaks for years; this is not a new problem. Some of the problems were discussed in the earlier section on sealants and it is scarcely surprising that weak spots appear when a 'van is towed along bumpy country lanes; as the saying goes, 'prevention is better than cure'.

Checking for damp

Owners are strongly advised to have an annual damp test carried out on their caravan. Whilst this is normally included in a full service schedule, some caravan workshops will also conduct a damp test as an individual service item.

At a specialist service centre an owner is often given an owner is given skeleton drawings showing all 36 checking points where damp test meter readings are taken.

Inexpensive damp test meters are also being sold at DIY stores, and some owners carry this work out themselves. However, a few of the cheaper testers are far from reliable. If you try one on damp wooden fence posts in your garden, you can get a clue about its level of sensitivity.

A professional meter used at many service centres is from the Protimeter range – a Company that makes no secret of the fact that inexperienced users don't always understand the full diagnostic scope of the instruments. There's no doubt, damp testing might be best entrusted to staff at your service centre. In fact during a warranty period, this is essential.

The wisdom of arranging regular damp tests using a meter is indisputable, but it is also prudent to make periodic visual checks as well. For instance you can:
• remove the screws from ventilators and check the sealant is achieving a good bond;
• look carefully at surface-mounted grab handles which have more pull and push threat to their bedding sealant than anything else;
• look around road lamp fittings. This is a common point of water ingress, especially if a neoprene washer behind the lens starts to deteriorate;
• use your nose inside! A musty smell is always the 'give-away' that mould is developing in the damp behind the wall panels;

If you unscrew a vent, it will adhere firmly against the caravan if the bedding sealant is still flexible.

• check the route taken by water discharging from the front and rear slope of the roof on a dewy morning. A critical point is the horizontal trim strip above the windows which covers the join between moulded front (or rear) panels and the lower edge of the roof cladding material. If you see water disappearing behind this strip and not re-appearing underneath, it is a certain sign that water is draining via an attachment screw into the void

Check carefully around light fittings; water can penetrate the body when neoprene washers lose their resilience.

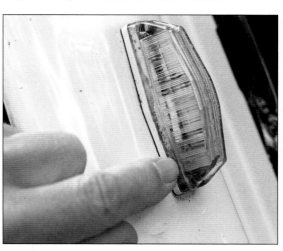

Rust marks in the lens of this light show that rain is making a forced entry.

Taking a regular check with a damp meter is a wise precaution.

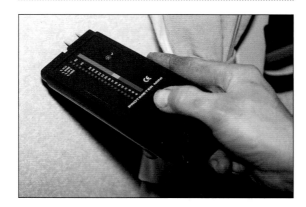

behind. If you remove the trim strip, rusty screws usually confirm the points of entry;

• check around the side windows. Rainwater can also creep behind the horizontal strip from which a plastic window is suspended and it then spreads all around the aperture.

Results of water ingress

If rain does get into the caravan, the outcome is serious as the accompanying photographs illustrate. In many cases appalling degradation occurs because of a failure in the bedding sealant behind decorative trim strips and the awning rail. Note too, that a caravan built using bonded wall panels is just as susceptible to damage as an older caravan which has a void between the inner and outer cladding.

However, it is the front and rear walls of a caravan that often fail first because this is where most of the water discharging from a roof is channelled. The accompanying photographs show work at Crossley Coachcraft and the recurring problem of front-end damage from damp.

Results of rainwater damage

Outside: Failed sealant on the trip strips and awning rail has led to severe damage.

Inside: Water has rotted wood in the walls and the polystyrene is also very damp.

(Photographs courtesy of Sika Ltd)

Before re-building part of the timber sub-frame, a caravan front must be completely taken apart.

The rotted part of the frame will be cut away and replica sections made.

The timber was badly rotted around this window and a new framework had to be fitted.

Exterior body maintenance

It is wise to check under trim strips every few years and to apply a fresh bed of mastic sealant if necessary.

When ribbon mastic is applied, a protective backing paper has to be removed before the fitting is reinstalled.

Precautionary measures

Whilst early-warning readings on a damp meter show that damp is present, many owners take steps to ensure this problem doesn't happen in the first place. The above photographs show a trim strip being re-bedded on fresh ribbon sealant which is a comparatively easy DIY task.

In addition it is often suggested that awning rails should be re-bedded every five years or so. The sequence opposite shows a re-bedding operation where Sikaflex 221 is being substituted for a conventional mastic. Although a few screws are initially needed to hold a rail in place while the Sikaflex adhesive cures, the product achieves an exceptional bond without a need for screws.

Structural damage

Two things bring about a need for major repair work: stress fractures arising from a design fault and the more common problem of accident damage. Major structural damage would normally be undertaken by a specialist in body repairs but some DIY enthusiasts have the background experience and resources to tackle some of the work.

Design faults

This problem is uncommon, but in the early years of sandwich wall construction, a number of caravans were built with a rear kitchen and a rear door. Some models subsequently developed aluminium stress tears above the door aperture. The condition was aggravated by the weight of kitchen appliances and the fact that they were located at the very back of the living area. On a rough road, the pitch and toss of towing soon finds weak spots.

If there's merely a polystyrene core above the door opening, this creates a point of great weakness and shearing is inevitable. The cure is to insert and bond a timber lintel into the core.

Then the upper part of the wall is overlaid with a new aluminium skin to hide the area of repair.

Suffice it to say, a timber lintel is now always fitted in caravans at the time of construction.

Accident damage to GRP

It is distressing to visit a body repair specialist like Crossley Coachcraft at their branches in Leyland and Darlington, but experienced coachbuilders can bring back wrecked caravans from the very brink of a breaker's yard.

Surface damage to GRP is not so worrying and many DIY car owners will be familiar with products sold for repairing rotted car sills, damaged wings and so on. Examples of products include:

Isopon P40 (Trade version U-Pol B)

This is a polyester resin paste containing a mulch of chopped glass fibre strands to give strength to a weak or damaged panel. It can be used to repair splits in GRP as a first-stage operation – thereby giving a material strength before a finishing filler is applied later. To repair a small split in a GRP fairing cover, for example, you would:

i) remove the cover and gouge deep scratches in the roughened rear face with an old chisel or wood rasp
ii) support the splits by applying Sellotape or brown parcel tape on the shiny side
iii) apply a mix of Isopon P40 to the rough side of the moulding with a decorators' knife.

A product like Isopon P40 is prepared on a scrap of plywood by adding a catalyst paste to the polyester/glass compound. Given temperatures around 16C° (60°F), the mix ratio is a 'blob' of P40 the size of a golf ball with three 'blobs' of catalyst paste the size of garden peas. The two items should be mixed thoroughly on the board and a decorators' knife is useful. The catalysed mix should be used promptly and applied with the knife to the unseen side of the fairing.

Re-bedding an awning rail

1. Once the screws are removed, the rail is removed as a unit.

2. The mastic shown here is still in reasonably good condition, but there are places with poor coverage.

3. Remains of the old mastic are removed with a cleaner; white spirit is often effective.

4. The aluminium seam is meticulously cleaned as well.

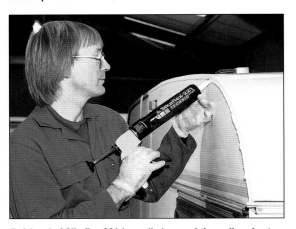

5. A bead of Sikaflex 221 is applied around the wall perimeter.

6. A further application of Sikaflex 221 is injected around the rail, before it is remounted and held with self-tapping screws.

Photographs courtesy of Sika

Acetone cleaner can be purchased at modest cost to clean the mixing knife; alternatively, and at risk of reprimand, you can use expensive acetone nail varnish remover obtainable from any well-equipped handbag.

Isopon P38 (Trade version U-Pol Extra)

This is a filler paste used to recreate a smooth surface on a damaged area of GRP. It lacks the strength of P40 but is applied to the outer side of a panel to recreate an attractive finish.

Using the damaged fairing as an example, once the P40 is set, the tape on the shiny side of the panel is removed. Any stray material is smoothed off with coarse glass paper and the shine is removed from around the repaired section. The filler is mixed in a similar manner to P40 and then knifed over the prepared area to recreate any contours.

When it has cured (a term meaning hardened) the filler is rubbed down with abrasive papers using progressively reducing grades of coarseness. Once the surface is smooth, the filler is finally painted.

Polyester resins and chopped strand mat

More ambitious repairs are often tackled by DIY enthusiasts who have experience of glass fibre laminating work. Anyone who has built or repaired a GRP canoe, for example, will be fully conversant with the way a glass fibre panel on a caravan can be re-constructed.

A specialist like Trylon in Northamptonshire, has supplied the DIY builder/repairer with the necessary materials for over thirty years. The Company supplies polyester laminating resins, gel coat resin, filler powders, colour pigments, reinforcing chopped strand mat, catalyst, acetone cleaner, brushes, laminating rollers and instructions about safety, storage and use.

Guidance given by Trylon about the use of these materials is invaluable, and a number of practically-minded caravanners have found that seemingly irreparable GRP caravan fronts or backs can be successfully rebuilt.

As regards less serious surface abrasion, the

A GRP front can be repaired successfully by anyone familiar with lamination techniques using products supplied by a specialist like Trylon.

Surface damage to this GRP skirt can be fully repaired using either a filler paste, followed by matching paint, or using a pre-coloured gel coat.

outer surface known as 'gel coat' may get damaged in a minor collision. Pre-coloured gel coat resin suitable for surface repairs is sometimes available from a caravan manufacturer's after-sales department. This is mixed with a catalyst, applied to the damaged area and then immediately covered with Sellotape.

The adhesive tape retains the gel in place which is especially necessary on a vertical surface but it also keeps air from the resin while it cures and if you don't do this the gel coat can remain tacky on the surface. Around 24 hours later the tape is removed and the surface smoothed with wet-and-dry papers of diminishing coarseness until a shine is achieved.

An alternative to gel coat is to use surface filler like Isopon P38. This subsequently has to be painted, and many car repair suppliers have paint-mixing facilites so that an exact colour match can be achieved. The specially mixed paint will even be put in an aerosol can if required.

Repairing a split in an acrylic-capped ABS panel

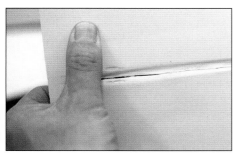

1. Holes are drilled at the ends of the split to prevent further stress damage; the damaged area is also deepened in order to accommodate the repair compound and roughened with P80 grit paper to achieve a key.

2. Surface cleaner is applied to the damaged area, wiped over with a lint-free cloth, and left to dry. Primer Adhesion Promoter is sprayed on next and allowed to dry for 30 minutes.

3. Self-adhesive fibre reinforcing tape is cut to size and stuck to the rear of the damaged panel.

4. A two-part bonding filler is dispensed from a standard sealant gun through the spiral nozzle supplied so that the components are blended. This is applied to the split, to finish just below the surface.

5. When the bonding filler has fully cured, the area is rubbed down so that no filler appears above the surface.

6. Primer adhesion promoter is applied to the surface once again in readiness for the addition of a final top filler.

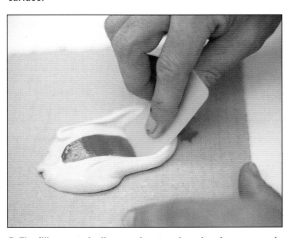

7. The filler paste is dispensed on to a board and a measured amount of red catalyst is mixed in thoroughly with a plastic applicator.

8. The filler is applied over the damaged area using the applicator and feathered off at the sides. This will be smoothed off when dry with abrasive paper; a matched etching paint suitable for this material will be applied and a colour-matched top coat added finally.

Accident damage to acrylic-capped ABS

Rather surprisingly, the procedures for repairing ABS panels are not particularly dissimilar from the methods of repairing GRP. On the other hand, the chemicals are certainly different.

The photographs show a repair carried out just prior to the launch of Gramos Microfil Extreme ABS plastic repair system in 1999.

Note: *Gramos repair kits are now available to the general public and can be purchased from Kingdom Industrial Supplies. At the close of 1999, new repair kits were also launched by Bradleys whose specialism in the repair of ABS materials has been well established in the car industry. Bradleys also manufactures special paints for application to this type of plastic surface (see Appendix addresses for these contacts).*

73

Blistering on the aluminium skin all along the side of this caravan is an example of advanced delamination.

Delamination

The strength in a piece of plywood is achieved because its layers are all bonded firmly together with adhesive. If the glue fails, the weakness of the individual laminates is demonstrated in no uncertain manner.

It's exactly the same with the bonded panels used in caravan construction. Individually the 3mm ply or sheet aluminium forming a wall is flexible and fragile; and the block polystyrene used in the core is as brittle as a biscuit.

When bonded the strength is remarkable but if the layers start to come apart, there's a serious problem, and delamination will occur.

In practice it is delamination of floor panels that is the more common failing. If you hear creaking in the floor and notice a spongy feeling in certain areas, take immediate action. Typically delamination is most common in areas of heavy use – just inside the door, and around the area of the kitchen sink. Some owners find that small areas on the inner section of plywood rise up like a blister.

The condition might develop later in the life of a caravan, but there are cases reported of delamination starting in a floor panel on a caravan's very first trip. This is covered, of course, within the warranty but it proves that newer models are not always free from failure.

Fortunately repairs are not only possible; they are even completed successfully by confident and determined owners.

Procedure

Re-bonding is achieved by injecting special adhesive into the delaminating area. Repair kits are produced by Apollo Chemicals Ltd and plastic syringes are supplied.

The procedure for dealing with delamination in the outer aluminium skin on a wall is shown in the diagrams below.

On a floor, the carpet must be removed and holes then drilled around the faulty area to match the exact size of the nozzle on the syringe. This is around 4mm, but check first because a tight fit is important. If surplus adhesive oozes out of a hole, it sets rock hard, so once the injection is complete, wood screws are inserted into each hole to act as plugs. If the adhesive still creeps out on to the surface, the surplus has to be removed with a rag as soon as possible.

The adhesive is a two-part epoxy resin and in the Apollo Chemical range this is AX8136 Part A and B.

Having injected the adhesive, you must then apply pressure over the entire damaged area. On a floor, lay some paper, a sheet of thick ply and heavy items like house bricks. On a wall, wedge a block and a small piece of ply against the aluminium skin as shown in the drawing. If you wish to hasten the curing process, a hot air gun can be judiciously directed at an aluminium panel, but this isn't essential.

Procedure for dealing with delamination in the outer aluminium skin on a wall

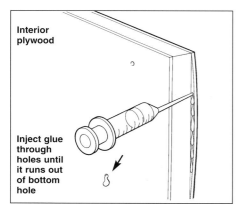

Interior plywood

Inject glue through holes until it runs out of bottom hole

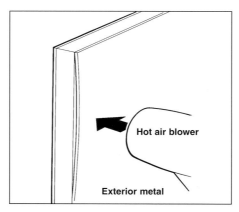

Hot air blower

Exterior metal

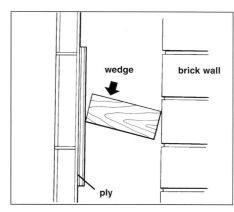

wedge

brick wall

ply

Exterior body maintenance

Applying a new aluminium skin

This is really a job for a specialist body repairer. Once bent, aluminium sheet cannot be beaten flat again because the material stretches. So if a caravan wall is dented on the outside, a recessed area has to be filled and Apollo A5045 two-part adhesive is often used. This doesn't react with the polystyrene core in a bonded wall – which may happen if a polyester resin-based filler is used.

Having restored a flat surface, the entire area has to be overlaid with another sheet of aluminium. The fact that caravan walls are usually divided up with trim strips means that a small section can often be applied rather than the entire side.

The specialist will remove the awning rail and all the trims, apply masking paper where necessary, and then spray both surfaces with several fine applications of a product like Apollo A11. When the new pre-painted aluminium sheet is offered-up, a notable bond will immediately be achieved. What's more, the fact that there's a wall section covered with a double skin of aluminium is seldom discernible.

Pressure then needs to be applied and various wedges can be arranged by parking the caravan adjacent to a wall. However, Crossley Coachcraft has developed a large inflatable mattress which is mounted to a vertical wall inside the Leyland factory. When a freshly skinned 'van is parked close to the wall, the mattress is inflated with a compressor. It is a clever arrangement because it ensures that a sustained pressure is exerted uniformly over the entire side of the caravan.

Once all the trim pieces are reinstated, it is then only a day or so before the owner can be enjoying his or her caravan once again.

When a hole is torn in the side or a major strengthening repair has been carried out, the entire area will be overlaid with a new aluminium panel.

A completely new middle section of aluminium has been bonded on top of a damaged panel. Later the 'van will be parked closer to the wall and the black mattress will be inflated to apply consistent pressure to the entire area while the adhesive is setting.

(Photograph courtesy of Crossley Coachcraft)

Interior maintenance and improvements

Interior design is an important factor when choosing a caravan. In the first part of this chapter the focus is on furnishings; in the second part, attention turns to the furniture.

The interiors of most British caravans have traditional styling and offer a high level of comfort. They are frequently finished with fitted carpet, velvet curtains and patterned upholstery. Whether the proliferation of florid fabrics is to everyone's taste is a matter of debate.

In contrast, Continental interiors are less ornate and their designers are clearly conscious of campsite reality. For instance vinyl floor coverings are more common than carpet. Bearing in mind that caravanning in the countryside inevitably brings mud, grass cuttings and other elements into your living space, this carries a certain logic.

Interior furnishing materials

Whether to opt for a plush interior or one that lends itself to an active lifestyle depends on the purchaser. Either way, keeping it clean and comfortable is appropriate and a knowledge of furnishings and fabrics is helpful here.

Foam

Most caravans are supplied with foam interiors in the seats and seat backs. Upholstery specialists often refer to these collectively as 'cushions' and openly admit that the foam supplied with some new caravans is not of particularly good quality. The seats may seem reasonably comfortable at first, but after a few seasons, the foam inside loses its resilience and the cushions start to 'bottom out'.

This is apparent if you sit down abruptly. Poor resistance offered by the foam causes you to bump against the plywood base underneath. One remedy is to replace the original foam with a high density product. Though costly, this provides good support and will retain its elasticity for many years.

Another solution is to have an extra top-up layer bonded to the original foam. Several specialists offer this service and since the existing foam has lost its resilience, the thin extra layer can often be added without making alterations to the covers. In effect, a number of 'sandwich' constructions are possible to suit particular situations and this alternative approach is included in the box below on foam classifications.

Some upholsterers also recommend an addition of 'fibre wrap'. This soft polyester padding is a thin material which softens sharp, angular edges on cushions. It undoubtedly improves appearances although it only makes a minimal contribution to comfort.

Foam classifications

Foam: Typically this is a synthetic product manufactured to different specifications. High-density foam is guaranteed to retain its shape and comfort for a long period. Foams are available in soft, medium or firm grades and these designations relate to the amount of support provided. As a guide:

Soft **is suitable for backrests but is not advised for use as a seat or bed base.**

Medium **is sometimes specified for backrests or, possibly, as a mattress for a child. It is unlikely to provide sufficient comfort or support for an adult.**

Firm **is usually too hard for back or arm rests, but is the best choice for a seat that will also be used as a mattress. It is both comfortable and durable. It is possible to combine any of the above grades to meet individual preferences. A good specialist can produce a sandwich mix – for example a bonded three-layer cushion which has a hard centre section and layers of softer foam on either side.**

Dunlopillo **uses latex which is the sap from rubber trees. It is naturally fire-retardant and non-allergenic. Though costly, Dunlopillo is a superior foam offering excellent support, long life, durability and good ventilation properties. It is commonly used in domestic furniture but is seldom seen in caravans.**

Hard and soft foams can be bonded together to meet specific requirements.

By covering foam with a thin stockinette, the cover will slip on much more easily.

Upholstery specialists can fit spring interiors as an alternative to synthetic foam.

On the subject of comfort, the fact that seats also have to double-up as beds introduces another difficulty. Some seats are contoured with a raised portion on the forward edge known as a 'knee roll'. They may be heavily buttoned, too. Neither feature is helpful when the seat changes its function to that of a mattress.

As regards the depth of foam, this varies considerably and anything from 50mm (2in) to 150mm (6in) is used. Foam for a sleeping base intended for adults is usually 100mm (4in) deep, but there is a growing tendency to specify 150mm (6in) foam on more expensive caravans for the master bed. On bunk beds made up using 'split folding' units, the foam is generally 50-75mm (2-3in).

Irrespective of dimensions or densities, all foam used for furniture has to achieve a 'combustion modified' designation for reasons of safety. See the box below for details of legislation.

As a further addition, many upholsterers recommend that foam is covered by a layer of thin stockinette material. This addition makes the task of fitting a cover much easier because it greatly reduces the friction of the foam against the inner face of the fabric.

Spring interior cushions

In response to owners' comments, several caravan manufacturers now offer spring interior cushions as an alternative to a foam filling. Spring interior units may also be fitted at a later date by an upholstery specialist. However, the cost is quite high and owners often restrict the alteration to those seat cushions which will be used for the double bed. Moreover, there is another reason for this strategy.

There is no doubt that spring interior cushions are fine for a bed, but when used for seating, there is sometimes a tendency for the forward edge to lack rigidity. Poor support behind the knee joint can be unsatisfactory and this point should be checked before replacing foam fillings.

Interior fabrics

Various fabrics are used for cushion covers although velour has been especially popular in recent years. However, tweed materials and cotton-type products

have had varying moments of popularity, too.

In addition to the main fabric there's also variation in the type of edging strip used around upholstered cushions. Terms like ruche and piping are explained overleaf in the box entitled, 'Trade terminology'.

Where covers are stitched in place, cleaning becomes more complicated and you are obliged to deal with them *in situ*. In the event, several cleaning chemicals are effective although there's an obvious advantage if covers are fitted with a zip so that dry cleaning can be carried out.

As regards curtains, velvet with a stitched-in

Furniture legislation

Compliance with the *Furniture (Fire Safety) Regulations 1988* has focused attention on foams as well as fabrics and the ability to meet ignitability tests is confirmed on a product's labelling. As the DTI publication, *A Guide to the Furniture and Furnishings (Fire) (Safety) Regulations, May 1995* pointed out, regulations apply to upholstered furniture supplied with new caravans sold from 1st March 1990. In response, manufacturers use a fire-resistant product described as 'combustion modified' foam.

However, the regulations do not apply to furniture in second-hand caravans. Caravans built prior to 1st March, 1990 are unlikely to achieve the same level of safety and some owners therefore decide to have the foam replaced.

Covers have to possess a resistance to cigarette or match ignition too, and new caravans carry a label verifying their integrity. Sometimes this resistance is lost after dry cleaning although there are products which can be reapplied to reinstate these qualities.

The term 'ruche' refers to the different types of edging trims.

Stretch covers

At one time, stretch covers were made from rather poor materials, but nowadays there are attractive, thicker, high quality examples at competitive prices. Modern fabrics and improvements in the manufacturing processes mean that stretch covers have a more permanent and more striking appearance.

Some stretch covers offer two wearing sides – an advantage for distributing areas of wear and tear; many are also machine washable. So some caravanners use them as a way of protecting the original coverings – especially if they have children at the 'sticky finger' stage or if they own a dog.

If you order stretch covers, zip fastenings are often available, but remember to specify zips at the time of ordering because tie tapes are quite common. The minor problem of covers slipping out of place is easily overcome if upholstery buttons are fitted – and many specialists supply DIY buttoning kits. The buttons have a long tail with a

lining material seems to have continuing popularity even though many caravanners don't draw their curtains when blinds are fitted. A lining material enhances their appearance, but can lead to washing difficulties because one of the fabrics might shrink slightly more than its partner. Dry cleaning would be preferred, but most caravan curtains are made with sewn-in plastic attachments and these are not accepted at most dry cleaners. So if curtains have to be washed, a popular answer is to stitch them into a pillow case and then run them through a washing machine on a very cool wash programme.

Note: *Many fabrics are treated with stain-resisting and fire-retarding treatments. Depending on the product, these are likely to retain their properties for one or two dry-cleaning operations. Thereafter, re-proofing can be undertaken by many upholstery specialists. Alternatively, products are available in spray cans for DIY application. Scotchgard is one of the well known treatments.*

Many stretch covers are machine washable.

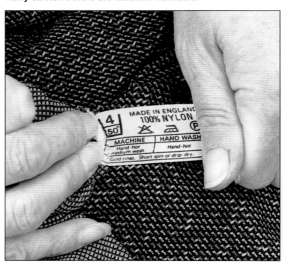

Trade terminology

Bottoming out: When foam loses resilience a caravanner will often feel the wooden base underneath when sitting down abruptly.

Raised front cushions: Also known as knee rolls or graduated cushions, these products have a foam section bonded along a forward edge to offer a raised profile. It can add to the comfort of a seat but is less pleasant when the cushion forms part of a bed.

Piping: Cord stitched around cushion edging gives protection from excessive wear. Straight piping is plain and purposeful; a twisted cord is more ornate.

Ruche: Serving the same purpose as piping, ruche is a decorative tape. The fluffy edging trim often seen in caravans is referred to as 'cut ruche'.

Top stitching: A decorative feature accomplished by stitching through both the outer fabric and a thin backing layer to delineate shapes in a patterned material such as flowers or leaves.

Buttoning: When covered in matching fabric, buttons are decorative features but they also help to prevent covers from slipping out of position.

Split folders: The term refers to cushions that open up like a book in order to form a wider unit – typically to make a bed width.

Fire retardant foam: Since 1990, all foam used in furniture has been required to meet a British Standard in order to achieve a minimum fire rating.

Fire retardant fabric: A treatment mandatory on all fabrics since 1991.

Zips are better on caravan stretch covers than tie tapes.

When ordering by post, an accurate paper pattern showing precise measurements is crucial.

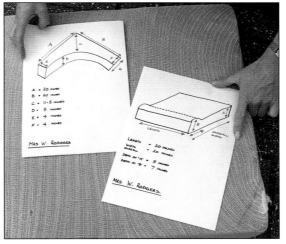

Diagrams showing unusual shapes and their dimensions are recommended when using a mail order service.

'T' tag which has to be driven right through the cushion using an upholstery needle. Whilst this addition serves a practical function, it adds a decorative detail as well.

Note: *When measuring-up prior to placing an order, confirm with the manufacturers that they will be making the allowance for stretch when the covers are made.*

Ordering new covers

Manufacturers of made-to-measure covers can usually supply tweeds, cotton print fabrics or velour. If you send for samples, it is immediately apparent that a remarkable selection of fabrics is available. Indeed it's not unusual to recognise some patterns as the ones being used in current caravans.

Bear in mind that the choice of fabric is only one consideration. Further decisions need to be made about points of detail. Top stitching, buttoning, piping or cut ruche add individual features that combine decorative effects with practical performance.

If you decide to have your caravan re-upholstered, some specialists are able to work from information and measurements supplied by the customer; others prefer to have the cushions available in order to guard against inaccuracy in the finished product. If using a mail order supplier, you should supply carefully cut pattern pieces and precise measurements for each cushion.

Methods of ordering and despatch vary; some companies use carriers whilst others operate a 'callers only' service. Several companies can also supply replacement foam, spring interiors and 'extras' such as curtains and scatter cushions.

Making and fitting covers is an involved operation and completion may take a full day. As part of their service, some upholsterers allow you to park and stay overnight in a factory car park while the work is being undertaken.

Unless specified at the time of ordering, the majority of covers are supplied with a plain lining

material for the underside of the cushion. This should be non-slip, durable and will help to reduce costs – though you can't rotate the cushions to even out the wear. Dark fabrics are preferred because any rust stain from bed box hinges is less discernible. Don't forget to indicate clearly on all patterns which are the top, sides, or fronts of the cushions. Clear line diagrams can help here.

Many covers now have concealed zips along the back edge, although tapes and envelope ends can be provided upon request. Some companies will stitch the covers in place; but this makes removal for cleaning more difficult.

DIY approaches

Many upholstery specialists supply materials to customers who want to tackle their own refurbishment work. In fact stretch covers are successfully made-up by many experienced owners.

However, making your own *permanent* covers is a different task altogether. Owning an industrial sewing machine is essential and tasks like fitting ruche edgings can be extremely laborious. A few

A number of specialists will sell surplus cushions bought directly from the caravan manufacturers.

some manufacturers are recognising that many owners enjoy active leisure pursuits like cycling, fishing, walking and water sports; in response to this, several caravans, e.g. models from the Swift group, are supplied with removable carpet sections, which in turn overlay a vinyl flooring. These have stitched edges and are easy to remove for cleaning. It is a far more flexible arrangement. If the forecast for a weekend predicts rain and a farm site has been booked, it makes sense to leave the carpet pieces at home for that particular trip.

indomitable DIY upholsterers achieve good results, but not many match the standard of the professional who has the advantage of industrial machinery.

If you are renovating an older caravan, another strategy is to buy manufacturers' surplus cushions, and companies which specialise in surplus stock often have trade stands at major caravan rallies. Firms like Magnum Mobiles & Surplus Stock and O'Leary Motor Homes Sales & Hire are examples.

Carpets

It was mentioned earlier that in British caravans, fitted carpets are the usual type of floor covering. When a caravan is manufactured, carpet is laid on the plywood floor surface and the furniture is then built on top.

Although this is the more common approach,

More manufacturers are supplying removable carpet – which is much more practical than a fitted carpet covering.

Removing stains

Everyone spills something or brings in dirt from outside at one time or another. The golden rule is to deal with the damage immediately and there are several points to keep in mind:

■ Apply a stain remover as soon as possible – if a specific treatment is available rather than a general purpose cleaner, so much the better.

■ If in doubt about the way a fabric might react with a cleaning chemical, use the product on a small corner first to check compatibility.

■ Always remove individual stains before washing an entire item.

■ Keep an emergency cleaning kit in your caravan.

■ Always apply a treatment with a clean, white cloth – like an old piece of sheet. If you use a patterned cloth, dye can run into the fabric you're cleaning.

■ If there's a surface deposit, scrape this away using a blunt knife before applying the cleaning compound.

■ When removing a mark from a velour fabric, always work in the direction of the pile to avoid surface damage.

■ Be gentle in the approach using a dabbing action where possible. Fabric fibres can be damaged if a rough, rubbing action is employed.

■ Be sparing when using fluids and keep the area blotted periodically to lift marks and to avoid deep penetration into the material.

■ Try to remove as much of the cleaning treatment as possible. Some chemicals leave a mark of their own.

■ If a trace of water is needed on the area of damage, a mist spray bottle is ideal. These are sold at garden centres.

■ Safety advice: wear surgical gloves, open windows to release fumes, extinguish flames (some chemicals are flammable), keep cleaning chemicals in labelled containers, and never mix chemicals together – the result might be explosive.

Tackling common stains

In many cases, stains can be removed using kitchen products and the list that follows describes typical problems. The recommendations presume the mark is dry.

Beer

Using a solution of one part white vinegar to five parts cold water gently sponge the area. Blot well before repeating with cold water. Allow to dry naturally; don't apply heat because this can permanently set a beer stain.

Blood

Brush the stain lightly to remove surface deposits. Sponge using salt water solution followed by a mild ammonia and water solution before finishing with clear water. Blot well at every stage and avoid heat when drying.

Chocolate

Gently scrape away any residue. Any remaining blemish should respond to washing powder that you've mixed into a paste with water – apply with the knife in your cleaning kit and leave for thirty minutes, then carefully scrape it all away.

Egg

Scrape off any dried residue; then apply a paste of biological powder and water and leave for thirty minutes. Brush off before thoroughly sponging with clean water and blotting well. This is another case where you should avoid heat because it can set the stain permanently.

Grease

This is a stain whose remedy can cause colour problems. As a rule it's best to use a recognised grease solvent first, such as Mangers De-Solve It or K2r Spray before shampooing the area. Be prepared to re-treat the area at a later date – grease spots have a habit of reappearing.

Ink

Gently dab the area with either clear methylated spirits or a proprietary ink remover. Blot frequently throughout the treatment to avoid spreading the mark and take care in case fabric colours run. Finally use a suitable fabric shampoo.

Jams and marmalade

Soften stain by applying glycerine for up to thirty minutes. Sponge away with clean water then follow up with a solution of one part white vinegar to five parts water. Blot well throughout.

Sauces and ketchup

Soften with glycerine; remove excess then sponge with a 50-50 mixture of white vinegar and water.

Biological washing powder and water may help to remove any remaining dye marks but be prepared for problems; some sauce stains are exceptionally hard to remove.

Tar

Where possible, remove any surface deposits before applying glycerine to soften the remaining mark. Leave for about an hour before blotting and then apply a proprietary product such as Mangers De-Solve It. Be careful not to drive tar further into fabric fibres; use a gentle lifting action instead. Incidentally, a product traditionally used for removing tar is lighter fuel, but this is highly flammable.

Urine

This is a difficult mark to remove successfully and professional help may be needed for any lingering odours. To loosen the stain, soda water can be applied and then blotted thoroughly. Follow this by using a proprietary product. Work even harder on the potty training.

Vomit

Gently but thoroughly sponge the area with water into which a few drops of ammonia have been added. Apply a paste of washing powder and water, leaving this for thirty minutes. Brush off the paste, then rinse and blot the area with fresh water.

Wine

Remove as much colour as possible using a white vinegar and water solution. Alternatively if you can't get white vinegar, prepare a mix of lemon juice and salt. Then apply a washing powder and water paste and leave for around thirty minutes. Brush this away before continuing with clear water.

Note: *Professional advice is available on customer help lines operated by manufacturers of proprietary stain removers. Check details on brand labels.*

Cleaning kit

A cleaning kit might include the following:

1. **A general purpose cleaner from a chemists or hardware shop.**
2. **An aide-memoire listing household products which can be used for stain treatment. Examples include: ammonia, biological detergent, clear methylated spirits, glycerine, lemon juice, salt and washing-up fluid. White vinegar also removes some stains – and relieves wasp stings as well.**
3.
4. **A nylon scouring pad**
5. **A small nail brush**
6. **White absorbent cloth**
7. **An old house knife with a blunt-ended blade.**

Car Interior Shampoo from AutoGlym is sprayed on to the face of a cushion.

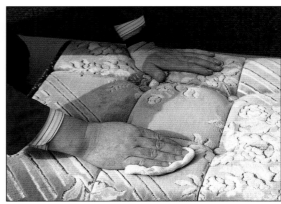

After gentle agitation with a soft nylon brush, the shampoo – and dirt – is removed with a clean cloth.

Seasonal cleaning

Several products are suitable for cleaning caravan covers. Many are used to clean car seats as well, bearing in mind that velour is not unknown in vehicles.

Where possible, try to plan any shampoo work on a hot day so that the cushions will dry as soon as possible. Although some padded wall sections may be difficult to remove for cleaning, most cushions can be taken to an outdoor table for attention.

Many cleaners are easy to use. For instance, Car Interior Shampoo from AutoGlym is sprayed on to the cover, agitated cautiously with a soft nylon brush, then removed with a clean, white, absorbent cloth.

Interior furniture

To be successful, furniture in a caravan should be:

- structurally sound
- light in weight
- attractive in appearance.

Sometimes the quest to save weight leads to a compromise in strength. Furthermore, when a caravan is being towed, interior fixtures are submitted to relentless stress. So occasionally there may be a need to carry out some running repairs.

Construction

The need to keep everything light means that there is little similarity with the kind of furniture used in our homes. For instance, veneered or laminate-covered chipboard is not used because it is much too heavy.

To minimise weight, caravan manufacturers use extremely thin (3mm) decorative ply. This is finished with a white surface for use on walls or ceilings; alternatively it is faced with a paper that has been printed with an imitation wood grain. Unfortunately the product can normally only be purchased through a caravan accessory specialist or from a manufacturer spares section direct.

There is no doubt that the caravan cabinet maker employs great guile in disguising the product. All doors are usually built with a hollow construction and their apparently 'heavy' appearance is a clever illusion.

The fixings used to hold constructions together will vary, but staples predominate. These can be applied quickly and are less damaging when a framework is being assembled or clad with a covering. Paradoxically, the sudden impact from a staple gun is likely to be less damaging than

The black veneered chipboard is considerably heavier than the hollow door below.

A 3mm decorative lightweight ply is used extensively in caravans.

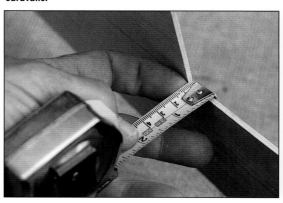

repeated blows where a hammer is used to drive home panel pins.

Making alterations

It is not unusual to find that a few alterations are needed in a caravan. Perhaps a shelf would be useful; or maybe the kitchen could be modified to make space for a microwave oven or a larger capacity fridge. Many practically-minded owners make successful alterations, but it is crucial not to add unnecessary weight to the caravan. The 'user payload' limit which defines how much equipment can be loaded into a caravan is often surprisingly restrictive. So bear in mind that an increase in weight through modifications will correspondingly lead to a reduction in the amount of holiday equipment you can carry in your caravan.

To fulfil the requirements of weight saving, a number of strategies can be followed. A first step is to approach surplus stock specialists who travel to outdoor shows; two specialists have already been mentioned in the section on replacement upholstery on page 80. Lightweight doors, work-top lids and other items are often on sale and frequently you can recognise which models they were used in originally.

Altering hollow doors

In addition to buying from surplus stock dealers, you can sometimes purchase hollow doors from a caravan manufacturer – especially unwanted

spares from an obsolete model. They might not be the right dimension but as the accompanying photographs show, you can reduce them in size quite easily. However, the process is speeded up and the finish is likely to be more satisfactory if you own a precision saw bench.

Edging strips

Doors, shelves and work tops are usually finished around the edges with either a thin strip or a more substantial moulding. Strip veneers that are applied using a domestic iron are not usually long-lasting; nor, for that matter, do they offer much protection against knocks.

A protective lipping is much better and this is one place where hardwood might be permitted even though it is likely to be slightly heavier than a softwood.

If you own a precision saw bench fitted with a tungsten carbide tipped (TCT) blade, preparing lipping is easy. Whilst an edging strip might be 6mm (¼in) or more, it can be prepared even thinner.

Anything of 6mm or thinner can be attached with an impact adhesive like Evo-Stik. But it still helps to support this with a mechanical fixing. Steel panel pins are one possibility and so are brass pins sold at marine chandlers. However, veneer pins are even less visible and provide a neat finish.

Whichever fixing is preferred, they all have a tendency to split a veneer or thin lipping. The time-honoured tip is to nip off the point with pincers –

Reducing the size of a hollow door

1. Using a saw bench fitted with a TCT blade, a clean cut is made through this hollow door.

2. An insert has been prepared to an exact thickness and will be glued into place using woodworking adhesive.

3. The insert should be held firmly in place with a G cramp and left overnight for the adhesive to dry.

4. When the side has been planed down and squared off, a thin lipping strip is used to cover the edge.

83

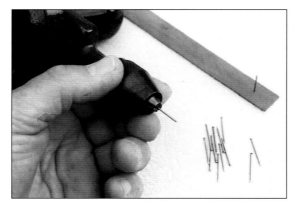

driving home a blunt point does reduce the chance of splitting the material. A better answer, however, is to drill a pilot hole and if you don't possess very fine twist drills, use a veneer pin as a drill in its own right. Nip off the head so it sits securely in the chuck of a hand drill and keep up the revolutions. The point of the pin won't penetrate as well as a twist drill and it's likely to get hot – but it will form a perfect pilot hole.

Adding a shelf

Another improvement job is to fit an additional shelf. Whether this is a small structure to hold little more than an alarm clock or something larger for cassette tapes, the construction should again create strength without unnecessary weight. Chipboard is out of the question.

Strength can be achieved in a number of ways and even something as seemingly flexible and fragile as 3mm plywood can be strengthened using battens and supports. The photographs below show a length of lipping that has been grooved in a circular saw in order to prevent the ply from flexing.

A hardwood lipping is prepared on the saw bench and grooved to house the light 3mm ply.

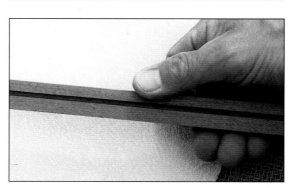

When glued to the front of the ply, rigidity is achieved without unnecessary weight.

If a further batten is fitted to support the rear of the ply and attached to a side wall, the resulting structure will be surprisingly sturdy. But its weight will be almost negligible.

Revisions to cabinets

Nearly all lockers, cupboards and cabinets are constructed with a skeleton structure of light timber and then clad with decorative ply. If obeche is available, this is an extremely light wood and yet it is strong. Otherwise, ordinary deal or a similar softwood can be used, but choose lengths with as few knots as possible.

To ensure a carcass framework is rigid, adjoining sections of timber should be glued and screwed, even if they are not jointed but are merely butted together. A woodworking adhesive like Evo-Stik Resin W (interior grade) is one of many suitable products and is easy to work with. When fastening structures to the floor or walls, you might decide to use a cartridge-injected adhesive like No More Nails or Evo-Grip. These products are now widely used in the building trade.

As regards fixings, twin-threaded countersunk 'Supascrews' are more rust-resistant than steel screws; equally, Reisser hardened steel screws are a delight to use. However, in locations where there's likely to be moisture such as a washroom, brass screws are more appropriate. A selection of G cramps is strongly recommended, too, so that support can be given to structures overnight while an adhesive is setting.

To save weight, all cabinets, lockers and bed bases are made with a skeleton framework

Several makes of cartridge-applied adhesive are available for anchoring structures to walls or floors.

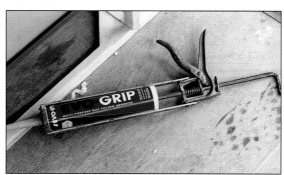

84

To achieve a clean edge, it is better to cut 3mm ply with a sharp woodworking knife than with a saw.

When a framework is completed, the addition of ply will not only enclose the structure; it will also serve as a bracing material which helps to hold the construction together. The best way to cut 3mm ply to size is to use a cutting scale and a sharp woodworking knife.

Catches, fittings and accessories

Some hardware items sold at DIY stores are suitable for use in caravans; others are not. Magnetic catches, for example, are less successful in a caravan since the furniture is subjected to so much stress movement.

Catches can often be purchased from a caravan accessory shop and the after-sales departments of caravan manufacturers can sometimes help as well.

When it comes to plastic vent covers, restraining catches and mainstream caravan items, CAK carries an extensive range of products. Many fittings used by manufacturers can be purchased using their mail order service.

Another mail order specialist is Woodfit, whose service to DIY cabinet makers is legendary. Woodfit's catalogue lists huge ranges of hinges, catches, door handles and so on. It also includes drawer runners, moulded cutlery trays, waste bins and the kind of wire baskets on runners that are fitted as blanket boxes and vegetable storage units in many 'up-market' caravans. If you are embarking on a major renovation project, the Woodfit catalogue is a worthy work of reference.

Bathroom units

If you decide to rebuild a bathroom or add a shower, some caravan dealers can supply plastic washbasins, cabinets, shower trays and so on. Or you can use the CAK mail order service and there are plenty of products in stock.

Equally, the specialists who deal in surplus stock bought from caravan manufacturers might be able to help. For example, Magnum Mobiles & Surplus Stock carries a wide range of items, as mentioned on page 80. These items may need adapting to fit your particular caravan, but it is presumed that anyone tackling a project of this magnitude has already recognised that radical alterations are going to be needed.

Kitchen improvement

Anyone buying an older caravan may feel the kitchen deserves modernisation. If the budget is limited, caravan breakers like Franks of Luton carry stocks of ovens, hobs, sinks and draining boards. Alternatively the ranges of smart sink fixtures imported by Alde are displayed at many major indoor exhibitions.

It doesn't take a lot of work to install a new sink and draining board, provided that the basic framework forming the kitchen units is sound. Fitting replacement cooking appliances is not difficult – at least as far as the woodwork is involved. But making connections into the gas supply system should only be tackled by a qualified gas engineer – as emphasised in Chapter Ten, *Gas supply systems and appliances*.

Interior blinds

Most models now include cassette blinds and fly screens. Sometimes they are easy to fit and the installation of a fly screen for a door is described in Chapter Twelve. The main requirement is sufficient clearance around the aperture.

One of the problems with a spring retractable blind, however, is the tendency for the spring to lose its tension. This happens if it remains under tension for prolonged periods – for instance when the blinds are lowered during winter storage. It is better for the spring if blinds are left in a raised position; but then the upholstery fades.

On most blinds, however, there's a spring re-tensioning screw at one end of the cassette. A turn with a screwdriver usually solves sluggish blind retraction, but gaining access to this adjuster often necessitates removing the unit completely. In fact it is sometimes necessary to remove pelmets, shelves or overhead cupboards as a preliminary operation. What a pity that some caravan manufacturers overlook the need to keep these all-important adjustment screws within reasonable reach of human hands.

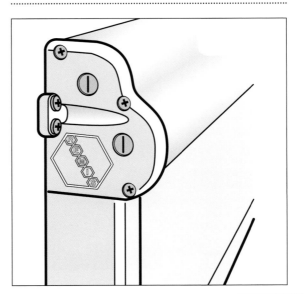

The spring on a blind has an adjusting screw on the end of its cassette.

The 12 Volt supply system

A caravan fitted with its own battery and 12 Volt supply system offers many benefits. However, a low voltage system needs to combine efficiency with safety. It is also important to keep a battery in a good state of charge.

It seems surprising that gas lamps were still being fitted in caravans in the early 1970s. However, this form of lighting became obsolete when Lab Craft, an electrical engineering specialist, found a way to run fluorescent lighting units from a 12V supply.

By boosting the Direct Current (DC) supply to around 130V and changing it to Alternating Current (AC), Lab Craft found it was possible to ignite a fluorescent tube. This economic and efficient way of providing lighting in caravans was immediately acknowledged.

Safety

Changing a faulty tube in a fluorescent light fitting is normally straightforward. But you must ensure the 12V supply is turned off at source; inside the casing of a fluorescent unit the supply is boosted to around 130V.

When the cover is removed, you will find that some tubes have tags fitted on their connection pins. More recent tubes are held in a slot with a push and twist arrangement. Either way, fitting a new tube is not difficult.

Single socket supply from the towcar battery

When caravans were first fitted with a 'strip light', this was the only component needing a 12V supply. Hence in 1970s caravans, Pin 2 on the black 12N socket (primarily intended for road lights) was allocated so that caravan lighting could be powered by the towcar's battery. Careful use meant that the battery would retain sufficient charge to start the engine after an illuminated evening in the caravan.

If you purchase a second-hand caravan built during this period, there is no reason why you shouldn't just use a 12N connection system – as long as your car is appropriately wired. Pin connections are given in Chapter 3, *Towcar preparation*. Unfortunately, however, the idea of having a fridge, a supply for a 12V TV, an electric water pump and a shaver point is an attractive proposition. But if these appliances are added, it is then necessary for a caravan to have:

- an independent battery,
- a fused distribution unit,
- separate supply circuits,
- battery charging facilities.

Once a 12V system is extended in this way, the wiring becomes far more elaborate. Moreover, an additional 12S socket will also have to be fitted to the towcar to support the system.

The 12S (supplementary) socket

When legislation required caravans manufactured after 1st October, 1979 to have a rear fog-lamp, it was decided that Pin 2 on the black 12N socket, hitherto used for caravan interior lighting, would provide its electrical feed. This prompted the need for a second socket to supply interior services, leaving the 12N plug to deal exclusively with the caravan's road lights.

Named the 12S (supplementary) socket, this new connection is described in Chapter 3. Pin allocation is explained together with revised 12S connections applicable to caravans manufactured after 1st September, 1998 in response to European Standard EN1648-1.

In summary, a 12S connection provides:

• a permanent live feed from the towcar's battery to power interior appliances;
• a feed to run the refrigerator on 12V which is live when the engine is running;
• a feed from the alternator to charge the caravan battery when the engine is running;
• an earth return (two earth returns in the case of post 1st September, 1998 'vans).

In addition, the 12S socket has one road lamp connection – Pin 1 – to operate reversing lamps, although these are not fitted on many caravans.

Circuit designs

Starting at the towcar, when the grey multicore cable from a 12S plug has been taken along a caravan's draw bar, it usually terminates in a forward locker. In most caravans the individual feeds from the multicore cable are then separated and wired into a connecting strip. This marks the starting point of the internal wiring system.

In caravans built in the last twenty years, a 12V circuit draws its supply from one of two sources – *either* the vehicle battery via the 12S connection, *or* the caravan's own auxiliary battery. A switch is also fitted into the system so that a caravanner is able to choose which battery will provide the power. A three-position rocker switch is usually chosen in which the central position isolates the supply completely.

In practice the preferred supply is from the caravan battery (often referred to as a 'leisure' battery on account of its unique construction). The vehicle battery should be regarded as a temporary provider since over-use may mean that vehicle starting is affected.

A supply fuse should be fitted, too, in order to

When the supply is provided by either the car or the caravan's own auxiliary battery, a selection switch is needed in the circuit.

■ A 12V circuit *must* be protected from an overload situation by an in-line fuse connected to the feed coming from a battery's positive terminal. It should also be close to the source. However, since a leisure battery is usually installed in a ventilated locker, electrical engineers recommend that the fuse is positioned *outside* the enclosure. This is because a battery sometimes gives off an inflammable gas (hydrogen) while being charged. Since a fuse often sparks when it fails, it is therefore wise to fit the fuse holder *outside* the battery compartment away from the discharging gas.

■ The rating of a battery supply fuse varies. Plug-in-Systems recommends that a 15A fuse is usually appropriate. However, some manufacturers e.g. Swift normally fit a 20A fuse. A few manufacturers fit 25A fuses which is a questionable strategy. It is based on the fact that if all the 12V appliances in a well-equipped caravan were operated at once, a total current of 25-30A would be drawn. In truth, this situation is unlikely.

guard against overload; this is described in the Safety box above.

Having obtained a 12V supply, this is then divided up into separate routes like the branches leading away from the trunk of a tree. Each branch is independently protected by a switch and a fuse, the rating of which is appropriate for the appliances being served. For instance a radio/tape player has a particularly low consumption, so it is normally protected by a 5A fuse. On the other hand, a water pump has a higher consumption, and a 10A fuse is usually fitted.

The purpose of having a switch to control each branch is to offer separate control within the system. For instance if you needed to look at a troublesome water pump on a dark evening, you could switch off this part of a 12V supply without having to interrupt the feed to your interior lights. Some caravan control units do not have separate switches, but a supply can usually be isolated by

Recent caravans are fitted with a built-in battery box and the control panels are often mounted behind the container.

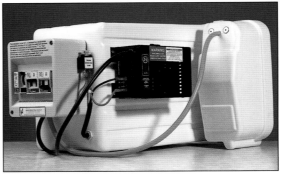

The mains consumer unit and charger are mounted on the rear of this Zig battery box.

(Photograph courtesy of Zig Electronics)

87

withdrawing its fuse from the control panel instead.

The subdivision of the main supply into separate routes is achieved using a fused distribution unit. In the United Kingdom, the units are usually made by BCA Leisure, Plug-in-Systems or Zig Electronics. Some are conspicuous in location; others are more discreet and may be mounted behind a hinged cover. In some instances, a fused control unit forms part of a purpose-made battery locker – the Zig PowerMate and the BCA Power Centre are examples.

Another feature included in the circuit is a battery condition indicator; some units are stand-alone items whereas others form part of the fused distribution unit. This provides warning when re-charging is needed.

Some condition indicators show a battery's state using a meter although many distribution units are fitted with two light-emitting diodes instead. A green light on the panel confirms the battery is in good condition; a red light warns that recharging is needed.

Finally, the interior supplies of caravans built after 1st September, 1998 now have to comply with a new standard, EN 1648-1. One of the requirements is that all electrical appliances, *with the exception of the refrigerator*, will cease operation when the caravan is being towed. The reason for this requirement and the way the supply is automatically disabled are described later.

Typical low voltage systems

Even if the broad theory behind a 12V supply seems straightforward, an assembly of multicoloured cables presents a daunting prospect to most owners. In order to clarify the layout, a major supplier of components, Plug-in-Systems, takes a large display board to selected outdoor caravan rallies. This shows key components and these are coupled up on the display just as they would be in a caravan – albeit with abbreviated wiring.

As a further guide, the Company's wiring diagrams clarify the installation shown on the display board. The example reproduced below shows typical wiring in caravans manufactured prior to 1st September, 1998 before the implementation of EN1648-1.

A clear wiring diagram is always useful and it is regrettable that some caravan manufacturers fail to include this information in their owners' handbooks.

Revisions in 1999 models

In order to comply with a new European standard, EN 1648-1, caravans manufactured after 1st September, 1998 incorporate two important revisions. The decision to cease using a charging cable via Pin 2 in a 12S connection was discussed in Chapter 3 and has necessitated changes in the caravan 12V wiring. So too, has the decision that the 12V circuits should be disconnected when a caravan is being towed – with the exception of a 12V supply to the refrigerator.

The reasons behind these changes are related to the problem of Electro-Magnetic Compatibility (EMC). This is described in the box opposite.

It is important to note that whereas changes were effective from 1st September, 1998, some

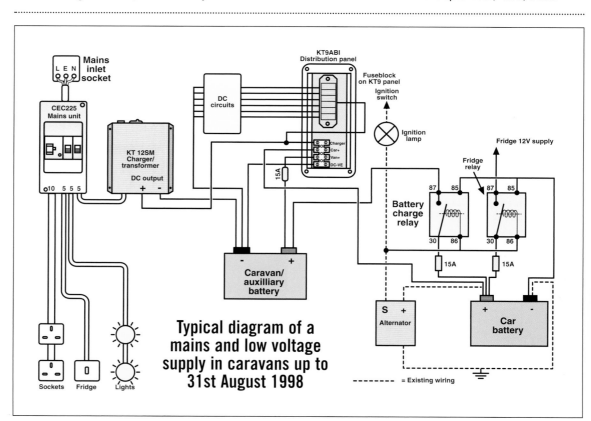

Typical diagram of a mains and low voltage supply in caravans up to 31st August 1998

manufacturers implemented the anticipated revisions *even earlier*. For instance Bailey Caravans had different 12S plug wiring in 1996 models; Elddis and ABI models had changes appearing around 1998, as their Owners' Handbooks revealed.

The changed system operates as follows: when the towcar is coupled up and the engine is running, the caravan refrigerator should receive a 12V supply via Pin 6 of the 12S socket in keeping with the well-established practice. This feature has not been altered.

Moreover, this supply to the fridge provides the signal to a 12V circuit that the caravan is in tow. In electrical terms, the fridge feed triggers an automatic switch known as a relay and it is this component which disconnects the live feeds going to all other appliances – light units, water pump, 12V sockets and so on. A typical wiring circuit containing this relay is shown below.

Most of the latest caravans have a second relay, too, which controls the new double function of Pin 4 on a 12S connection. Note that the dual role of Pin 4 could be controlled by a battery selection switch but to prevent a caravanner having to remember to set this manually, manufacturers are fitting a relay to switch the function automatically.

When a car and caravan are coupled up, under the latest régime, Pin 4 on a 12S plug operates as follows:

Electro-magnetic compatibility (EMC)

Anyone who has flown recently will know that airline operators strictly forbid passengers from using certain electronic appliances during the flight. It appears that a magnetic field might be created by some products which could upset the aircraft's crucial control systems.

As motor vehicles become increasingly controlled by electronic control units, similar fears are being expressed about cars. Important devices like engine management systems and ABS brakes are undoubtedly reliant on electronic circuitry. So the subject referred to as electro-magnetic compatibility is important.

These concerns about circuit interference are partly behind the latest European standards applicable to touring and motor caravans. Some caravan electrical experts claim that this is one of the reasons why caravans built after 1st September, 1998 carry one less current-carrying cable in the 12S socket. Pin 2, previously assigned to provide a charge to a caravan battery, is now left spare.

In addition, as soon as a post 1998 caravan is coupled up and the tow car engine is running, 12V appliances, with the exception of the fridge, are automatically disabled.

1. When the engine is not running, Pin 4 is the route whereby a 12V supply can be drawn from the towcar's battery as an alternative source to the caravan battery.
2. When the engine *is* running, Pin 4 provides a charging supply to the caravan battery.

Relay locations

A relay is a miniature switch which is activated by an electric current. Most types contain a small coil

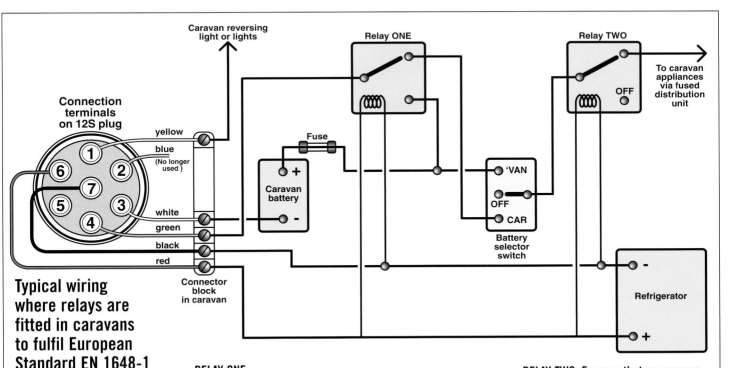

Connection terminals on 12S plug

yellow
blue (No longer used)
white
green
black
red

Connector block in caravan

Caravan reversing light or lights

Fuse

Caravan battery

Relay ONE

Relay TWO

OFF

To caravan appliances via fused distribution unit

'VAN
OFF
CAR
Battery selector switch

Refrigerator

Typical wiring where relays are fitted in caravans to fulfil European Standard EN 1648-1

(Models post 1st September 1998 and some caravans built prior to this date)

RELAY ONE:

When engine is not running – allows the car battery to supply caravan appliances when required via Battery selector switch.

When engine is running – ensures that a charge from the car's alternator is fed to the caravan battery automatically.

RELAY TWO: Ensures that no caravan 12V appliances other than the fridge will operate when the engine is running IRRESPECTIVE of battery selector switch position

that becomes an electromagnet as soon as it receives a current. In its magnetic state it pulls a tiny contact lever which acts as a switch to make, break or divert the flow of current in a circuit.

Occasionally relays develop a fault and need to be replaced which isn't a difficult task. A more testing problem is finding out where the relays are located.

In the case of caravans fitted with the BCA Power Centre – e.g. Coachman and Fleetwood, the relays are fitted in the control unit itself. In some Compass caravans, relays are fitted in a socket mounted in a forward bed box. Some

Elddis caravans will shortly be fitted with an electric module containing the relays, which will be easily accessible in a forward locker.

Suffice it to say, there is little standardisation at present and owners suspecting a fault are advised to seek help from either a main dealer or the caravan manufacturer's Customer Service Department.

Components in the system

Using the preceding information on circuit design, an owner wanting to add additional items or planning to rewire and improve an older caravan

The small coil that operates an electro-magnetic switch is clearly seen in this relay.

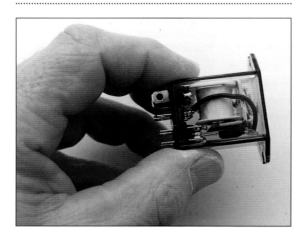

Sometimes caravan relays are fitted inside a control unit – as in the case of the BCA Leisure Power Centre.

It is easy to change a relay when the component is mounted on a connector that has been fitted in a locker.

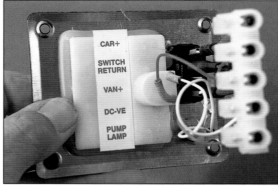

Connections on this Plug-in-Systems battery change-over switch are clearly labelled.

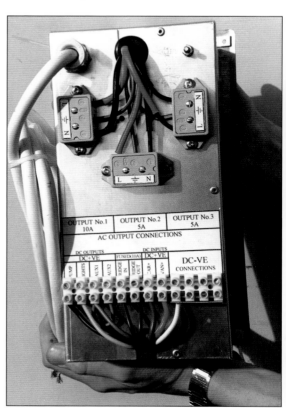

If you fit a fused distribution unit like the Plug-in-Systems PMS3, connections are distinctly marked on the rear.

will now understand modern systems. Most appliances have clear wiring instructions and control items like a battery selection switch or a fused distribution unit are clearly labelled on the casing. Nevertheless, if you plan refurbishment work of this magnitude, take heed of the safety points identified in the box opposite.

Cable

One of the potential weaknesses in caravan wiring is the problem of voltage drop. This is often caused by the use of unsatisfactory cable. Notice that the term 'cable' is used here in preference to the word 'wire'.

If cable is too thin, too long or a combination of both, there will be an appreciable drop in voltage. For instance if a fridge performs poorly in 12V mode when you are towing, one of the tests is to check the input voltage at the connector block on top of the appliance. This is done using a multi-meter when the towcar is coupled and the engine running. The reading should be at least 12V; if it is lower than this, the connecting cable needs to replaced with a thicker cable of higher rating.

A similar test is to take a check across the terminals of an auxiliary battery when it is being charged while the caravan is coupled to the towcar. The reading should be appreciably higher than 13V. In fact a poor charge rate is far more likely to be attributable to the length and rating of the cable than it is to a poorly performing alternator.

These examples affirm that it is crucial to use correct connecting cable.

To gain a fuller grasp of the system it is also helpful to understand a few electrical terms. The box below explains some key words.

Connecting accessories

When coupling up appliances, both the thickness of the supply cables and their length are significant. The previous section has pointed out that:

• a thick cable is needed to ensure there's a good flow of current. If the cable is too thin, there's a resistance to current flow and a safety risk, as explained in the accompanying box.
• cable length also needs consideration – the longer the run, the greater the drop in Volts. So if your leisure battery is situated a long distance from the base vehicle alternator, a significant voltage loss is inevitable when charging the battery while towing the caravan.

As regards the type of cable needed, a caravan 12V system is often wired using automotive cable. This has good flexibility because it is made from separate strands or 'filaments' and these have a standard thickness of 0.33mm². However, caravans wired with a custom-made wiring harness manufactured by BCA Leisure will have mains quality 12V flexible cable which has a thicker insulation sleeve. This is a more costly strategy but it means that in multiple cable runs, both 230V and 12V supplies are permitted to run alongside each other in a pre-made 'wiring loom' or 'harness'.

Automotive cable suitable for 12V wiring is sold at any well-stocked caravan accessory shop.

Safety

■ If you use a cable that is too thin for a high consumption appliance, e.g. a refrigerator, it may start to get warm as a result of the cable's resistance. If the rise in temperature then starts to cause the insulation to melt, there's a serious problem ahead. If several cables are strapped together, for example, melting insulation could lead to a short circuit.

■ A low voltage 12V supply doesn't pose the threat of electrocution like a mains supply. But a powerful spark is caused when there's a short circuit, so an acute fire risk accompanies a 12V system. Melting insulation on a supply cable is similarly dangerous. Fuses in a circuit are intended to eliminate danger situations but they have to be of the correct rating and appropriately located.

Electrical terms

When explaining electrical theory, many textbooks compare the flow of electricity to the flow of water. For instance, you can get a high pressure jet of water coming from a very narrow hose. Alternatively you can have a very large bore hose that releases water in huge quantities even though the pressure here may be much lower. If you combine the two and large quantities flow at great pressure, the rate at which water discharges from a pipe is impressive.

These three situations can be compared to the flow of electricity and the terms Volts, Amps and Watts.

Volts (V) – This unit of measurement is concerned with pressure. In a practical situation, a cable offers a resistance that can lead to a loss of pressure. Moreover, the longer the cable, the greater the drop in voltage.

Amps (A) – Amperes or 'amps' measure the amount of electricity referred to as the 'current'. In practical terms, a caravan fridge needs a large amount of electricity to work properly (8 amps). In consequence it needs a relatively thick connecting cable. In contrast, an interior strip light only needs a small amount of electricity (0.7 amps); so it works quite successfully with a much thinner connecting cable.

Watts – (W) This is the rate at which electrical energy is used and some appliances are more greedy than others. Watts are a combination of both the amount of current (amps) and the pressure of flow (volts). The formulae to remember are:

Watts = Volts x Amps   Amps = Watts ÷ Volts   Volts = Watts ÷ Amps

As regards cable rating, this is governed by the number of copper strands that make up the conductor, and whereas a low consumption appliance like a fluorescent light only needs a thin cable, a high consumption appliance, like a refrigerator, needs thicker cable.

Cable rating is indicated on its packaging and information is sometimes expressed in respect of its cross sectional area in mm^2. Alternatively the label might quote an 'approximate continuous current rating' in amps. On a practical note, if a label is missing, you can confirm cable rating by carefully counting its copper strands. This presumes they are of standard size. Table A below shows the use of different rated cables in caravans.

As regards the length of cable used, the simple advice is, 'the shorter the better'. Table B below expresses the implications in practical terms by quoting the maximum current in amps that a cable can provide taking into account the *total length* of the live and neutral cable connecting an appliance to the power source.

Connections

Sometimes additions are needed in a caravan. For instance you might want to fit a Whale diaphragm pump and the manufacturer is insistent that this is connected up using 2.5mm^2 cable. It would therefore be entirely inappropriate to connect this up to a 12V cable serving a lamp over the kitchen work top. As the accompanying table shows, light units are usually supplied with 1.00mm^2 cable.

In any case, an appliance like a water pump would need to be served directly from the water pump switch and fused supply on the 12V distribution unit. So the supply and return cable should be fed through from here, endeavouring to find the shortest practicable route.

On the other hand, if you want to add some reading lamps in your caravan or halogen spot lights, it is usually acceptable to couple these up to the supply cables feeding a nearby lamp unit. This will involve the use of a connector.

Of the many types of connector, three types are commonly used:

1. Snap locks (Scotchlocks).
2. Crimp connectors.
3. Block connectors.

In this context, electricians tend not to use snap locks. Crimp connectors are better and their overall size allows them to be discreetly hidden. On the other hand, a block connector is easily disconnected and joints can be reformed without difficulty. The final choice is likely to be determined by the location.

Once an appliance is added using the correct type of cable, the run should be discreetly hidden and carefully secured. Where access is achievable, clips should be fitted as follows:

- On horizontal runs – at intervals no greater than 250mm (10in).
- On vertical runs – at intervals no greater than 400mm (16in).

Table A – Confirming cable rating

No of strands	Cross sectional area in mm^2	Current rating in amps	Application in caravans
14	1.00	8.75	Interior lights.
21	1.50	12.75	Wire to extractor fans, but check the model.
28	2.00	17.50	Feed to fridge (minimum) See note.
36	2.50	21.75	Feed to battery from a charger. Feed to a diaphragm water pump e.g. Whale Evenflow.

Note: *For a number of years, Electrolux installation manuals stated that if 2.0mm^2 cable is fitted, the cable run mustn't exceed 8m. Longer cable runs – between 8 to 10.5m – need 2.5mm^2 cable to avoid an unacceptable drop in voltage. More recently, however, Electrolux is strongly recommending 2.5mm^2 cable as a minimum in order to be certain of good refrigerator performance.*

Table B – Maximum current (amps) permitted for cable of different cross sectional areas on the basis of length

Cable size	Maximum cable lengths (supply and return)		
	4 metres	8 metres	12 metres
1.00 mm^2	9.4A	4.7A	3.1A
1.5 mm^2	14.1A	7.0A	4.7A
2.0 mm^2	18.8A	9.3A	6.3A
2.5 mm^2	23.5A	11.7A	7.8A

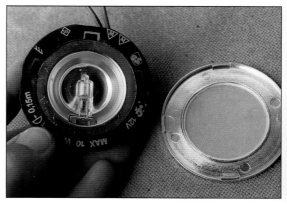

Spotlamps fitted with halogen bulbs are popular now and can be easily added to your caravan.

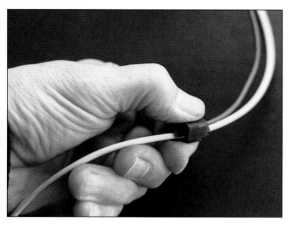

One way to couple a new cable to an existing supply is to use a snap lock.

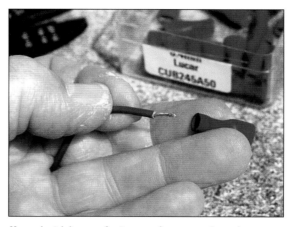

Many electricians prefer to use crimp connectors when adding accessories.

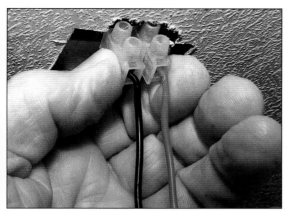

A standard screw coupling is used here for an additional ceiling lamp.

Leisure batteries

A caravan 'leisure' battery should not be regarded as a 'fit and forget' accessory. On the contrary, a battery needs periodic attention and special measures have to be taken if it is likely to remain unused for an extended period.

There are also important differences between a 12V leisure battery and a 12V vehicle battery. In summary:

A vehicle battery is designed to produce a surge of power to operate a starter motor. This is a demanding task, but once the engine is running, the battery gains an immediate recharge from the vehicle's alternator.

A leisure battery has to provide current over an extended period – and some time might elapse before recharging is possible. However, a recharge mustn't be delayed too long. Battery manufacturers also strongly advise owners not to discharge a battery completely – this can cause permanent damage.

The continued pattern of charge/discharge (referred to as deep cycling) is something that a *vehicle battery* cannot endure for long. The lead plates will soon get damaged and the all-important

paste held within them can fall away. In a *leisure battery,* the plates are constructed with separators which retain the paste more effectively. This is reflected in the price although in the long term a leisure battery is a more economic proposition.

In Elecsol leisure batteries, carbon fibre is used in the plate construction as well. This is an unusual development and early indications suggest that Elecsol batteries will give notably long service. Without doubt, the inclusion of a five year warranty is proof of the manufacturer's confidence in the product.

Guidance on use

To get the best from a leisure battery, the following recommendations are put forward by manufacturers:

• The electrolyte must be checked periodically and if the level falls below the top of the plates, it should be topped up with de-ionised water. This is available from car accessory shops.
• A battery must not be left in a discharged state; ignoring this is likely to leave the battery irreparably damaged.
• If a caravan is parked for an extended period, its leisure battery must be kept in a charged condition. To achieve this it is usually removed and

When the level of the electrolyte falls, it should be topped up with de-ionised water.

93

■ The stated capacity of a battery, expressed in Amp hours, presumes the temperature is 25°C (77°F). For every 1°C (approx.) drop in temperature, there's a 1% fall in battery capacity. So when a battery which is nominally rated as 60Ah is operating in a temperature of 15°C (60°F) it effectively becomes a 54Ah battery.

Problems are even more acute for winter caravanners. Not only will a battery work harder to provide lighting and fan-assisted heating on long, dark evenings; the actual capacity of the battery is considerably less than its Ah rating might suggest.

■ Performance between charges deteriorates as a battery gets older.

■ If several appliances are used simultaneously, the faster rate of discharge reduces the effective battery performance still further.

It is recommended to smear battery terminals with a thin coating of grease.

transferred to a bench for charging. Alternatively some owners use a trickle charger like the Airflow or Carcoon products which are left permanently connected.

• Completely sealed non-spill gel electrolyte batteries e.g. the Varta Drymobil, are less common and you should seek the manufacturer's advice about care and maintenance.

• When removing a battery, disconnect the negative terminal first: when installing a battery, connect the negative terminal last.

• The terminals should be smeared with grease, like Tri-Flow, or petroleum jelly (Vaseline).

Checking condition

Battery condition is usually checked with a meter although specific gravity testing is an alternative. A voltage reading is best taken directly from the battery terminals, but several points need to be born in mind:

• It is recommended to use a digital voltmeter since these are easy to read and the level of accuracy is usually good. Voltmeters of this type used to be expensive but that is no longer the case.

• Make sure *all* appliances are disconnected. Even a permanently connected clock can falsify a reading.

• If a battery has just been disconnected from a charger, or you've recently been towing your caravan, the reading will not be a true indication of battery condition. It is necessary for the battery to settle before taking a voltmeter reading and this

means waiting for at least four hours. The reason for the delay is that an elderly battery has a problem holding its charge; if you can wait even longer, e.g. 12 hours, the voltmeter will provide an even better indication of battery condition.

• Whilst a battery is described as providing a 12V power supply, the description is misleading. In fact a reading of 12V indicates the battery is completely discharged. The state of charge is as follows:

Voltmeter reading	Approx. charge state
12.7V or over	100%
12.5V	75%
12.4V	50%
12.2V	25%
12V or under	Discharged

Battery life between charges

The 'capacity' of a battery is expressed in Amp-hours (Ah) and this indicates how long it can provide an output before needing a re-charge. As a rule, the external dimensions of a leisure battery are related to its Ah capacity and whilst a 90Ah battery product needs a re-charge less frequently than a 60Ah version, there isn't always sufficient stowage space. In some purpose-made battery boxes fitted to caravans, there is only space for a 60 or 75Ah version.

In practice, this may not present a problem. If you tour with your caravan and are regularly on the move, the periodic charge received from the towcar is very beneficial. However, if you tend to site your caravan on a pitch for a week or more, a 90Ah battery has clear practical advantages, particularly if there is no mains hook-up.

To assess how long a battery will provide power between charges, a simple calculation makes a rough, but helpful estimation. The procedure is:

1. Establish the wattage of appliances. Typical examples: A single tube strip light – 8W; a spotlight – 10W; a water pump – 50W; a colour TV – 50W.

Note: *The wattage of colour TV sets varies so check the label. Some models such as the Goodmans Compact 510 are as low as 21W max.*

2. Work out how many hours (or fractions of an hour) the appliances will be used in a 24 hour period.

Calculating Ampere hours

Equipment	Rating in Watts	Hours in use	Watt hours
Two 8W lights	16	5	80
Two 10W spot lights	20	1	20
Water pump	50	0.2	10
Colour TV	50	5	250
		Total Watt hours	360

Divide Watt hours by Volts to get Ampere hours:

$$360 \div 12 = 30 \text{ Ah}$$

3. Calculate Watt hours for each appliance by multiplying Wattage by hours in use.
4. Add together the total of Watt hours.
5. Divide Watt hours by Volts to get Ampere hours (Ah).

So if your caravan is fitted with a 60Ah battery, at the rate of use shown in the table on page 94 (30Ah consumed in 24 hours), it will last for two days before a re-charge is needed. If a 90Ah battery is installed, it should last for three days. However, this is only a rough guide and the point was made earlier that running a battery to the point of total discharge is a bad practice.

Other factors play a part, too, as discussed in the technical tip box on the previous page.

Leisure battery location

The closer a leisure battery is to the towcar's alternator, the better the charge rate when you are towing.

The reason for this, as discussed earlier, is that a long run of connecting cable leads to a fall-off in voltage and a poorer charge rate. Admittedly a thicker gauge of cable helps to reduce voltage loss on long cable runs. But the long run of cable from the engine compartment of the towcar and the leisure battery in the caravan reduces charging efficiency very significantly. In fact the term 'trickle charging' is used to describe this situation.

To achieve a better charge rate when towing, some caravanners transfer the leisure battery to the rear of the car. This is coupled up to the vehicle as follows:

1. The battery's positive terminal is connected using a spring battery clamp and a 2.5mm² feed. The feed is connected up to the charging cable that connects either to Pin 2 of the 12S socket on pre 1st September, 1998 caravans or the cable to Pin 4 of the 12S socket on a post 1st September, 1998 caravan.
2. The negative terminal is coupled using 2.5 mm² cable to a sound earthing point in the towcar.

The battery must be secured so it cannot spill acid and it is strongly advised to arrange venting for the hydrogen relief tube. If anyone is smoking in the car when hydrogen is emitted during charging there could be a serious risk.

Since the cable run between the alternator and battery is now greatly reduced the charge rate is higher. This is referred to as 'boost charging'.

To make this transference of the battery to the car comparatively simple, Lab Craft produced the TP2 battery box which has been used by caravanners for many years. Whenever the car is used for a solo drive, TP2 owners transfer the battery in its carrying box to the vehicle, connect using Lab Craft's plug, and achieve a boost charge.

This is a thoughtful system and it's unfortunate that this notable product is no longer being manufactured. New regulations led to its withdrawal in 1999.

The TP2 portable battery box with its built-in mains charger has been popular with caravanners for many years.

Spring-loaded battery clamps are fully recommended; never use crocodile clips.

Other points regarding the location of a battery are:

• A battery should never share a locker with gas cylinders. Rather surprisingly some caravans made in the 1980s were built with a battery fixing point in the forward gas locker. (Gas cylinder valves can leak and a spark from a battery terminal could cause an explosion).
• The preferred location is in a purpose-designed locker, fitted with security straps and vented to the outside.
• Traditional bolt-on connectors sold in auto shops are recommended, although spring battery clamps sold at caravan accessory shops are better still. Avoid using crocodile clips on battery terminals. A clip might become dislodged and a spark across a poor connection can be powerful.
• A battery location must have ventilation. The reason for this is given in the safety box on the right.
• When adding an auxiliary battery in an older caravan, it may have to be fitted in a bed box or in the bottom of a wardrobe. All safety measures should be noted. Make sure the battery is firmly installed so it cannot tip over and ensure there is ventilation. The easiest answer here is to buy a battery with a gas venting tube and to feed this through a narrow hole drilled in the floor.

Charging

Methods of charging a leisure battery can be achieved using the following:

- a portable or fixed mains charger,
- the engine alternator,
- a petrol generator,
- a wind or solar system.

Mains chargers

As regards mains chargers, the following points are worthy of note:

- The amp output of a charger influences how quickly a battery is revived. Too high an amperage, however, is not good for a battery. As a rule of thumb, if you divide a battery's Ah rating by ten, this is the maximum recommended amp output rating of a charger.
- A leisure battery needs a different charging régime from that required by a vehicle battery. This is why an inexpensive portable car battery charger isn't recommended. On the other hand, some of the better types incorporate a selection switch; this provides the appropriate régime for either a car or a leisure battery.
- A battery can be 'over-charged' and when this happens, a situation inaccurately referred to as 'boiling' may occur. As a result, the water content of the electrolyte (diluted sulphuric acid) will start to evaporate. If this happens, the concentrated acid can damage the lead plates; so as soon as charging is completed, the battery must be topped up using de-ionised water.
- There are several separate cells in a battery, each of which has its own top-up point. Sometimes one of the cells will fail and this can upset an automatic charger's sensing system. Instead of switching off automatically when the other cells are recharged, it maintains its full output on account of the failed cell. This is another situation causing the battery to boil and the emission of hydrogen.
- When on a mains hook-up, some people keep a built-in caravan charger running all the time. This is acceptable with older chargers that incorporated a transformer. However, some manufacturers of 'switched mode' electronic chargers recommend

the charger is turned off when the battery level indicator shows a satisfactory condition. The charger from BCA Leisure forming part of the Power Centre unit is an exception and can be left on permanently without detriment.

- Bear in mind that a 12V supply should not be drawn directly from a mains-operated charger, *without* having a battery in place. This is because the output will fluctuate and some appliances *must* have a stable supply. Having a battery in circuit smoothes out irregularities and prevents damage to appliances.
- The charge rate on a gel-type battery (as opposed to one containing diluted sulphuric acid) should not exceed 13.8V.
- In spite of warnings, some caravanners still attempt to use a 12V supply without a leisure battery in circuit (i.e. by drawing directly from a charger as if it were a transformer/rectifier). Recognising this, manufacturers of built-in chargers limit their output to 13.8V as a safety measure. This introduces a problem with dilute sulphuric acid batteries as the next point emphasises.
- To start the charging process where a battery is in low condition, a number of battery manufacturers specify that a start-up output from a charger of 14.2 to 14.4V is essential. When the battery's voltage reaches a certain level, charger output should then fall back to a 13.8 'float' voltage. Some battery manufacturers assert that a discharged battery might *never* re-achieve its peak condition if a 14.2 to 14.4 start-up voltage cannot be delivered by the charger.
- The emission of hydrogen from a battery under charge (called 'gassing') normally doesn't start until a charger output is around 14.2V.

Taking the above points into account, the best type of charger is one offering 'stage charging'. This commences with an output around 14.4V, then dropping to 13.8V, and subsequently

The Guardian Leisure Charger is one of the few portable units that provide stage charging.

The BCA battery charger is a compact unit that can be left running when coupled to a mains hook-up.

The Carcoon trickle charger is designed to be left connected to a battery all through a lay-up period.

switching off automatically when the battery achieves a full charge. A product achieving this is the Selmar Guardian Leisure and Marine charger which is a portable unit. Similarly the Lab Craft BC126 and BC1210 variable output chargers that were fitted into the more recent TP2 battery carrying boxes offer stage charging.

Other useful products include the Airflow Battery Conditioner and the Carcoon Conditioner/Charger. These compact units are made for the classic car owner as a way of keeping batteries charged when a vehicle is laid up. Their use is now recognised by caravan owners. The products indicate battery condition via light emitting diodes (LEDs) and provide charging when connected to the mains. Electronic circuits monitor battery condition and activate the units automatically when charging is needed. In consequence these automatic trickle chargers can be left connected for the entire winter lay-up period.

The engine alternator

The charge from a vehicle alternator is high and can provide the needs of both the car and caravan batteries. When the caravan battery is left in the caravan, there will be a gentle (i.e. 'trickle charge') while the caravan is being towed via the 12S connection. However, it was mentioned earlier that a higher 'boost charge' is achievable by transferring the battery to the rear of the towcar.

Petrol generators

With the widespread use of 'switched-mode' battery chargers in caravans, the fluctuating supply that frequently comes from a petrol generator can present problems. A sudden surge is referred to as a 'spike' and further reference to this is made in Chapter 8. Difficulties occur if you plug the 230V output from a generator into your caravan mains system and then operate the in-built charger. It is much better to charge the battery *directly* by coupling up to the separate 12V terminals fitted to most generators.

On the other hand, older chargers built with a transformer, seem to be less susceptible to damage from supply irregularities.

Solar and wind generators

The idea of getting 'something for nothing' is very attractive. On the other hand, these types of generator will only provide a trickle charge for a battery.

If you park a caravan on an exposed site or at a storage location in a region known to have sustained windy weather, a wind generator would be able to provide a battery with a useful trickle charge. Marlec systems are well known. However, these appliances are more useful for marine applications than they are for caravanning.

On the other hand, solar panels are dependent on light rather than weather and you can certainly keep a battery topped up in favourable conditions if you purchase:

- a good quality panel,
- a voltage control unit, and
- the appropriate installation components.

Strictly speaking, the term 'solar' is inaccurate because photo-voltaic cells also produce some electricity in cloudy weather. They do not depend on sunshine, nor for that matter do they need heat. In fact the bright light in cold arctic locations is more effective than the hazy light often found in the heat of a Mediterranean location.

During a winter lay-up, a large roof-mounted solar panel may be able to keep a battery in fair condition, although shorter daylight hours do not help. In the longer days of summer, the output is very much better. In fact some users report that when a large panel like a Siemens SR90 5.30 a/90W panel is coupled up to a 90Ah battery, it is possible to be completely self-contained.

Several products are available, complete with installation kits, but both the weight and the initial cost of high output panels are substantial. Indeed the notion of 'something for nothing' is certainly not the case in this instance.

Solar panels are available from specialists such as A. B. Butt who supply caravanners with compact units for portable use or large high-output models for roof mounting. A control unit prevents a solar panel from over-charging and can also report both battery condition and solar output.

The mains supply system

Modern caravans are equipped with appliances that operate from a 230 Volts AC supply. This chapter explains in detail how a mains system is installed and used.

In 1977, The Caravan Club arranged to have twelve mains power sockets installed on one of its sites. The idea was unusual in those days and few caravanners would have imagined that twenty years later, most large sites would be similarly equipped. Some of the latest hook-ups even feature a credit card 'swipe' facility so you only pay for the electricity consumed during your stay.

Since these early trials, a lot has changed. For instance:

• it is no longer appropriate to speak of 240V; today the nominal voltage is 230V AC with a permitted variation of +10% and −6%.
• nearly all modern caravans are fitted with a mains system as standard.
• in caravans made from 1995 onwards, manufacturers have been obliged to include an approved hook-up cable.
• standardisation of items like hook-up sockets is happening throughout many European countries,

Some sites have hook-ups where the electricity used is shown on a digital read-out; payment is made using a credit card 'swipe' facility.

although an adaptor should still be taken abroad.

Notwithstanding the present popularity of 230V provision, many older caravans are not wired for mains; so the work entailed in fitting an approved supply system is described later in this chapter.

Also covered are the procedures for connecting safely to a supply, and the way to calculate what electrical appliances can be used without overloading a site's supply capability.

Assessing the appliances you can use

On arrival at a site reception office, enquire how many amps are available from the hook-up points. Occasionally you may even come across a two-tier provision and two pricing bands. To convert the information to Watts, multiply the current rating (usually expressed as Ampères or amps) by the Voltage (230V). In other words, a site offering 5A would be suitable for operating appliances whose total Wattage doesn't exceed 1150W.

Practical implications

The term 'amps' refers to the *amount* of current available whereas most electrical appliances are

Safety

In one of its technical leaflets, *The Camping and Caravanning Club* states that 'Electricity is a very good friend but an even worse enemy'.
This is an important reminder. Fortunately the standards of equipment in Britain and the practices adopted are generally very good, but in some parts of Europe you may come across less impressive arrangements. If a hook-up point looks doubtful, it may be wise not to couple-up to a supply.
Be careful too, if you see slender lengths of twin flex cable coupled into mains hook-up points. Some may be merely joined with insulation tape and when you take into account the sudden downpours that characterise Continental thunderstorms, the situation becomes more worrying still. Always exercise vigilance; you will find some sites that have rudimentary installations whereas others exemplify the very best in electrical standards.

rated in Watts – which refers to their *rate* of consumption. For instance a light bulb might be rated at 60W whereas a Carver water heater is rated at 600W. A conventional domestic kettle used at home may be rated as high as 2500W – typically expressed as 2.5kW where 'k' refers to a thousand. As a general rule, the Wattage of appliances is shown on a label – or marked on the glass dome of a light bulb.

The remarkable difference in the rate of consumption between a light bulb and a conventional electric kettle is very clear. Bearing in mind that some sites only provide a maximum of 5A, it is immediately apparent why you have to leave normal domestic appliances like kettles, pop-up toasters, and deep fat fryers at home. If you want an electric kettle on holiday, the answer is to buy one of the special caravan types rated around 750W. Low Wattage kettles or heating jugs work well – they merely take longer to boil.

However, what will happen if you exceed the stated limit of a hook-up? Happily, there's unlikely to be a danger element if the installation is safe. Should you overload the supply, the site's safety cut-out comes into operation, leaving you with no electricity at all. The only recourse then is to seek the help of the site staff who will have to reset the supply to your hook-up – recognising that they're unlikely to respond in unsocial hours.

With this in mind, you can carry out a simple calculation to ensure you don't trip the site's overload switch. The procedure is to:

- establish the amp supply at your hook-up point.
- multiply this by 230 to establish the rate of consumption in Watts, as mentioned in the previous section,
- check the Wattage of all mains appliances in your caravan,
- monitor what you have running at any one time, adding up the total Wattage of each appliance and confirming that you are keeping well within the site's limit. *But note the later section on problems that can occur at times of peak demand.*

A rough idea of typical power ratings are given in the box above.

Problems at peak periods

Caravanners have been quick to grasp the benefits of having a mains supply, so it is hardly surprising that manufacturers have responded by offering water heaters, space heaters, fans, chargers, air conditioners and other appliances that operate on 230V. This hasn't been without its problems.

It is true that some sites can offer a hook-up output as high as 16A from an individual supply pillar. But this presumes that all visitors are not hoping to run an array of appliances *at the same time*. In winter when the evenings are dark and temperatures low, more and more caravanners switch on an electrically operated space heater, a colour TV, an array of lights, and keep the hot water storage heater and fridge running on mains as well.

Assessing what appliances you can use

Remember that some sites provide as little as 5A – some are even lower. On the other hand, some offer up to 16A from their individual hook-ups and several Caravan Club venues are examples.

As regards electrical appliances and accessories, these are typically:

Light bulb	60W
Small Colour TV	50 W
Battery charger	100 W
Refrigerator	125 W
Microwave oven	1300 W
Domestic kettle	2,500 W

When adding up the Wattages of the appliances in use *at any one time* make sure you don't overlook items like an unseen battery charger, a refrigerator, a hot water storage heater or a Fanmaster heat distribution unit.

When this happens, the supply is simply unable to cope and posters recently displayed at Caravan Club sites have urged members to exercise careful vigilance over the draw on current.

In reality, if a site is full in winter and if caravans are coupled into the hook-ups on *every* pitch, the *actual* supply available is far lower than 16A at each hook-up point. It has even been stated that a simultaneous demand of *5A* from every hook-up is likely to lead to a site supply failure.

Whilst it is true that the cabling and components could be upgraded to provide a true 16A from every supply socket simultaneously, the cost of the installation would run into millions of pounds.

Coupling procedure

For safety's sake, a strict procedure should be followed:
1. Check that the site supply pillar looks safe and doesn't have an array of badly coupled cabling and adaptors. On some sites abroad, adherence to safety standards in the height of the season leaves a lot to be desired.
2. Ensure the switch on the caravan's mains control unit is OFF.
3. Unwind the cable into large, loose coils and trail it towards the coupling pillar making sure it lays flat on the ground. Never leave it tightly wound on a drum because it might get hot and in extreme cases the insulation can melt.
4 Couple the blue female plug (with recessed tubes) into the input socket of your caravan. *Connect this end of the cable first.*
5. Then couple the other end of the cable to the site supply. On some of the Caravan Club sites the plug has to be inserted and then rotated clockwise to engage the contacts.
6. Stow any surplus cable out of the way in loose coils under the caravan to ensure it doesn't get in the way.
7. Switch on the supply at the mains Consumer Unit in your caravan, and then test the trip button to confirm that the residual current device is responding by switching off instantly. Reset the safety switch.

Operation of the safety cut-out, called an RCD, can be confirmed by pressing a test button on the Consumer Unit.

A polarity tester from W4 Accessories is available from most caravan accessory shops.

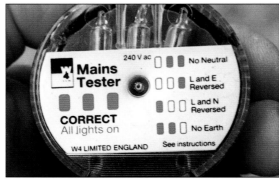

On some sites, it is necessary to depress a release button before withdrawing the hook-up connector.

8. Having coupled up, it's wise to check polarity – there may be a warning light on your Mains Supply Unit. Failing this, you can purchase a polarity tester and the product from W4 Accessories is stocked at most caravan accessory shops. Fit this into one of the 13A sockets, switch on and check the display lights in conjunction with the information on the tester's label.

9. If it is confirmed that the polarity of the supply is reversed, refer to the later section which describes the implications of this reversal.

Disconnection

1. Switch off the supply at the caravan mains control unit.

2. Disconnect the cable from the supply pillar. On some sockets – especially on Caravan Club sites – you have to press a red release button in order to withdraw the coupling plug

3. Recoil the cable and disconnect from the caravan.

Polarity

In the UK, it has been traditional for switches to create a break in the live cable serving an appliance or lamp fitting. In other words when a light is switched off, current is prevented from reaching either the bulb or its socket. On the other hand, the neutral wire remains permanently connected to the lamp fitting.

On the Continent the arrangement is different because the switches used abroad create a break in both live *and* neutral connections, a system known as double-pole switching. This is undoubtedly a very safe arrangement. It means that if the live and neutral feeds are reversed – a situation referred to as 'reverse polarity' – the

supply current is still unable to reach an appliance or a light fitting.

Unfortunately reverse polarity can be very dangerous for the UK tourist whose caravan is normally only fitted with single-pole switches. When you switch off an appliance it is true that it ceases to function. But if we take a lamp as an example – *the light fitting remains live* because polarity reversal means that the switch creates a break in the neutral cable which leads *out* of the unit.

In a situation of reversed polarity, the usual advice is to cease using a supply – just in case you accidentally touch a live connection.

To overcome the problem, some caravanners take a second Continental adaptor intentionally wired up with reversed connections and duly marked with a bold label to indicate the reversal. This effectively remedies the problem at the supply point itself.

As a result of IEE regulations, caravans manufactured since 1994 now have a double-pole switched RCD and double-pole MCBs so the level of protection is improved. Regrettably however, 13A sockets with single-pole switches are still fitted

Some caravanners buy a second Continental adaptor and change over the live and neutral cables to suit hook-ups which have reversed polarity.

Markings on the reverse side of 13A sockets in the Concept range from W4 confirm they are double-pole switched.

in spite of the fact that double-pole sockets are now available in the UK. The Concept Range, sold by W4 Accessories, is an example and their double-pole switching is verified in the moulded plastic lettering on the reverse of these units.

If double-pole switched sockets, together with a double-pole switched RCD and double-pole switched MCBs are fitted, the danger posed by a hook-up with reversed polarity is now eliminated as far as the caravanner is concerned. On the other hand, some appliances, e.g. lap-top computers, might be polarity-sensitive, in which case damage could occur.

Mains system components

Bearing in mind that a towed caravan is subjected to some destructive movements on bumpy roads, the specifications for a mains system are different from those which apply to wiring in our homes.

If you decide to wire up an older caravan to accept a mains supply, the kit from Powerpart provides all the items you need.

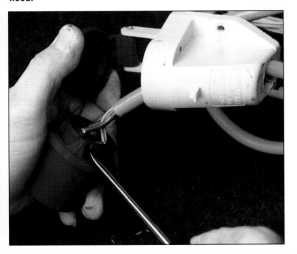

Only the correct components for caravan installations should be used. So if you purchase a pre-owned caravan which contains a DIY mains installation, it is imperative that this is checked by a qualified electrician before being put into commission.

As regards owner installation, some very good kits are available and enable a competent and careful practitioner to install a mains supply where one hasn't already been fitted. Kits from suppliers like Powerpart or W4 Accessories, for example, are stocked in many caravan accessory shops. Purchasing a full kit of parts in this way ensures you have components of the correct type and quality.

Many people would entrust this work to a qualified electrician, of course, but *some* DIY enthusiasts undoubtedly have the knowledge and ability to fit one of these kits themselves. Simple electrical connections will have to be made but a lot of the work only involves carpentry.

As regards the provision itself, this should comprise:

1. A caravan hook-up cable with couplings.

The couplings are 16A industrial products which have to be blue in colour and compliant with BS EN 60309-2. Plugs and sockets of this pattern are often seen on building sites and at other industrial locations. Hook-up points on caravan sites in the UK have been equipped to receive these couplings for many years and this pattern is now required at new sites in European Member States.

In addition, the coupling lead has to be heavy duty three-core flexible PVC shielded cable in which the cross sectional area of each core is 2.5 mm^2. This coupling lead should be 25m long (+ or −2m) and should meet BS EN 60309-2.

A longer cable should not be used, nor for that matter is it deemed acceptable to link up more than one extension lead.

Note: *If you want to connect the supply lead to a 13A socket at home – perhaps to pre-cool a fridge prior to departure – you'll need an adaptor. Similarly another adaptor is needed to connect into many of the hook-up pillars used abroad.*

101

If you want to couple up a caravan supply lead to a 13A domestic socket at home, you'll need a special adaptor.

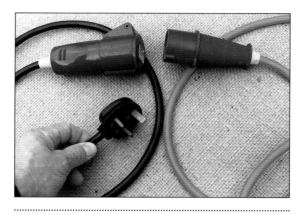

Wall-mounted inlets sometimes include a release lever which has to be depressed in order to withdraw the connecting plug.

2. Caravan Inlet

At the caravan end of the supply lead, the blue plug is designed with deeply recessed tubes to eliminate any chance of making accidental contact with the live connectors. The caravan itself will correspondingly be fitted with a 16A inlet to meet BS EN 60309-2.

The location of the inlet socket should not be higher than 1.8m above the ground. Curiously in some mid-eighties caravans (e.g. imported Homecar models) the socket was often positioned above head height which was most inconvenient.

A surface-mounted input socket is no longer

considered suitable if installed below the floor. Even if fitted with a protective cap these sockets are easily damaged by road dirt and debris. However, if you don't want to cut into the wall of your caravan to have a boxed socket with hinge lid fitted, a face fitted socket can be installed in an exterior locker as long as it is not a locker used for gas cylinders or gas supply pipe.

As a point of interest, some sockets now feature a retention catch and a release lever to prevent the plug from being accidentally withdrawn.

Even when there's a protection cap, face fitting inlet sockets are no longer considered acceptable for installation below the floor.

To afford good protection, some face fitting sockets are located in a locker – but never use a locker containing gas cylinders or supply pipes.

3. A permanently installed connection to the caravan consumer unit

The first length of cable inside the caravan which runs from the inlet socket to the mains consumer unit is *not* protected by the Residual Current Device (RCD). Only the wiring runs, sockets and appliances that are in the circuit *after* the RCD are protected by the safety trip switches.

For this reason the run of cable here should be continuous and as short as possible. In any event it shouldn't exceed 2m and it must either be installed within conduit or attached to the structure securely using insulated clips. These should be no further apart than 0.25m on a horizontal run and 0.40m on a vertical run.

This part of the internal system should be carried out using 3-core PVC flexible cable in which each core has a cross sectional area of 2.5 mm^2. This is the same as the cable specified for the outside coupling lead.

4. Consumer Unit

To meet regulations, a mains control or 'consumer unit' has to fulfil several functions. It should be fitted with:
• an isolating switch,
• over-current protection (achieved by miniature circuit breakers or MCBs),
• a double-pole residual current device (RCD) to comply with BS4293.

A number of products meet these requirements although there are several variations in design. For instance many caravans are fitted with a stand-

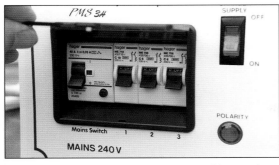

The RCD and 3 MCBs shown here are integrated into a unit which also houses a battery charger and fuses for the 12V supply system..

alone consumer unit. Products from Hager are well-known examples. On the other hand, there are also instances where the mains consumer unit is integrated into a larger control system which incorporates controls and fuses for 12V systems as well. This is the case with the Power Box from BCA Leisure and the Power Management (PMS3) from Plug-in-Systems.

Further variations will be found in respect of the MCB provision. Many units are fitted with one MCB rated at 5 or 6A which protects lighting circuits, battery charger circuits and fridge circuits from overload situations. A second MCB rated at either 10A or 16A is designated to afford protection to the socket outlets fitted in the caravan. In some installations a third MCB is included as well.

5. Bonding requirements

To meet the regulations, a bonding cable no less than 4mm² has to be connected from the RCD earth to the chassis and to any other conductive parts with the exception of the aluminium wall panels on a caravan. So if a metal sink is fitted, this must be bonded – just as it should be in a modern house.

The cable will have a green and yellow sheathing and the point of connection should bear a warning tag advising users not to disconnect it.

Note: *Some caravanners express concern that although an earth wire is attached to the chassis, corner steadies are often lowered on to wooden or plastic blocks, thus preventing earthing to the*

A mains system in a caravan must include an earth bonding wire which is connected to the chassis and marked with a warning tag.

ground. However, earthing via this route is not necessary – earthing is carried out via the earth pin on the hook-up socket in accordance with the procedure detailed in BS 7671:1992.

6. Internal connecting cable

Connections from the consumer unit to appliances, e.g. the refrigerator and the 13A sockets, must be made with 1.5 mm² *flexible cable*. To fulfil IEE regulations, this has to be fixed permanently and whereas running it within conduit is acceptable, clips are more commonly used. These should be spaced no further apart than 0.25m on horizontal runs and 0.4m on vertical runs.

The reason for specifying *flexible* cable whose conducting wires are multi-stranded is the fact that it is more able to absorb jarring movements at points where connections are made. The twin and earth flat PVC sheathed cable used for connecting up 13A sockets in our homes should *not* be used for connecting up the 13A sockets in a caravan. Its single strand copper conductor is not sufficiently resilient.

Normally the cable runs will be unbroken. However, if there is a need to connect lengths of cable in the installation, this should be achieved using a junction box fitted in an accessible location.

7. Switches, sockets and spurs

The 13A sockets in a caravan are fitted into either a flush fit or surface-mounted box. It is important that the plugs on appliances carry a fuse of the correct rating. Many 13 plugs are sold with a 13A fuse, but if you are using this for a table lamp, it is important to change this for a
3A fuse – as you should at home. Manufacturers of appliances like TV sets and hair dryers will similarly specify the fuse needed in the plug.

As a rule, the switched sockets fitted in caravans are seldom double-pole switched types. In view of the recurring problem of reversed polarity experienced on many sites abroad this is a pity. Sockets from the W4 Concept Range are double-pole switched and are well worth considering in an upgrading project.

Where an electric space heater, an electric water heater and a refrigerator are fitted, these should be coupled directly into their own fused spur socket outlet. These usually carry a red neon

Safety

■ A mains system should be checked annually by a qualified electrician and a written certificate issued to verify the installation is safe.
  Periodically check your RCD operation by pressing the test button. This should switch off the system instantly – just as it should if anyone accidentally touched a live wire.
■ It's best to use only double insulated appliances in your caravan. The BEAB approval sign is affixed to appliances fulfilling this safety requirement.

Double-pole switched
sockets in the Concept
range from W4 Accessories
can also be purchased with
12V and TV aerial sockets in
the same unit.

indicator and this switched control should be as close to the appliance as possible.

Normally a battery charger is fitted into a mains system as well and if one of these is added in an upgrade project, the manufacturer's instructions regarding connections should be followed. Some are stand-alone items whereas other chargers are built into a mains and 12V fused distribution unit.

The Consumer Unit supplied with a Powerpart Mains Kit is pre-wired in order to make the installation much easier.

Installation requirements

If you have purchased an older caravan and want a mains installation, the easiest way to do this is to purchase the Powerpart Mobile Power Unit. This is a self-contained product that offers three 13A sockets and the unit is pre-connected with hook-up cable. It carries the full complement of protective devices like the RCD and MCBs that would be found in permanent installations. But not only can you take this portable product with you when selling a caravan: it is a protection system you can also use whenever operating DIY power tools at home.

However, if you want to fit a permanent mains system, it is recommended that a kit is purchased. Some have pre-connected consumer units in which the input supply cable, output cable for the sockets and earth cable are already coupled up and hanging from the box. In reality, you still need to take off the front casing to gain access to the screw fixing holes, but a pre-connected unit certainly simplifies the installation.

When fixing the consumer unit, choose a

location where it is easy to see and where its control switches are accessible. In addition you will almost certainly need to strengthen the wall panel or furniture panel on which it is going to be located. This is easily done by glueing and screwing a base piece of 9mm (⅜in) plywood to the surface as a reinforcement. Cut this to the size of the consumer unit and use an impact adhesive like Evo-Stik.

A similar strategy is likely when fitting 13A sockets. The standard 3mm decorative ply used in caravans is not sufficient to provide a stable base. Nor does it offer sufficient depth for the threads of the fixing screws.

When the installation is complete, you should have it checked by a qualified electrician before putting it into commission.

In order to screw a Consumer Unit in place, the cover has to be removed to reveal the fixing holes on the back plate.

The Powerpart Portable
Mains Unit is ideal for use
in an older caravan when
the owner doesn't want to
fit a permanent installation.

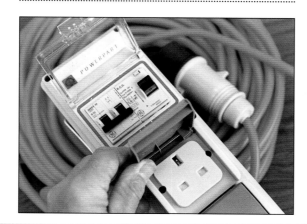

Portable Generators

In a remote location a generator can be extremely useful; but on a crowded site its noise is undoubtedly intrusive.

A portable generator's output is also limited and there are usually power surges when the load on the engine changes suddenly. This happens, for example, when a timed cooking period on a microwave oven reaches completion. The resulting surge can damage appliances like a battery charger that is connected up to the generator's mains supply when the microwave oven cuts out.

Nevertheless, there are several surprisingly silent models available and the Honda EX650 is a good example. Like other similar machines this compact machine produces a maximum output of 650W at its 60Hz setting. However, when selecting the 50Hz setting to run voltage-sensitive appliances the maximum output is lower. In effect the scope is fairly limited and the Technical Tip box on the right regarding microwave ovens should be checked.

Perhaps the biggest problem has been in respect of battery charging arrangements. In the last few years, caravans have been fitted with switched-mode chargers instead of the earlier transformer-type chargers which were heavier. Since the switched-mode charger is permanently wired into the caravan's 230V system, should you decide to draw a mains supply from a generation, a power surge is likely to damage the electronic circuits in the charger.

Fortunately the older transformer-type battery chargers fitted up to the early 1990s are less likely to sustain damage. However, this is the reason why several portable mains generators also have a 12V outlet. This enables you to by-pass your caravan charger altogether by coupling the 12V

terminals on the generator *directly* to the terminals on the leisure battery as shown on page 97.

Limitations aside, generators have a useful part to play and if you prefer to use remote farm locations rather than large holiday parks, they are worthy accessories to consider.

Inverters

Another way to gain mains power is to draw current from the 12V system and to convert it into a 230V supply using an inverter. Models like the Xcell from Driftgate 2000 and the Sterling inverters from RoadPro are well-respected. Other models like the PROwatt are popular, too.

Permanently installing a product like the Xcell is extremely easy. It should be located near the battery, fixed securely and connected to the live and neutral battery terminals. The device can then run mains appliances providing their Wattage doesn't exceed the rating of the inverter. Larger inverters designed to run high Wattage appliances are also available in the Driftgate 2000 and Sterling ranges.

Without doubt, where lighting and low wattage appliances are concerned, an inverter is excellent, but its supplying battery effectively limits the possibilities. For example a 250W inverter – even if 100% efficient – would draw more than 20A from a battery when working to its limit. In consequence a 60Ah battery would be completely discharged in less than three hours.

Note: *In practice, no inverter is 100% efficient, so the discharge rate is also affected by unavoidable power loss.*

On the other hand, you often want to use an appliance for a short spell and since a sound battery has a self-recovery element, using an item like a hair dryer or shaver is unlikely to create difficulties. Even comparatively high wattage appliances can be used briefly with some inverters without necessarily discharging a battery totally.

To enjoy the benefits of mains lighting, and to run low wattage appliances, the value of an inverter is unquestioned – especially if you have a 90Ah battery in your caravan.

A Consumer Unit should be located where it is easy to see and control – but the recommendation was not followed in this 1999 model.

The Xcell inverter from Driftgate 2000 converts 12V DC from a battery to 230V AC mains power.

A growing number of caravanners are interested in microwave ovens and hope that one of these appliances will run from their generator. Unfortunately it is seldom possible – unless you have a large output generator. This confuses many people, especially if they own a generator offering a 650W output when their microwave oven is rated at 500W.

The point to note is that if your microwave oven is rated at 500W, this figure relates to the oven's *output* as opposed to the *input* it requires. To establish if your generator can run a microwave oven, the advice from specialist suppliers Phoenix Power & Equipment is to double the oven's quoted wattage and then deduct 10%. Hence a microwave oven rated at 500W, would need a generator producing at least 900W. Regrettably this is creeping into the small industrial size units which are considerably noisier and less compact than the 'leisure' models.

Contents

Carver Products

Throughout this chapter there are references to Carver water products which have been fitted in many caravans. Since this 3rd Edition was written the Company has closed the division manufacturing components for caravans and motorhomes. However, spare parts, accessories (like water filters), and similar products are available from Truma UK whose address appears in Appendix C.

Water systems

In order to carry out servicing, repairs and precautionary winterising jobs, it is important to know how a caravan's supply and waste systems work.

Like many services in a modern caravan, the water system has become increasingly sophisticated. Electrically driven pumps are standard nowadays and nearly all new caravans have a hot and cold water supply.

At the same time, some features are disappointing. Even when a high quality pump is fitted, the connecting supply pipes cannot always be described as 'state of the art' plumbing.

In waste water systems, for example, it is not unusual for water to empty from a sink or basin at a sluggish rate – a feature that can so easily be improved. Curing a problem like this is discussed later and recommendations for improvements are proposed throughout the chapter.

Moreover, to ensure that owners of a wide range of models can identify the system they have fitted, the chapter also looks at the different components installed over the last thirty years or so.

Fresh water supply

As caravans became more sophisticated, one of the changes was the move away from manually operated pumps. Electric pumps are now a standard feature. This change was prompted by a desire to provide hot – as well as cold – water at the sink, coupled with a decision to introduce hot showers in caravans. Running a shower is not something that can be achieved using a footpump!

Notwithstanding the benefit of these creature comforts, the earlier manual systems undoubtedly had their merits.

Pre-electric systems

Many 1970s caravans are still in use and few will be fitted with an electric pump or a water heater. These 'cold water' caravans rely either on a hand-operated pump mounted on the sink – like the Whale Flipper, or a foot pump fitted at floor level – like the Whale Tiptoe model.

In the case of foot-operated products, water is delivered from a faucet – the name given to a permanently-open outlet. This is different from a tap which has a mechanical system for physically arresting the flow of water.

As a rule, hand or foot pumps are very reliable and continue to be used in cabin cruisers as well as caravans. Parts are therefore available for the more popular models. As regards the rest of the system, it merely comprises the supply pipe – though there may also be a non-return valve fitted near the input point.

A non-return valve is a small component fitted within a run of pipe. It is connected up so that water will only pass in one direction, namely towards the sink outlet. Its purpose is to prevent water from draining back through the system every time you stop using the pump.

If we look at the pipe needed in a system driven by a foot pump, there are only two lengths. These are:

- a feed pipe to the pump that couples to the inlet point on the caravan,
- a run from the output side of the pump to the faucet on the sink.

The sheer simplicity of the system is its attraction. Anyone owning an older model who uses sites equipped with a washroom and who doesn't mind boiling a kettle to get washing-up water might be advised to make no changes to the arrangement. There is hardly anything to go wrong in a cold water system.

Electrically pumped systems

Hot and cold systems require *many* more components. These include:

- an inlet socket,
- a non-return valve,
- an electric pump,
- a battery to power the pump (*see* Chapter 7),
- a switch to activate the pump,
- a pipe system,
- a drain down point,
- a water heater (*see* Chapter 10),
- taps and shower controls.

This is a simplification, however, and several *different* types of electric pump are in use. Accordingly this has an influence on the type of inlet socket fitted. Equally there are three types of switches for setting a pump in motion. These are:

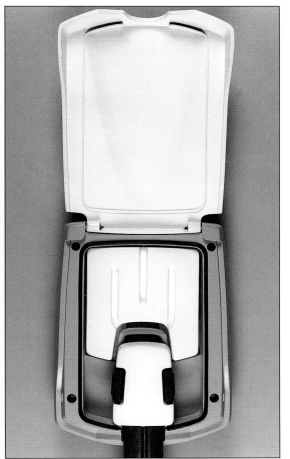

Many recent models are fitted with a Carver Crystal MkII wall-mounted inlet.

- a button switch (e.g. Whale BS7204) or a foot switch (e.g. Whale FS7210). In practice these are seldom used;
- switches built into each tap – one for hot, one for cold and referred to as 'microswitches';
- a pressure-sensitive switch located in one of three places – fitted in a supply pipe, integrated within an inlet socket, or built into the pump.

Although these are the main features fitted in caravans, you will often come across other arrangements as follows:

Winter inlet

Some owners fit an additional water input point inside a caravan so that the water container can be brought indoors when caravanning in sub zero temperatures. *Carver* used to supply an installation kit for this winterising arrangement. The water container would be placed in the shower tray and the alternative input mounted on one of the internal walls in the washroom. When two inputs are fitted a blocking plug must be inserted into the one not being used.

Direct coupling pitches

Using this system you can connect up permanently to a water supply point that exclusively supplies

Winter inlet conversion

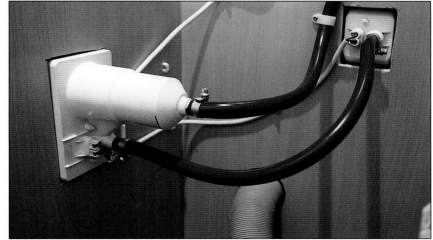

1. The additional socket on the right is mounted on an interior wall of the shower compartment.

2. When there's frost outside, the water container is placed in the shower tray.

3. A blocking plug has to be fitted on the exterior socket before water is drawn from the inlet inside the caravan.

your pitch. The provision is appearing on a growing number of the larger caravan parks and a special coupling hose is needed to take advantage of the service. For instance the Carver 'Waterline' unit was made for coupling into a Carver Compact inlet.

Alternatively the Whale 'Aqua Source' includes an adaptor so you can couple into either a Whale Watermaster socket, or a Carver Compact inlet. Both products feature a pressure-reducing valve so the mains supply will not damage the couplings in the caravan's plumbing system.

NOTE: *The supply hose is fitted* **in place of** *a submersible pump. If your caravan is fitted with an inboard diaphragm pump, the coupling cannot be used unless the plumbing is modified to bypass the pump.*

The Whale Aqua Source is one of the kits for coupling-up directly into a pitch supply pillar.

Taste filters must be changed periodically; this Carver cartridge is removed with a 'T' shaped key.

Inboard water tank

Some caravans are fitted with an inboard tank and the 1999 Bessacarr Cameo is an example. The arrangement is common in motorcaravans since they are more easily driven to a water point for refilling. On a touring caravan – which is less convenient to move to a tap – a long coupling hose is needed to refill the tank. Alternatively you could take a portable water container for replenishment, but this rather defeats the object of the system.

In-line taste filters have to be unclipped and disconnected from the feed pipe.

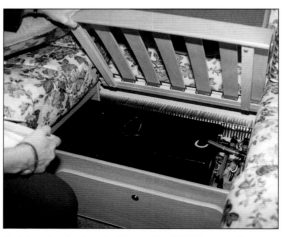

An inboard water tank is fitted on the 1999 Bessacar Cameo.

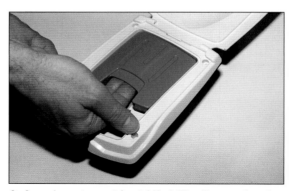

On Carver's most recent Crystal Mark III wall connection, the filter can be removed by hand, though a sustained pull is needed.

Taste filters

In recognition of the unpalatable characteristics of some types of tap water, many caravans are fitted with a taste filter. This should not be confused with the grit filter fitted on many pumps. Nor should it be confused with water treatment units in which bacteria are killed by an infra red lamp. Taste filters are normally fitted with charcoal and they must be changed at periodic intervals.

Having looked at variations on the basic theme, it is helpful to have a clearer understanding of pumps, taps and pipes.

The rear of Carver's most recent filter shows the red 'O' rings that achieve a water-tight fit; they can be coated with vegetable oil to couple up more easily.

Centrifugal pumps

One of the earlier types of electric pumps is the Whale GP74. The Mk5 version weighs only 245 grams (8oz) and can achieve a maximum output of 11 litres (2.42 gallons) per minute. This is normally fitted in a cupboard below the sink and it is a type of pump that has to be primed before it delivers water.

Priming means that air has to be expelled from the casing and water introduced in its place before pumping can take place. Once primed, a small paddle wheel or 'impeller' then pushes water along the supply pipe and a good flow rate is usually achieved.

Devices using an impeller are often referred to as 'centrifugal pumps' – or by the more descriptive title, 'pusher pumps'. These are not used solely in caravans. For example a centrifugal pump with an impeller is normally used for emptying a domestic washing machine. However, since the pump is installed below a washing machine's drum, the effect of gravity means water being emptied from the machine dispels air in the pump automatically. In a caravan where a GP74 pump is fitted, you could achieve the same effect by putting your fresh water container on the roof.

This is completely impracticable, of course, so caravans fitted with a GP74 pump also have a foot pump alongside such as the Whale GP51.

Every time air gets into the system – such as during towing, or if you draw every bit of water from your water container – you need to operate the foot pump to re-prime the pump. This should only require a few foot strokes, after which the system will keep on working until air is pulled into the pump again.

The system was fitted in many early 1980s caravans and one of its advantages is that if the auxiliary battery completely discharges, you can still pump water to the taps using the foot pump on its own. This is because water can be driven *through* the casing of a centrifugal pump, even when its impeller is stationary. This is not the case with diaphragm pumps (the self-priming devices mentioned later).

In spite of the benefits offered by an inboard electric pump such as the GP74, it is no longer fitted in new caravans. The submersible pump has taken its place.

On many older caravans it is not unusual to find a GP74 electric pump coupled up with a GP51 foot pump.

Submersible pumps

The previous section has explained the purpose of pump-priming, and the characteristics of a centrifugal or 'pusher pump'. In effect the submersible pump is much the same as the inboard GP74 previously described.

For instance the casing of both pumps houses a 12V electric motor which drives a small impeller or 'paddle wheel', protected by a filter.

The clever feature about submersible units, however, is the fact that they become automatically 'primed' merely by dropping them into a water container, but occasionally air bubbles can get caught in the casing and water doesn't flow as it should – a point explained in the box below.

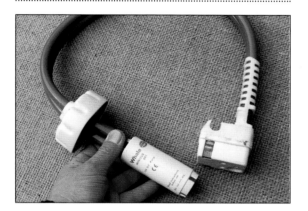
Submersible pumps have become very popular in the last few years.

A blue impeller is located directly below the removable filter on this Carver submersible pump.

Technical tip

When a submersible pump is lowered into a water container, air bubbles sometimes remain caught in the casing. Even though the motor turns at its usual speed, you find that water isn't delivered at the taps.

To dislodge the bubbles, disconnect the feed pipe from the caravan's input coupling where this is possible. Keeping the pump below the surface of the water, swing the feed pipe so that the unit bumps several times against the side of the water container. This helps to dislodge trapped air which is then released through the upper end of the disconnected hose or from the lower end of the pump.

Trapped air is not unusual and in newer submersible units like the Whale 881, an air release hole has now been included in the top of the casing.

Without doubt, a good quality submersible pump will give unfailing service for many years. However, cheap units have been supplied in the past in a bid to keep caravan prices down. The problem with low quality pumps is that if the casing becomes damaged, water finds a way in and ruins the electrical components. In practice, successful repairs are seldom possible and the product has to be thrown away.

For this reason, anyone embarking on a long and important holiday abroad is always advised to take a spare. If your pump fails while you're away, finding a replacement with the correct type of coupling is often very difficult.

As regards the coupling-up procedure, the favoured system today is to have a socket mounted in the wall of the caravan and a mating plug on the feed pipe from the pump. When withdrawing the connection it may demand a firm pull. This is because there are both electrical terminals to release as well as a leak-free water connection. To ensure there are no leaks, a rubber 'O' ring is fitted and this is why the coupling is tight.

Having a detachable pump is current practice. However, around 1990 many caravans were fitted with Carver's Mk1 Crystal system. It features a permanently connected roll-away double core hose. Water flows along one channel, the electric cables run through the other. When leaving a pitch, there's nothing to disconnect and the whole unit is simply rolled up and stowed in a compartment fitted in the side of the van. It's a clever idea although repeatedly rolling up the hose eventually leads to damage.

In practice a replacement isn't needed often and this type of double core flexible hose is usually available from accessory shops. Alternatively, there is a conversion kit available from Carver, which will upgrade to the later version where the pump is detached and stowed somewhere inside the caravan.

The water-tight socket and the electrical connection are shown on the rear of this coupling.

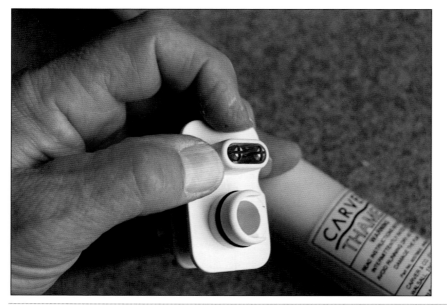

Booster pumps

A product that few caravanners are aware of is a booster pump, such as the Whale Superline 99. At first sight, this looks like a submersible pump except that it has an inlet nozzle at one end of the casing and an outlet at the other. Since it features an electric motor which drives an impeller, the pump has to be primed before it can push water through its casing.

Operating on its own, the Superline 99 has a maximum output of 12.3 litres (2.7 gallons) per minute and fits into very restricted spaces. Provided it is used in conjunction with a foot pump for priming, it can take the place of the slightly bulkier GP74.

However, a particular strength is its ability to work *in conjunction with* a submersible pump. By fitting it within the water supply pipe and by connecting it up to the same switched supply cable that activates the submersible unit, the two units will operate together. This can boost an otherwise sluggish flow – though a better strategy might be to dispense with centrifugal pumps altogether and to fit a high quality diaphragm pump.

Diaphragm pumps

More expensive caravans are often fitted with a self-priming diaphragm pump rather than a submersible unit. Instead of its electric motor operating an impeller (i.e. a paddle wheel), it drives what is known as a 'wobble plate'. As this plate revolves, it bears against tiny pistons which are pushed up and down in turn. Adjacent diaphragms follow the movement and operate a valve assembly.

The reciprocating action of the pistons is very small – usually around 3mm – so it is essential that grit doesn't get into the mechanism. This is why a diaphragm pump is always fitted with a grit filter and its gauze should be periodically inspected and cleaned as shown in the accompanying photographs.

Diaphragm pumps are well-engineered products and are considerably more expensive than submersibles. Normally they give fault-free service although there are after-sales repair and overhaul facilities to cure problems that can arise. For instance *Leisure Accessories* undertakes repairs of Shurflo pumps, a product manufactured in the United States. Similarly there's an equivalent service operated by Whale for the Evenflow and Clearstream models.

If you do find the motor doesn't operate, carry out the following check procedure before sending the pump away for repair:

1 Check the pump switch on the main control panel is *on*.
2 Switch on some of the other 12V appliances to confirm the battery hasn't become totally discharged. Even better – put a 12V meter on the battery terminals to confirm its condition.
3 If the control panel has a separate fuse for the water pump, check that it hasn't 'blown'.

Removing the grit filter from a Whale Clearstream pump

1. A wide-bladed screwdriver is used to undo the filter cover on the Clearstream pump. It is usually a tight fit.

2. The gauze is easily removed for cleaning – and the water pipe does not have to be disturbed.

Removing the grit filter from a Whale Evenflow pump

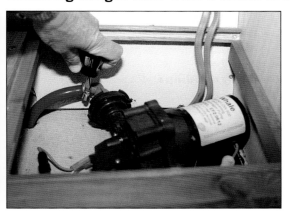

1. On an Evenflow pump, the hose has to be disconnected from the filter.

2. When a plastic collar has been removed, the two sections of the filter housing can be parted.

3. The mesh filter is seated in the middle of the casing.

4 Open a couple of taps to ensure the switching is activated and leave them open.
5 Locate the pump and see if there's an in-line fuse on its live lead. Inspect the fuse and change if necessary.
6 Put a test lamp across the terminals of the pump – or better still, use a meter.

7 If the power is definitely reaching the pump, then it can be deduced that it is the motor that requires attention. Using the appendix address list at the back of this book, contact the supplier to find out about repair services.

Note: *If the motor operates, your supply vessel is full, but no water is delivered at the taps, it might be caused because a sealing 'O' ring in the pump chamber is perished, stretched or damaged. If air gets into certain parts of the assembly, a pumping action cannot take place. Sealing washers can fail occasionally and this is not an unusual source of pumping problems.*

The diagram on the next page shows the components in a typical Shurflo unit and spares are available. However, repair work is not normally a DIY option. It is true that dismantling this type of pump is fairly straightforward but putting it all back together again can be a particularly testing task!

As regards performance, diaphragm pumps are impressive. For instance both the Evenflow 600 and 1000 models self-prime and lift water from a container positioned up to 2m (6ft 6¾in) below the

111

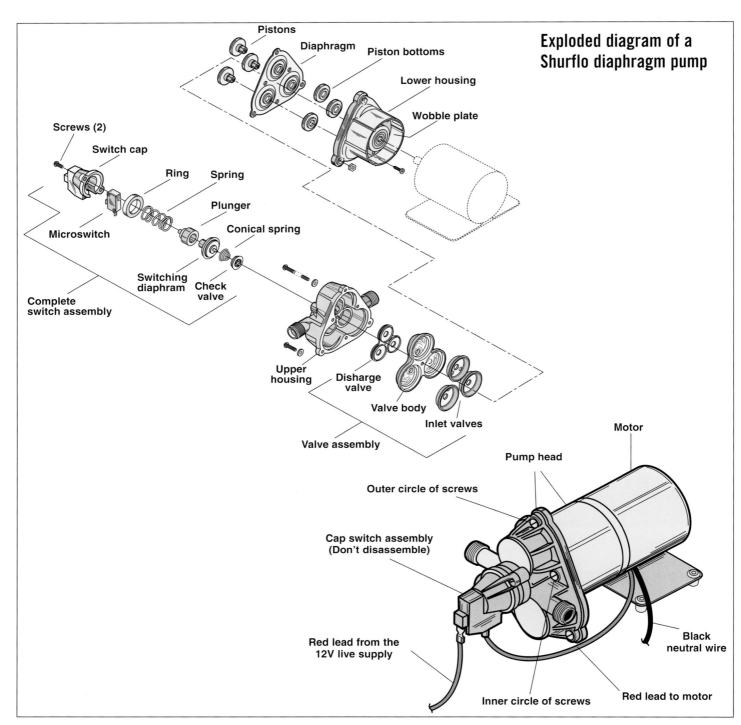

Exploded diagram of a Shurflo diaphragm pump

Pistons

Diaphragm

Piston bottoms

Lower housing

Wobble plate

Screws (2)

Switch cap

Ring

Spring

Plunger

Conical spring

Microswitch

Switching diaphram

Check valve

Complete switch assembly

Upper housing

Disharge valve

Valve body

Inlet valves

Valve assembly

Motor

Pump head

Outer circle of screws

Cap switch assembly (Don't disassemble)

Red lead from the 12V live supply

Black neutral wire

Inner circle of screws

Red lead to motor

All major parts are available to repair a Shurflo pump and the manual gives exploded diagrams and part number listings *(courtesy of Leisure Accessories Ltd).*

unit itself. The Clearstream will lift water up to a metre (3ft 3in) above the level of the container.

Another benefit is that if the motor is left running accidentally and in a dry state, it is unlikely to overheat. This is not the case with a submersible pump which is soon damaged if left running.

However, there are disadvantages, too. Unlike in-line and submersible non-priming pumps, it is not possible to drive water through the chambers of a diaphragm pump. This means you cannot fit a back-up foot pump to provide an alternative service if the battery fails.

Equally, when preparing for winter, a diaphragm pump will not permit water in the pipework on the

'tap side' of the system to be drained off via a low level drain cock. In other words, to release residual water from 'upstream' pipes, you either need to fit a second drain cock or disconnect the supply pipes on the outlet side of the pump. You can generally confirm which is the outlet connection by reference to a flow direction arrow moulded on the casing.

Noisy operation is another regular complaint and the tip box opposite explains how this can often be reduced.

Finally, the delivery of water is sometimes subject to surges because the motor might produce irregular pulses due to battery condition. To resolve this, a surge damper is often built into

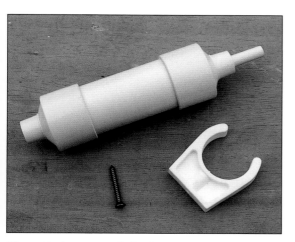

When a diaphragm pump is fitted, a surge damper is often added to smooth the delivery of water.

the pipe supply. This helps to smooth out the flow of water and if you fit one yourself, make sure it is mounted vertically with its connection at the bottom.

Pump switching

The two most common ways to switch a pump motor into operation have been mentioned earlier. As a general rule, caravans fitted with submersible pumps usually have a microswitch fitted within the tap assembly – though there are exceptions.

To confirm that a water pump is activated by microswitches in the taps, look under the sink or basin. Normally there will be microswitches on both the hot and cold supplies so look for one pair of cables connected to the microswitch for the cold tap outlet and a second pair of cables serving the microswitch on the hot tap.

Pressure-sensitive switches are situated in one of three places:

1. Within the mechanism of a diaphragm pump as shown in the photograph below.

2. In-line – meaning the switch unit is mounted within one of the main supply pipes.
3. As an integral part of a wall connection socket – as in the case of the Whale Watermaster coupling.

As a point of interest, there is no obligation to use the pressure-sensitive switch in Whale's Watermaster unit. Other terminals on the product allow a coupled submersible pump to be triggered by a microswitch on the tap instead. In other words, if your caravan has one of these couplings, it is possible to make a change from one type of switching to the other without too much alteration to the wiring.

The operating principle of a pressure-sensitive switch is described in the box overleaf. In addition there are two further points to keep in mind.
1. The sensitivity of the switch is usually adjustable to compensate for a battery losing its power and also to reduce sensitivity in a supply system that has tiny air leaks in some of the pipe connections. In the case of the in-line version, there is usually a turn wheel on the top for making fine adjustments. On the diaphragm pump and on

Different locations of pressure-sensitive switches

1. Some are built into the casing of a diaphragm pump.

2. This in-line switch and a filter are fitted in a bed box.

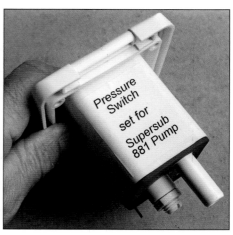

3. The Whale Watermaster wall socket contains a pressure-sensitive switch.

Pressure loss

A pressure-sensitive switch is able to detect a drop of pressure in the water supply pipes.

As soon as the tap is turned, the opening creates a loss of pressure in the pipes which is detected at once, whereupon the pump is automatically set in motion. This generally works well. However, a small pressure loss can also occur at a faulty connection in one of the pipes. This might not be serious enough to cause a water leak, but it sends a false message to the pump which briefly comes to life.

Locating the leak and re-forming the joint is the best answer, but you can often cure the problem by making an adjustment to the setting control on the switch to make it less sensitive.

To alter the sensitivity of the switch in a Watermaster socket, there's a setting screw on the rear of the unit.

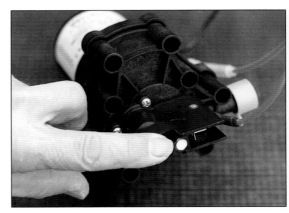

The setting screw to alter switch sensitivity on the Evenflow pump is behind a silicone bung.

the Whale Watermaster socket, you need a slotted screwdriver to fine-tune a threaded screw. This is hidden below a white plug of silicone sealant on a Whale Evenflow pump and beneath a cover cap on the Clearstream model.

2. The slightest drop in pressure in the water pipes will often cause a pump motor to trip into action for two or three strokes. This can be rather distracting, especially at night, so the caravan manufacturer normally includes a pump isolating switch – usually mounted on the 12V fused distribution and control unit. It thus becomes a habit to turn off the pump last thing before going to bed.

Changing the microswitch on a Whale Elegance mixer tap

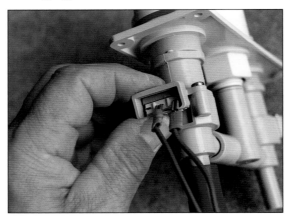

1. Reaching under the sink, locate and slip off the rectangular spring collar.

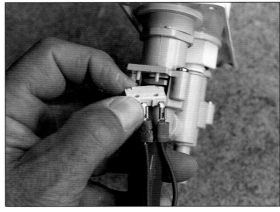

2. Leave the terminals in place, but ease the switch from its mounting pillars.

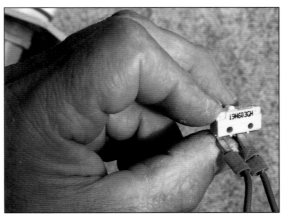

3. When you are in a more comfortable position, detach the electrical terminals – they can be fitted either way round.

4. The forefinger shows the tiny switch button on the casing; modern microswitches are usually sealed units.

Microswitching versus pressure – sensitive switching

So which is the better system – pressure-sensitive switching or a microswitch arrangement? In truth, neither is fault-free. The false 'tripping' of pressure-sensitive switches has already been mentioned; also microswitches sometimes get damp in the casing and the motor is switched into action without even turning the tap.

Caravanners often report that their battery becomes mysteriously discharged whenever they've been out for the day. Not unusually this is because the pump has been running intermittently and unnoticed for prolonged spells due to false switching.

Changing a faulty microswitch fitted to the side of a tap is shown in the sequence photographs on the previous page. It is much easier on recent designs of tap even though

gaining access beneath a sink or basin demands a measure of human flexibility. With this in mind, it is pleasing that changing a microswitch on the latest Elite taps from Whale is wholly done from above the worktop.

Changing the microswitch on a Whale Elite mixer tap

1. To take off the operating lever, remove the hot/cold indicator to reveal an attachment screw.

2. With the tap lever removed, lift off the switch activating plate, *noting its position very carefully.*

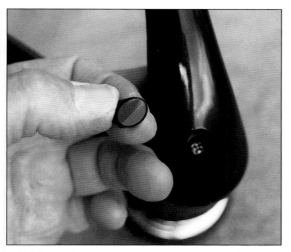

3. Use a small screwdriver to prise the microswitch from its location.

4. Ease the switch clear, so that the connecting terminals can be reached.

On older taps, the design included a soft connecting hose that was squeezed by a clamp to arrest the flow of water.

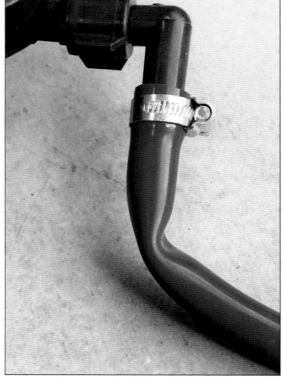

The disadvantage with flexible hose is that kinks easily develop.

Handy tip

If your caravan has a microswitching system and the pump doesn't operate when one of the taps is turned on, there's an easy way to establish if the fault lies in the switch. This presumes the tap is one where the terminals for the switching cables are easily accessible and you've established that the pump is activated when any of the other taps are used.

1. Ensure that the pump circuit is switched on at the main control panel.
2. Disconnect the two wires that go to the faulty tap.
3. Touch their terminal tags together whereupon the pump should immediately respond.

In effect you are simply doing the job of a switch by creating continuity in the supply cables. If the pump still doesn't respond, you've established that the microswitch cannot be blamed for the fault.

Taps

In some of the latest caravans, taps look much the same as the fittings used at home. However, if the flow rate on a pump is modest, full-size domestic taps are rather disappointing when delivering water.

In reality, smaller and less pretentious fittings are used in the majority of caravans and these display a more appropriate feeling of scale. It is interesting to note that the Elite taps from Whale adopt a lever operating system – currently fashionable in domestic situations – but these are appropriately scaled down to suit the caravan setting.

As regards principles of operation, whenever there is more than one tap in the system, each unit must have a physical means of arresting the flow of water. Whilst a faucet is fine for a single outlet, as described earlier, you cannot fit two faucets in a caravan since both would deliver water at once whenever the pump starts to operate.

To achieve a mechanical closure, taps used in the 1980s have a short length of soft hose connected to the delivery nozzle. This is merely pinched by a sliding bar in the same way you would pinch the neck of a balloon to prevent it losing air. It seems rather rudimentary, but it works surprisingly well. Since then, more sophisticated mechanisms have been employed.

On taps which operate a microswitch to activate the water pump, the best examples are those where changing the switch is straightforward. On a few imported taps, the microswitches are sealed inside the unit. This is wholly unsatisfactory because if one of the microswitches fails, the entire tap unit has to be replaced.

Pipes and fittings

One of the most disappointing features in a fresh water supply system is the use of flexible hose and clipped joints. Whilst this may prove adequate in the short term, kinks often develop in pipe runs after several seasons. With the passing of time, hose becomes less flexible, kinks become permanent, and flow rates are affected.

Many caravanners then blame the pump for the poor flow of water. But if all the pipe runs are carefully checked, there will usually be a kink – typically at a point where the pipe has to negotiate a sharp corner. On older caravans, this frequently occurs where the pipe comes from underneath the 'van and takes a sharp upward turn through the floor.

Leaks can be another problem. Couplings formed using worm-drive clips (Jubilee clips), can have variable success. Where cheaper substitutes are used, the integrity of joints is often poor.

The black channelling supports semi-rigid pipe so that it doesn't kink when turning a 90° bend.

Many caravans are not built with a drain-down tap in the supply system, so frost can cause damage to pipe joints or key components e.g. an in-board pump. Since residual water is held in pipes on account of the systems non-return valve it is therefore necessary to disconnect a pipe to drain off the water before the onset of winter.

Fitting a Whale drain-down tap is a much better answer and this should be positioned 'upstream' of the non-return valve. As a rule, these one-way valves are usually situated near the main input point. Moreover, in a caravan fitted with a diaphragm pump, a drain-down tap is needed on the 'up-stream' side of the pump as well, for reasons explained in the earlier section describing these units.

Several reputable caravan manufacturers still persist with this primitive form of plumbing which is surprising. A much better system is available. Semi-rigid plastic pipe and push-fit couplings have been available in the caravan industry for several seasons. But the product has a much longer history. Food quality semi-rigid pipe was used behind bars in pubs and clubs as long as thirty years ago.

Now it is being used by some caravan manufacturers as well, though sadly not all. The system is not difficult to install and a range of components are available. Push-fit drain-down taps, in-line taste filters, right-angle channelling for preventing kinks, adaptors for linking up with traditional connections and a full range of couplings are available. Push-fit components are included in the water component ranges from both Carver and Whale. A similar system was also used in ABI caravans several seasons ago although the 10mm bore size of the pipe was narrower than Whale's 12mm product.

Replacing flexible hose with semi-rigid pipe is an improvement job that many DIY owners successfully carry out. If it proves easier to retain part of an orginal hose system because of access problems, you can fit a combined arrangement using adaptor couplings.

Waste water removal

Criticisms of the plumbing for waste water were voiced at the beginning of the chapter. There is no doubt that the rigid PVCu waste and cistern overflow pipes available from a builders' merchant provide a much better system than one constructed with a narrow flexible hose. Indeed a domestic pipe is used under the sink of current Vanroyce caravans, together with a trap for keeping smells in

The waste hose in this 1999 caravan is level in places and its ridged construction will certainly trap food particles.

the pipe from seeping into the caravan. It is most pleasing that an idea described and illustrated in the First Edition of this Manual in 1993 has finally been adopted by a caravan manufacturer.

But this installation in current Vanroyce caravans is unusual. For many years, caravans have been fitted with 19mm (¾in) convoluted flexible hose and its pronounced ridges catch grains of rice, peas and other water-borne debris. During a winter lay-up this decays, with the result that smells enter the caravan via the sink, basin and shower tray outlets.

Furthermore, if you look under caravans, you will often find the waste hose has pronounced sags between the fixing clips. This helps residual water to collect and stagnate.

Equally if you inspect the hose in kitchen and bathroom cupboards, you will sometimes see that sections of the run are installed with scarcely any fall. It is little wonder that water can be so slow to discharge from a sink or basin.

To improve the situation, manufacturers are starting to use a larger 25mm (1in) diameter waste hose. Moreover, in a few of the very latest caravans the hose is coupled up with lengths of rigid pipe; but this has a small bore which is too narrow to achieve an efficient outflow.

One of the better products introduced recently is a convoluted hose which has reinforcing ridges on the outside but a smooth-walled finish on the inside. This is being installed in a number of coachbuilt motorcaravans. Yet it doesn't appear to be fitted in many trailer caravans at the moment. The enthusiastic DIY owner could easily fit this type of waste hose as part of an improvement project and it is available from CAK, a specialist in water components for caravans.

Undoubtedly the best answer, however, is to fit a completely new waste water system using domestic PVCu waste pipe.

General improvements

A number of alterations can be made to either the fresh or waste water systems. Changing your pump or altering the pipe arrangement is unlikely to present problems.

117

Installing a diaphragm pump

If you want to upgrade your system to include a diaphragm pump, this is generally straightforward. The instructions supplied with the new pump are usually comprehensive.

One of the points to bear in mind relates to the supply cable. The problem of voltage drop due to using a cable of an incorrect rating was discussed in Chapter 7. Avoiding a drop is especially important with this type of product and the minimum gauge of cable recommended for Evenflow pumps is 2.5mm^2.

There will also need to be a wiring alteration if the previous pump was controlled by microswitches. To do this, start by isolating the battery. Then disconnect the pair of wires going to a microswitch and join them together with crimp connectors. Repeat for all microswitches. This would effectively keep the original pump running continuously when everything was switched back on again. However, both the live and neutral cables supplying the former pump should now be detached from their previous connections, re-routed, and connected to the terminals of the replacement diaphragm pump instead. In future, pump activation will now be achieved by the integral pressure-sensitive switch of the new product rather than by microswitches.

A disabling switch should also be fitted into the live feed so that the pump can be switched off at night. The importance of this was emphasised in the earlier section on diaphragm pumps. Alternatively you may have an existing pump switch on the 12V control panel which would serve the same purpose.

An in-line fuse will also have to be fitted near the pump and this would normally be rated at 10A.

As regards the fixing itself, remember that this type of pump can create a considerable noise if the screws holding it in place are over-tightened – a point made in the Tip Box on page 113.

Finally, you will usually find that several pipe couplings are supplied with the pump. For instance its inlet and outlet connections may be threaded to accept ½in BSP couplings but there are likely to be unions supplied to accept a flexible hose as well. Adaptors are similarly available to suit push-fit connections so that the pump can be coupled into a system that uses semi-rigid pipes.

Overall, the installation is something many experienced DIY owners complete without difficulty although discreetly hiding the pipe runs often takes more time than fitting the pump!

Installing fresh water pipe

If you install hose and clip plumbing during cold weather, you often find the plastic pipe lacks resilience. This makes it quite difficult to create leak-proof joints because Jubilee clips cannot pull tightly into the cold, inflexible material.

This problem is easily overcome if you heat the end of pipes before coupling up and tightening the fixing clip. A good way to do this is to dip the end of the pipe in a mug of boiling water. It will become remarkably pliable and if you tighten the clip without too much delay, the coupling will be much more likely to achieve a sound connection.

As regards push-fit systems, it is always important to make sure you cut the pipe squarely and cleanly. To help you make a good job of this, Whale includes a pipe cutting tool in the product range.

When forming the joint, make sure you push the inserted pipe fully home. The coupling is notably

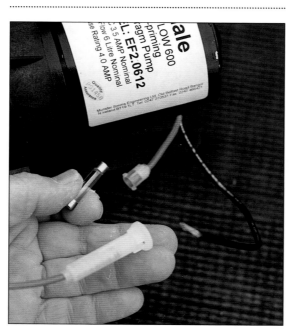

An in-line fuse is fitted on the live feed to this Evenflow pump.

Be careful not to over-tighten the fixing screws when installing a diaphragm pump.

effective and you can pull hard on coupled sections without being able to disconnect them. This is because a small component called a collet grips increasingly tightly on the pipe as you attempt to detach it from the coupling.

However, if you push the small exposed section of the collet into the coupling at the same time as you pull the pipe in the opposite direction, it then becomes possible to withdraw the pipe. This is a helpful feature. But you do not want accidental disconnection during the pitch and toss of towing, so it is wise to complete the joints by adding a protective cover cap. This hides the collet and maintains the integrity of the joint.

Waste water upgrade

If you decide to replace the original flexible waste hose with PVCu pipe, start by parking the caravan completely level. This means that a fall in the pipe can be introduced when fitting the system. It also means that the fall will be apparent every time you level-up your caravan in future.

Rigid 32mm (1¼in) pipe is ideal and this is available from builders' merchants, together with a jointing adhesive called 'solvent weld'.

To make a waterproof joint it pays to roughen the mating surfaces of the pipe using glass paper to remove any shine. The solvent tin has a brush in the lid, so it is easy to apply the adhesive next on both roughened surfaces.

When you insert a coated section of pipe into a coupling, give it a small twist in one direction followed by a twist in the other. Then leave the adhesive to set, and make sure that water isn't put down the pipes for at least 24 hours.

As regards the pipe layout underneath the floor, you will need to work around chassis members. This may commend creating a different drainage outlet position from the one originally fitted. You will also find you can couple up sections with a dry run first of all, offering up fairly large assemblies in order to confirm that everything is correctly measured before finally applying the adhesive.

When fastening lengths of pipe to the underside of the floor, use the clips sold for domestic installations. However, by adding small blocks of wood of different thicknesses you can create a gentle fall in the pipe which significantly improves the efficiency of the system. Where the pipe terminates, fit a piece of car radiator hose with an elbow curve to steer water into your waste container.

There is usually only one problem point and this is directly below the sink or basin outlets. The outlet itself is obviously made for a smaller bore hose but no attempt to change this is necessary. All you have to do is to cut the original hose leaving a short tail under the sink of about 150mm (6in). This will then hang vertically within the replacement downpipe and a good overlap should be created. The junction of the two pipes can then be sealed with builders' foam.

Admittedly the 'tail' constitutes a narrower section within the system, but since the remaining large diameter pipes feature a carefully created sloping run, you'll be amazed how quickly water discharges into the waste water container. This improvement project is well worth your time and the cost of the components is modest.

When connecting semi-rigid pipe, ensure it is pushed fully into the couplings.

The red and blue cover caps on this push-fit coupling ensure the pipe cannot become accidentally dislocated.

This waste system is being constructed in sections before the components are offered up underneath the caravan.

Gas supply systems and appliances

Gas Standards

Information on the revised gas standards are detailed on page 168

Liquefied petroleum gas (LPG) is heavier than air, non-poisonous and easily transportable in steel cylinders. It is a convenient fuel for cooking and heating but caravanners should be mindful of safety whenever the gas is used.

Even though electricity is exclusively used for lighting, gas is the caravanners' fuel for cooking and heating. Some motorcaravans are now being fitted with central heating units driven by diesel fuel, but the development is unlikely to extend to tourers. The convenience of gas is indisputable.

Characteristics of the gas

Many caravanners are surprised to learn that in its natural state, liquefied petroleum gas (LPG) is odourless. This could be a dangerous feature because leaks might pass unnoticed, so the suppliers add what is known as a 'stenching agent' and its unpleasant smell soon warns of a fault in the supply system.

Another important feature about LPG is that it is heavier than air. In other words if gas leaks from a faulty cylinder valve or a poor connection in a supply pipe it will start to accumulate at floor level. This is potentially very dangerous.

To ensure leaking gas escapes, low level ventilators are installed in caravans. There are also escape outlets referred to as 'drop out' holes situated directly under gas appliances. It is most important that these vents are unobstructed.

The same provision must be made in gas lockers and the escape outlets should be situated at *the lowest point*. It is a matter of considerable concern that some manufacturers have failed to observe this requirement; occasionally you will come across caravans where ventilator grills are only fitted in the *sides* of locker doors. This is wrong; at least one outlet *must be* at the lowest point of the enclosure.

A further point to recognise is that there are two types of LPG: butane and propane. However, as long as a regulator of the appropriate type is fitted, both are suitable for use in a caravan. The need for a different regulator is due to differences in pressure and provided the correct type is fitted, all appliances in a British-built caravan should work as normal. However, some caravans built abroad may need to have different jets fitted in their appliances before they can be run on LPG sold in the UK.

The two types of LPG are different in a number of other respects as well:

BUTANE

■ **Butane** has a higher calorific value than propane which means it is a more efficient heat producer. Accordingly butane is the preferred choice when conditions are suitable.

■ **Butane** does not change from its liquefied state to a gas vapour if temperatures fall below 0°C (32°F) at atmospheric pressure. The liquefied gas freezes in the cylinder – so it is not the preferred gas of winter caravanners.

■ **Butane** is heavier than propane. Although the smallest Calor Gas cylinders for the two products are the same size, the propane version holds 3.9kg (8.6lb) whereas an identically sized cylinder of butane holds 4.5kg (10lb) of liquefied gas.

PROPANE

■ **Propane** changes from a liquefied state into a gas in temperatures as low as −40°C – so it is ideal as a winter fuel. Regrettably, many Continental gas suppliers only sell butane, though some processing companies add a small quantity of propane to butane cylinders in order to give improved cold weather performance.

120

The higher calorific value of butane makes it a more efficient heat producer than propane.

- ■ **Propane** in its liquefied state is lighter than butane. That is why in two cylinders of identical size, there is less propane by weight than butane.

- ■ **Propane** has a vapour pressure around five times that of butane and it is for this reason that different regulators are needed for the two gases. Accordingly if you change from one gas to another, you must change the regulator. Regulators are discussed in a later section.

Supply cylinders

Portable LPG cylinders are sold in a number of sizes, some of which are more suited to the needs of touring caravanners than the requirements in a domestic installation. Strictly speaking, you do not 'buy' a Calor cylinder but commence a hire agreement, paying a fee when using these products for the first time. In effect this means that ownership of the cylinder remains with Calor Gas Ltd. If you cease being a Calor customer, you can reclaim the hire fee provided the original hire document can be produced. In contrast, the arrangement with Campingaz is different – you do purchase the first cylinder and merely exchange it, when empty, for another.

One advantage with the Calor Gas system is that the Company normally permits changes of gas type – hence you can exchange an empty 3.9kg propane cylinder for a 4.5kg butane one. Similarly you can usually change a 4.5kg butane cylinder for a larger 7kg cylinder. Occasionally there are restrictions, depending on shortages.

Suppliers of LPG

In the UK, Calor Gas is widely available and is sold in several different sized cylinders. Both butane *and* propane are sold under the Calor brand name but unfortunately the Company doesn't operate abroad. Equally the gas valves on European cylinders have different thread patterns.

Campingaz is another product available in the UK but the largest cylinder (the 907) is only a modest size (2.72kg/6lb). Moreover, you cannot buy *propane* in Campingaz cylinders.

When travelling abroad, Campingaz is available in over 100 countries although prices vary enormously. It is notably *inexpensive* in Spain because butane cylinders are used in many less affluent homes – so it receives a heavy subsidy from the Spanish Government. As regards propane in Spain, this is normally only supplied for commercial vehicles.

Whereas Campingaz is sold in many European countries, it is not available in Finland or Sweden, and is also seldom stocked in Norway.

Other products are available abroad too, and in Germany there are several examples such as SKG 5kg propane cylinders. However, higher operating pressures are employed in Germany so before using this product a different regulator and coupling is needed. It is also prudent to seek advice from the technical departments of the Caravan Clubs before changing LPG supplies.

Calor cylinder sizes

3.9kg (8.6lb) propane
4.5kg (10lb) butane
6kg (13.2lb) propane
7kg (15.4lb) butane
13kg (28.7lb) propane
15kg (33lb) butane,
19kg (41.9lb) propane
- Calor Gas butane cylinders are painted blue
- Calor Gas propane cylinders are painted red.

Note: *The larger cylinders, notably 13kg propane, 15kg butane and 19kg propane are often used on permanent pitches but are normally too large for safe transport. Locker compartments are not designed to accommodate cylinders of these sizes.*

Campingaz cylinder sizes

0.45kg (1lb) butane
1.81kg (4lb) butane
2.72 kg (6lb) butane
Campingaz cylinders are painted blue.

Note: *Only the Type 907 Campingaz 2.72kg butane cylinder is a practicable proposition for the caravanner. The two smaller cylinders might be kept for emergency back-up to operate a cooker burner but they are really intended for camping use.*

The 907 cylinder holding 2.72kg of butane is the only Campingaz cylinder of practicable use; the small 901 cylinder is intended for camping.

121

The product known as Camping Gaz has been internationally available for many years. However, in late 1997, its identity was changed to 'Campingaz' and a new identification logo has been launched.
Throughout this manual we refer to the product using its new title.

Storage arrangements

The design of a caravan gas locker should incorporate an effective way to secure two cylinders. In fact if you caravan in Autumn or Spring, it is not unusual to take one cylinder of butane and another of propane.

As mentioned already it is most important that the locker incorporates a substantial drop-out ventilator at the lowest point of the enclosure.

The traditional storage location for gas cylinders has been on the draw bar. In the late 1960s, the cylinders were clamped on this part of the chassis and exposed to the elements. Locker boxes mounted on the draw bar came later and were fitted in the 1970s and early 1980s. However, by 1986 almost all caravans were built with an integral forward locker which is aesthetically more pleasing. The only problem is that some owners overload this with a number of weighty holiday items, thereby exceeding the permitted nose weight of the caravan.

More recently, manufacturers have seen the wisdom of situating the gas locker much closer to the axle. This has much to commend it in respect of weight distribution and models from manufacturers such as Avondale sometimes adopt this strategy.

A point of importance made in the earlier chapter on 12V systems is that a gas locker should never be used to accommodate electrical appliances – particularly a leisure battery. Leakage can occur at a gas cylinder valve and if a spark is generated when you are coupling wires to the terminals of a battery, an explosion could easily occur.

On return home, many owners remove gas

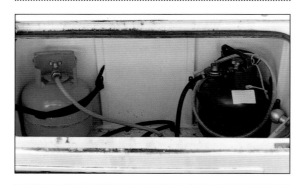

Many caravanners take both butane and propane cylinders on holiday in Spring and late Autumn.

Side-located gas lockers situated near the wheels contribute to good weight distribution.

■ Before taking to the road, it is important to turn off the gas supply at source. Although there are gas cocks in modern caravans to cut off the supply to different appliances within the system, the best precaution is to turn off the supply *at the cylinder*. This should be part of every caravanner's routine prior to departure.

■ Always transport a cylinder in its *upright* position. If a cylinder is laid on its side, the liquefied gas *might* escape from a faulty valve. When it is acknowledged that in the transfer from liquid to vapour there's approximately a *two hundred times increase in volume*, the potential hazard is clearly apparent. A tiny quantity seeping through the valve becomes a very large amount of gas.

cylinders from the caravan as a precautionary measure. This is fine, but storage of the cylinders at home presents new problems. Under no circumstances should cylinders be left in a cellar, for example, since leaking gas would have no means of escaping. In fact the *Gas Safety (Installation & Use) Regulations* state clearly that propane cylinders must not be stored inside any dwellings. Nor should they be stored anywhere that lacks low level ventilation outlets. An outside shed or outhouse might prove suitable; but it's safer to adopt the practice of the suppliers whose cylinders are kept in a roofed storage cage situated well away from any source of flame.

Pressure regulation and supply control

When you buy a brand new caravan you will immediately have to purchase a regulator for the gas supply. These components are not normally included in the sale, even though they are essential items. A gas regulator fulfils two functions:

1. It ensures the delivery of gas from a cylinder is at a stable and constant pressure to suit the needs of the appliances. It thus smoothes out the tendency for a full cylinder to deliver gas at a higher rate than one which is nearing exhaustion.
2. It incorporates a union so that the flexible feed pipe to the supply system can be coupled up safely to the cylinder without likelihood of leakage.

Note: *a) Some regulators also incorporate an on/off control – sometimes called a 'gas cock'.
b) The couplings on butane and propane are intentionally different thereby ensuring that pressure regulation is appropriate for the type of LPG in use.*

To connect to a propane cylinder the regulator is manufactured with a carefully machined and threaded insert *(male)* which achieves a tight fit within the receiving socket *(female)* of the cylinder. No washer is involved – merely a close metal-to-

The sealing washer on regulators intended for Calor's 4.5kg butane cylinder must be changed regularly.

An adaptor allows a Campingaz cylinder to be connected up to the coupling nut of a Calor 4.5kg butane regulator.

metal register. The coupling method is the same on *all* Calor Gas propane cylinders and you'll need to keep a spanner handy. An inexpensive open-ended spanner to suit the coupling is sold at caravan accessory shops.

Regrettably butane couplings are less straightforward because there are several different types. For instance on a 4.5kg Calor cylinder, there's a threaded female nut; this has to be positioned over the threaded male outlet and tightened *anti-clockwise*. The reverse thread often surprises newcomers to caravanning and a spanner is needed once again. Moreover, there's a small washer held within the regulator coupling nut

which *must* be changed periodically. Spares are available for a modest sum from any Calor specialist.

On both the Calor propane cylinders and the Calor 4.5kg butane cylinders a robust turn wheel on the top opens or closes the gas supply valve. However, when caravanners find it necessary to use Campingaz, it is normal to purchase an adaptor that screws into the top of the butane cylinder. This also incorporates a control valve and now enables the type of Calor butane regulator

Disconnecting a 541 regulator from a 7kg Calor Gas butane cylinder

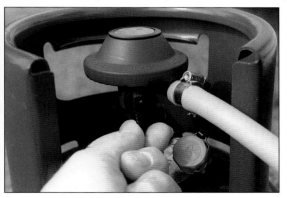

1. When the switch is in the 6 o'clock position, the gas supply is ON.

2. Turn the switch to the 9 o'clock OFF position to close down the gas supply.

3. With the switch in the OFF position, the disconnecting lever can be fitted and the regulator removed.

4. The orange safety cap must be replaced on the cylinder even if it's empty.

Technical tip

Since the Third Edition of this book was published, a growing interest has developed in re-fillable gas cylinders. However, many gas specialists have strong reservations about the safety of some products. For example a vehicle running on LPG draws gas in a liquefied form from its tank; in contrast, caravan appliances have to draw gas in a vapourised state. For that reason it is critically important that a refillable gas cylinder for use in a caravan is never filled beyond 80%. Accordingly the cylinder should have: a) an automatic fill-stop device, and b) an over-pressure relief valve. Unfortunately some cylinders have been sold which lack automatic fill-stop devices – hence the concern about safety.

Gaslow has produced a better answer by developing cylinders complete with overfill cut-off devices and designed for fixing as a permanent installation in a gas locker. The cylinders have a stainless steel hose which couples to an automotive filler installed on the side of a caravan. Replenishing the caravan's fixed cylinder is therefore just the same as refilling an LPG powered car.

Overall, refillable products for caravanners are in an early stage of development and safety standards are being discussed in several European countries. Meanwhile, some fuel forecourt operators have decided to forbid customers from replenishing portable, re-fillable caravan cylinders at pumps which dispense fuel for LPG-powered vehicles.

already described to be coupled into a Campingaz supply.

It is the larger butane cylinders from Calor Gas that adopt a different coupling method. The regulator needed now has to have a special clip-on coupling. Moreover, the on/off control now forms part of the regulator itself whereas on the smaller 4.5kg product the turn wheel was part of the cylinder.

To summarise, if you use different types of cylinder, you need to buy three different regulators – plus an adaptor if you want to connect up to a Campingaz cylinder. These are:

1. A Calor screw-on propane regulator – with open-ended spanner.
2. A Calor screw-on butane regulator to suit 4.5kg cylinders – with open-ended spanner.
3. A Calor 541 clip-on butane regulator to suit 7kg cylinders.
4. Either an adaptor to enable a Campingaz 2.72kg cylinder to be coupled up with a Calor screw-on butane regulator, or a Campingaz regulator with on-off control.

Technical tip

■ Remember to buy a supply of sealing washers if you use a Calor screw-on butane regulator. Contrary to popular belief, the washer that comes in the black screw-on blanking cap that you get with a new cylinder must not be transferred for use in a regulator. It is not made of the correct composition.

■ A butane regulator is rated at 11.2in water gauge (28m bar); a propane regulator is rated at 14.8 inch water gauge (37m bar). So if a service engineer connects a glass 'U' tube holding water to a butane supply, the pressure is sufficient to force the water 11.2in up the tube; propane would force the water 14.8in up the tube. Nowadays, however, most gas engineers measure this with a gauge.

■ A regulator is set at the time of manufacture and must not be dismantled. A diaphragm inside moves up or down to adjust the flow of gas and a lever mechanism monitors and regulates its operation. There is nothing to service and the units are sealed at the time of manufacture; a regulator should be renewed periodically and certainly at three year intervals.

■ A regulator has a tiny hole in the casing. If this becomes blocked, the diaphragm is unable to move inside. The problem sometimes occurs when a caravanner stays on a site for a prolonged period during the winter and positions the gas cylinder alongside the draw bar. This strategy is followed when a large cylinder is used to supply heating appliances. If moisture gets into the 'breather hole' and then freezes, the diaphragm can get stuck in the fully open position. Should you find that the flame on a cooker becomes far higher than normal, this 'over-gassing' situation is nearly always the result of regulator malfunction. To avoid this either devise a suitable cover or position the regulator so that the vent hole points downwards.

■ Regulators sold abroad often work at different pressures and cannot be used on UK caravans. In Germany propane appliances run on 50m/bars and if a regulator is fitted to serve UK appliances which run at 37m/bars there will be combustion and safety problems.

Cylinder state

Assessing the amount of gas remaining in a cylinder can be difficult. There are several devices intended to give a clear indication of the fill, including weighing accessories.

Some owners monitor consumption by weighing a full cylinder on bathroom scales before it is put into commission. The information is noted down or recorded on a sticky label which is then attached to the cylinder. Since the quantity of gas in a full cylinder is expressed in weight, it is easy to calculate what proportion of the gross figure is gas and what proportion relates to the weight of the empty cylinder (called the tare weight).

Furthermore, when embarking on a trip with a part-used cylinder, a further check on the bathroom scales will indicate how much weight has been lost since the cylinder was new – and correspondingly, what weight of gas is remaining.

Perhaps a more convenient way to monitor the amount of gas in a cylinder is to purchase one of the gauges from Gaslow. Some of these are sold as separate units whereas others are integral with a Gaslow regulator. The gauges also serve a further role as leak detectors – a feature explained later.

To assess the condition of a cylinder using a Gaslow gauge, the system *must* be in operation with at least one appliance in use. Taking into account the load imposed by the appliance(s), a Gaslow gauge then indicates if the supply is in: a good state; a mediocre condition; or approaching exhaustion. Earlier gauges used a needle which pointed to 'traffic light' segments on the dial; the red section warned of a nearly empty cylinder whereas a green segment indicated that all was well. On the latest gauges it is the segment that moves and to achieve even greater accuracy there are separate read-outs for use on 'cold days', 'cool days' and 'hot days'. A Gaslow gauge is undoubtedly useful, but you should bear in mind that it only gives an indication of cylinder condition when appliances are being used.

Some Gaslow gauges are separate units whereas others are fitted as part of the regulator itself.

This manual changeover from Gaslow is intended for use with Calor 4.5kg butane cylinders.

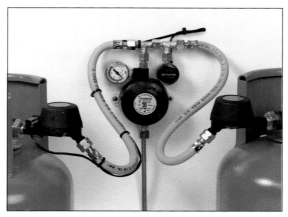

The Triomatic gas regulator from Truma was introduced in the UK in 1998.

Changeover systems

Running out of gas is always inconvenient. Even if there's a back-up cylinder, the business of disconnecting the regulator and coupling up to a new one is a nuisance, especially if it's raining. The job is even more annoying if it happens when a meal is being cooked or it is the middle of a cold night when the heating system is crucial for comfort. This is why a butane supply changeover system is so useful – especially one which is completely automatic.

Note: *Some gas specialists assert that propane changeover systems intended for locker installation are not recommended on account of the greater pressure of the gas.*

The simplest and least expensive types, like the Gaslow manual changeover, merely involve turning off the failed cylinder and opening the valve on its replacement. Since both connections are already coupled-up, the task takes only seconds to complete.

Automatic types are even more convenient although you obviously need to monitor progress periodically so that steps can be taken to remove and replace an emptied cylinder. In many systems you can disconnect the exhausted cylinder and take it to a dealers for exchange without upsetting the one that's operating; there is no risk of gas leaking during the changeover.

One of the specialists supplying automatic changeovers is Truma and the Triomatic which operates with propane was introduced in the UK in 1998. Other models are available too, and the Truma Duomatic L includes a control panel for mounting in the living quarters. This allows you to check cylinder condition without having to go outside. There is also a defrosting arrangement which ensures the Duomatic L doesn't ice-up in cold weather.

Pipework and installation

After LPG passes from a cylinder and through a regulator it enters the supply system through a flexible hose. Relevant points are as follows:

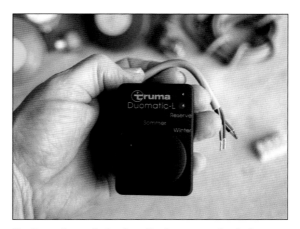

The Truma Duomatic L automatic changeover also features a control unit that is mounted inside a caravan.

• There should only be one flexible hose in the entire system – to couple up with the gas cylinder. Elsewhere, metal pipes have to be used and copper is the most common material.
• Until 1999 models, manufacturers fitted flexible hose in various lengths. Now its maximum is 400mm – around 16in.
• Where the hose is pushed on to ribbed unions, the standards recommend that hose clips are used.
• Flexible hose deteriorates very little when kept in stock at a suppliers. In use, however, it is affected by LPG and will need changing periodically. It is also affected by ultra violet light if a cylinder is used in the open air.
• The hose bears a date on the side to indicate when it left the factory; this may be a year or so *before* you make the actual purchase depending on stock turnover.
• It is important to note down the *precise* date when new hose is installed since it should be changed periodically. The Calor Gas Dealer Directory 1995 recommends this is done at five year intervals or more frequently if there's evidence of deterioration. For instance you sometimes find that it loses resilience and stretches at ribbed unions.

125

Safety

A competent and practically-experienced owner should find no difficulty in replacing the flexible hose on a gas supply system. However, fit *new* clips every time you replace the hose. Then check the two joints using a leak detecting fluid. Note: *Do not use clips whose drive serrations cut into the flexible hose.*

As regards the rest of the supply system, this should always be entrusted to a gas engineer who has been trained in the installation of LPG systems in leisure vehicles.

Flexible hose is connected to a bulkhead adaptor using a worm-drive (Jubilee) clip.

The inboard end of the flexible supply hose is coupled to a bulkhead connector using a clip.

On account of the risk of a serious accident, neither the rigid gas supply system nor the connections to gas appliances should be modified, repaired or coupled up by non-qualified DIY enthusiasts. In the Calor Caravan Check Scheme booklet (May 1995 Edition) it states, 'Gas installation is an expert's job and by law must only be undertaken by an experienced gas fitter.'

This view is endorsed here and technical descriptions about the supply system are provided for information only. In reality the task of connecting up copper gas pipe using a proprietary compression coupling is not difficult – particularly for anyone familiar with the similar pressure fittings used in domestic plumbing. But the inexperienced person will not know how much to tighten a coupling to achieve a leak-proof joint. Over-tightening can deform the pipe and a leak is inevitable – as it is if the coupling is under-tightened. So the instruction is clear: leave this to a qualified LPG fitter.

Technical Tip

For some time it has been stated that work on gas connections, flues and supply systems should only be undertaken by a competent gas engineer. More recently, however, this prescription has been deemed too vague and some advisers insist that only a CORGI registered engineer tackles this kind of work. Others assert that the requirement is even more stringent and state that a CORGI qualified person must be one who has successfully completed a course which embraces training in LPG installations in leisure vehicles. This caveat is added because some CORGI registered engineers are only trained to deal with domestic household installations. *Note: CORGI stands for 'Council for Registered Gas Installers'. Registration is a requirement for those who install and maintain LPG installations as laid down in the Gas Safety (Installation & Use) Regulations 1994.*

Copper pipe for gas systems is made in the following sizes:

5mm (³⁄₁₆in) outside diameter (OD) = feed to a gas lamp; seldom used today.
6mm (¼in) OD = feed to many types of appliance e.g. the fridge.
8mm (⁵⁄₁₆in) OD = main trunk feed in a caravan; feed for space heating appliances.

Pressure couplings are made to suit the pipe diameters, with reducers permitting branches to adopt different sized pipes from the main trunkway. The diagram opposite shows the key components such as the 'olive' and the 'cap nut'.

When a compression coupling is formed, it is pointed out in *The Dealer Information Booklet* published by Calor Gas that jointing compounds should not be used. In spite of this, some gas engineers add a very small smear of Calortite jointing compound around the olive prior to engaging the cap nut. This is a dark red paste and any surplus compound around joints has a nasty tendency of getting on to your clothing.

Bending copper gas pipe is often done by hand; but for more precise work, especially when forming

Compression fittings feature three items: a cap nut, an olive and the component itself.

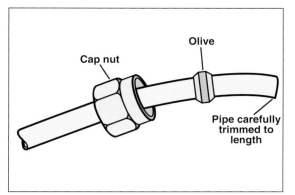

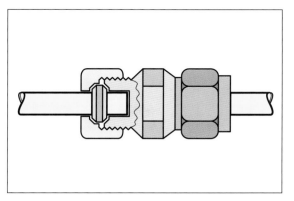

When connections are formed, the cap nut is fitted on the supply pipe first, followed by the olive. The pipe is then inserted into the coupling as far as the stop point and the cap nut tightened.

As a cap nut is tightened, the olive bears harder against the shoulder of the fitting and is squeezed inwards, gripping the gas pipe tightly.

For precise work, bending copper supply pipe is done with a pipe-bending tool.

Isolation valves (or 'gas cocks') are fitted in a gas supply system so that individual appliances can be controlled separately.

a tight bend, a pipe bending tool is used. This supports the walls of the pipe and prevents kinking. It follows the same principle of operation as a pipe bender used for domestic plumbing.

As regards the final coupling to appliances, this often employs a thread-to-thread union rather than a compression fitting. In this instance, a

special LPG jointing paste *is* required to seal the threads and Calortite is the usual choice.

In modern installations, it is also necessary for individual appliances to be controlled by a separate gas cock. If an oven were to give trouble on holiday, for example, you could completely shut down the supply to this appliance whilst leaving other appliances still useable.

Leak detection

Whilst work on a gas supply system should not be undertaken by a DIY owner, it is wise to keep a careful eye on the gas pipes – and a nose as well. The smell of leaking gas is easily detectable.

Many caravan owners also have a leak detector fitted and some types are available that an owner could fit themselves. In addition, if an owner wants reassurance that couplings are sound, there's no reason why he or she shouldn't check them using a leak detection liquid.

The procedure is to have the system switched on at the cylinder and to keep all appliances off. Cigarettes and naked flames must be extinguished. Couplings are then coated with either a proprietary leak detection product or a solution made of diluted washing-up fluid, but see the accompanying Technical tip box. Once it has been applied, check for bubbles – which indicate a leak. It is usual to apply the mixture with a small brush and to hold your fingers around the joint to prevent the fluid running away. If you find a leak, switch the system off at once and get the coupling replaced by a gas engineer.

A more convenient way to monitor a system is to fit a Gaslow gauge at the gas supply cylinder. These products were mentioned earlier because they have an additional function of indicating the amount of gas in a cylinder. Testing is carried out as follows:

1. Turn off *all* gas appliances.
2. Turn *on* the gas supply cylinder; the gauge should show a green segment.
3. Turn *off* the gas supply at the cylinder.
4. Provided there is no major leak, gas will be held

Technical tip

The use of washing up liquid for checking the integrity of gas joints is common practice. However, specialist engineers point out that it contains salts which are fine for cleaning dishes but these additives can corrode the components used in gas systems. If a proprietary leak detection fluid is unavoidable, washing up fluid MUST be washed off with clean water when a test is completed.

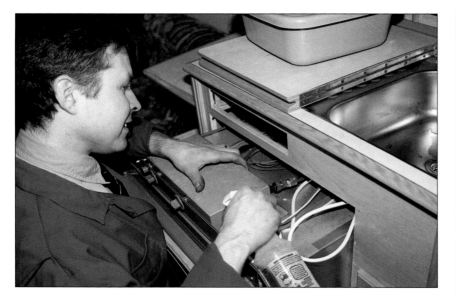

A gas engineer will confirm suspected faults in couplings using a leak-detection fluid.

Carver Products

In this section, there are several references to Carver space and water heaters; these appliances have been fitted in many caravans. Since this 3rd Edition was written the Company has closed the division manufacturing components for caravans and motorhomes. However, spare parts, accessories, and similar appliances are available from Truma UK whose address appears in Appendix C. In addition the Henry-GE Water heater was introduced in 2005 and manufactured along the lines of the Carver Cascade GE. Most of its parts are also claimed to be compatible with those of the Carver product. The complete product or individual components are obtainable from Caravanparts.net whose address is given in Appendix C.

in the supply pipes and the gauge will remain green for a prolonged period.

5. Using a standard Gaslow product, if the gauge remains green for at least a minute, the system is considered to be satisfactory.

6. Over a longer period however, the gauge will eventually return to the red sector.

Note: *Registered gas installers use much larger gauges and run tests over a 10 minute period. These trace even very small leaks in a system.*

Another way to keep a long-term check is to have an Alde leak detector fitted into the supply line by a gas engineer. This incorporates a small glass sighting chamber filled with a glycol liquid. To conduct the test you switch the gas supply on and turn all appliances off. When a red test button on the top of the detector is depressed, a regular flow of bubbles in the sighting chamber gives away the fact that gas is escaping somewhere in the system.

Different again are leak detectors that give an audible warning when a sensor detects gas. This

The leak detector from Alde is installed in the main supply pipe – bubbles in the sighting glass indicate a passage of gas.

■ Get a gas engineer with experience of LPG installations to check your caravan gas supply system once a year and to issue a dated certificate verifying its integrity.

■ Many engineers use a special pump to fill the supply pipes with air, whereupon the ability of the system to retain the air is checked on a gauge.

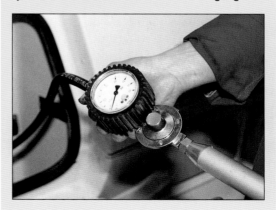

type of device *could* be fitted by a careful DIY owner. For instance the First Alert electronic alarm warns the occupants of a leak using a piercing 85dB siren. The unit has to be connected to a 12V DC supply and needs to be fixed to a secure base in an appropriate location. Recognising that LPG is *heavier* than air it needs fitting low down.

Cooking appliances

Cooking facilities in a caravan consist of a hob as a standard item; some models include an oven, too. In British models, a grill is also included as part of the hob.

Caravans built abroad are often different and a grill is not normally included. In fact the importers of foreign products often have to fit different appliances in order to make a kitchen more acceptable to the British public.

Technical innovation has been much in evidence in the last decade. For example, some cooker hobs fitted in the early 1990s were equipped with an electronic igniter on each burner, a facility now regarded as essential.

Since 1994, it has also been mandatory to have a flame failure device (sometimes called a 'flame supervision device') fitted to all gas burners. If the gas on a burner blows out, the device immediately cuts off its supply. You will see the small probe that projects into the flame of the burner; when this is hot, an electric current is generated. The current then flows to an electromagnetic gas valve that stays open all the time the probe is hot. However, as soon as the flame is extinguished, current is no longer produced, the electromagnet in the gas valve fails and a small spring closes off the supply. The only point to note with this system is that you need to override the gas valve when lighting the burner in order to give the probe time to heat up.

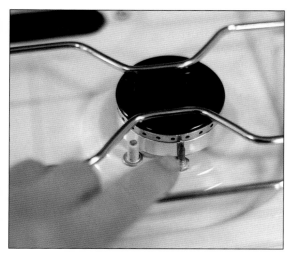

Since 1994, flame-failure devices have been fitted on each burner on a hob.

That's why a gas control has to be held down for a few seconds when igniting a burner.

Routine servicing and safety check

- Apart from cleaning, there are no servicing tasks on cookers that an owner can carry out.
- Like all gas systems, the cooking appliances *must* be checked by a qualified gas engineer in accordance with manufacturer instructions. This is one of the tasks that should come within an annual service check.
- If a gas flame flickers yellow and soot is left on saucepans, this is usually a sign of an incorrect

It is important for a gas engineer to test the operation of all cooking appliances on a regular basis.

gas/air mixture. The condition is symptomatic of incomplete combustion and when it occurs there may be a release of carbon monoxide. This can be serious so the appliance should be checked by a qualified gas engineer. Indeed the fault *must* be remedied before the burner is used again.

Space heating appliances

On the grounds of safety, an open burner 'gas fire' is no longer used in caravans for safety reasons. Unenclosed burners are considered dangerous because:
- something could fall on to the exposed flame,
- oxygen is taken from the living space while the heater is in operation,
- waste products are discharged into the living area as well.

Two air connections are fitted to room-sealed heaters – one admits air for combustion whereas the other is the flue for exhaust fumes.

129

The fins on this Carver heat exchanger help to release warmth created by the gas burner to the interior of the caravan.

In extreme cases there might be a risk of carbon monoxide poisoning, so appliances now have to be 'room sealed' and are referred to as 'space heaters' rather than 'gas fires'. Room sealing means the burners are housed in a chamber which is completely sealed off from the living area. Air for combustion is drawn directly into

On some of the heaters from Truma and Carver, the balance of air released into the ducts from the fan can be adjusted.

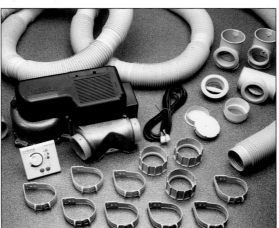

Many Carver and Truma heaters can be fitted with a blown air ducted system using one of the manufacturer's kits.

this sealed chamber from the outside and in a similar way, exhaust gases are returned outside via a flue.

Heat generated in the combustion chamber then has to reach the living area. The objective is achieved by directing the hot air through a 'heat exchanger' which is purpose-designed to release heat efficiently. Many heat exchangers are thus manufactured with moulded fins – rather like the fins on an air-cooled motorcycle engine.

In consequence it is the heat exchanger that warms the interior rather than the gas flames themselves. To assist in the distribution of heat, many appliances also have a fan which directs warmed air along a network of ducts. Outlets in this system then ensure that heat is distributed throughout the interior at low level instead of immediately rising to the ceiling. Closed rooms like a shower cubicle can also be supplied with warm air via the ducting.

On the rear of some Carver and Truma fans it is also possible to adjust the proportion of heat being directed along the two outlets served by the fan. So if one end of the caravan seems cooler than the other, the diversion lever offers the opportunity to adjust the distribution of heat as an adjunct to the butterfly control flap on the duct outlets.

Many practically skilled owners add a ducting system to their caravans; using proprietary components from specialists such as Carver and Truma, the task can be fairly straightforward. Hiding the ducting discreetly is the main challenge although it *is* possible to obtain specially reinforced sections to take routeways *beneath* the floor without too much loss of heat.

In 1994, Carver went one step further by introducing the Fanmaster which combined a 230V heating element within the heat distribution fan unit. With everything contained in the same appliance, a caravanner has the choice of either distributing warm air from the gas burners or creating warm air from a mains element. Both systems, however, should not be operated simultaneously.

The Fanmaster in which a 230V heating element is fitted inside its casing has a reset button to recommission a unit shut down through overheating.

In January 1995 this was made available as an 'add-on' appliance which could be fitted to a number of space heaters. Products like the Carver 1800, 2000 and 3000 heaters could be upgraded using the appropriate fitting kit. But with two heating levels provided by 1kW and 2kW elements, the 8.3A and 4.2A rating of a Fanmaster has implications for a site's hook-up capabilities.

Using this Fanmaster unit it is essential that at least one duct outlet remains open when the heater is running, but in the event of overheating, an automatic cut-out safety switch comes into operation. The device is reset as follows:

1. Wait until the appliance has cooled down.
2. Open all the outlets.
3. Disconnect the mains supply at the consumer unit.
4. Re-set the trip button by pressing the push switch on the side of the casing.

Unfortunately the reset switch can be difficult to locate and operate, especially when the casing is

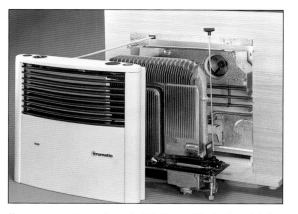

Key components are shown in this Truma Ultraheat model: the front casing; the heat exchanger with gas assembly; and the rear casing with mains heating elements.

mounted out of sight in the bottom section of a wardrobe.

As regards ignition, heaters installed in caravans in the 1980s and early 1990s like the Carver Trumatic SLP 3002 were fitted with a push button Piezo igniter. These are reliable but will not operate if the spark gap is incorrect or if the high tension cable from the switch has become damaged. Similarly, the push button assembly on the SLP 3002 sometimes fails. Spares are available, however, from Truma.

Note: *In the 1980s and early 1990s, Carver worked closely with Truma and heating systems shared many components. In 1996, however, Carver and Truma returned to their original position of independence; and manufactured high quality products under their own brand names. Then in Autumn 1999, Truma bought the gas manufacturing division of Carver. The effect of this on brand name use is currently unclear.*

It is also possible to replace the Piezo system on many Carver space heaters with an electronic auto ignition unit. This was introduced in May 1996

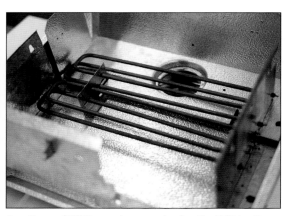

The Carver 4000 Fanmaster provides heat from either a gas burner or a mains element fitted behind the heat exchanger.

On a Carver 4000 Fanmaster space heater, the 230V heating elements are mounted within the main casing, to the rear of the heat exchanger.

Spiders' webs and dust in the trumpet shaped venturi affect operation of both the burner and the pilot flame.

and kits have been made for the conversion of 1800, 2000 and 3000 Carver models.

As regards more recent developments, both the Truma Ultraheat and the Carver Fanmaster 4000 are space heaters where the electrical heating elements are located behind the rear of the heat exchanger but within the main casing itself. In other words heating elements are no longer built into the fan housing.

In the case of the Truma Ultraheat, this appliance can be operated with both gas and 230V systems operating simultaneously. Variations in output are:

- one kilowatt from the electric element;
- two kilowatts from the electric element;
- three kilowatts from the gas burner;
- five kilowatts from the combined systems.

The appliance has been fitted into a number of larger caravans e.g. 1998 models in the Fleetwood range. However, to enjoy the full benefit of the 230V option, Truma points out that it is necessary to stay on a site where the hook-up offers a minimum supply of 10A – which is quite substantial.

In large caravans you will also find 'wet systems' in which radiators are used. The 3000 Compact central heating system from Alde, for example, is installed in high specification models like the Vanmaster. Reports from owners indicate that it is extremely efficient.

Routine servicing and safety check

Like cooking appliances, space heaters also need an annual safety check and service. This is not something the owner should tackle.

Several tasks will be carried out including

checks on the shape of the gas flames. The shape of a flame will inform the qualified and experienced gas engineer about operational efficiency.

One of the problems in caravans is that there are periods when gas appliances might not be used for an extended spell. This is when dust and cobwebs can accumulate. It often comes as a surprise to learn that the humble spider often upsets gas appliances. For instance filaments of a spider's web across a pilot light can distort the shape of the flame and prevent the main burner from igniting. Equally, a spider ball or a dead insect caught in the trumpet-shaped venturi through which combustion air is admitted to the burner is a common cause of flame distortion.

It is the same with the flue. Even a spider's web spun across a flue roof outlet can upset exhaust efficiency enough to prevent a space heater switching from pilot to main burner. So general cleaning is one of the elements of servicing and the labour charge for this is modest.

To summarise:
• There are no servicing tasks on gas heating appliances that an owner can carry out.
• Space heating appliances must be checked by a qualified gas engineer in accordance with manufacturer's instructions – an element that should come within a caravan's annual service check.
• In addition to checking the appliance, the flue will also be given a safety and efficiency check.
• Ensure that you are given a written account of the servicing work that has been completed.

Water heating appliances

Availability of hot water is a great asset and few caravans are built now without the inclusion of a water heater. There are three main types:

1. Instantaneous water heaters e.g. the Morco, the Rinnai.
2. Storage water heaters e.g. the Carver Cascade Rapide GE, the Maxol Malaga, the Truma Storage.
3. Water heaters integrated with a space heater e.g. the Trumatic C range, and Alde 3000 Compact.

Instantaneous water heaters have lost their popularity recently on account of the fact that the gas burner is exposed, a constructed flue above the unit is now a requirement, and the appliance takes up valuable wall space. On the other hand instantaneous appliances can produce hot water without any delay and continue to produce it all the time there's a cold water supply and gas to heat it.

Storage heaters have the advantage of being inconspicuous, can easily be mounted in a bed box and their operation uses a remotely sited control panel. Their balanced flue is discreet, too, and more recent versions incorporate a mains heating element as an adjunct to the gas burner; both can be operated simultaneously to speed up

If a Carver Cascade 2 overheats it has an emergency cut-out; a reset button is on the end of the casing.

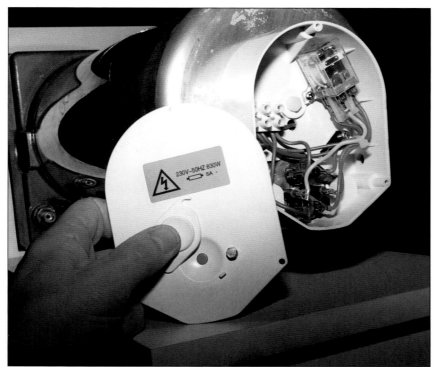

heating time. Notwithstanding the twin source of heat, the storage vessel still takes time to heat up from scratch and the quantity of available hot water is limited, too. There's also the matter of weight. Few people drain down the water before taking to the road and water is significantly heavy. A Carver Cascade, for example, holds 9 litres (2 gallons) thereby taking up 9kg (20lb) of payload capacity.

Since its debut in the mid-1980s, the Carver Cascade has undergone a number of improvements. In recognition of this, Carver manufactures upgrade kits for owners who want to improve earlier Carver Cascade models. For instance the Cascade 2 can be upgraded to achieve the faster drain-down of the Cascade 2 Plus using a special kit.

In addition, the Cascade 2 Plus GE includes a 660w mains heating element. However, the latest Cascade Rapide now has an 830W heating element and if you buy a tank repair kit this also includes a replacement 830W element. On recent models, the overheat re-set button is situated behind a cover flap.

Upgrades to older models can be carried out by your dealer, although many competent owners have also installed the components successfully, too.

While the Carver Cascades have been the most popular storage heater fitted in recent caravans, the Maxol Malaga and the Malaga E (which has an additional 230V heating element) have been fitted into a number of caravans including models in Fleetwood's 1995 range. Water heaters bearing the later name of the Belling Malaga were fitted in the Bailey Hunter-Lite range from 1997 onwards.

Routine servicing and safety check

It is important that a water heater is inspected and serviced regularly at an approved dealership. As with other gas-operated appliances, servicing and repair work fall outside the scope of DIY endeavour. Draining-down work, however, is an exception.

Frost will seriously damage a water heater. For instance in the Carver Cascade units, the water storage casing can be forced away from the heating section when freezing water expands in the chamber. In an instantaneous water heater like the Rinnai, extreme damage can be sustained within the labyrinth of narrow bore water pipes.

There are two ways to ensure this doesn't happen. One is to fill the entire system with potable anti-freeze. This strategy is favoured in the United States and a potable anti-freeze is now available under the Camco accessory range imported by Alde UK. All you have to do is to pump the recommended quantity into the system via your water container, leaving it there until the weather improves. The only point to bear in mind is that some manufacturers of water heaters, e.g. Carver, do not approve the idea of using potable

On earlier models, the drain down plug on a Cascade 2 had to be left open for a considerable time.

anti-freeze in case it leads to component damage.

The alternative is to drain down your system as described in the manufacturer's instructions. With a Carver Cascade unit the procedures are:

• Open all taps over sinks and basins;
• Remove the drain plug on the appliance;
• Leave the water to drain out completely – this may take an hour or more
• Replace the drain plug to keep out spiders and insects.

Early Carver heaters took an age to drain and it is wise to leave one of these units discharging water for a couple of hours if possible. More recent models release all the water at a much quicker rate and an air release screw is situated on the top left part of the external framework.

Instantaneous water heaters can also take time to drain down. If a receptacle can be left underneath to catch water for a day or more, so much the better. Time spent here is well rewarded; repairing frost-damaged appliances is a costly business.

Recent models of the Carver Cascade water heater achieve a faster drain down when an air release stopper is loosened.

133

Refrigerators

As well as being one of the most useful appliances in a modern caravan, a refrigerator is an important contributor to comfortable living. However, successful operation is only achieved if the appliance is correctly installed, used properly and regularly serviced.

Product identities

For many years, the refrigerators fitted in leisure vehicles were manufactured by Electrolux. However, in 2001, the leisure appliance division of Electrolux became an independent company and the name Dometic was adopted. This had been a brand name in the US for a number of years. In 2003, many appliances were still bearing both Dometic and Electrolux badges which was rather confusing. However, in 2004 the licence to use the Electrolux name expired. In this chapter both names are used because thousands of motorcaravans are fitted with products previously manufactured by Electrolux. Only more recent models have appliances bearing the Dometic badge, and because many of the Company's staff worked in the former Leisure Appliance Division of Electrolux, aftersales advice covers both products. Norcold is another manufacturer of absorption refrigerators. These products were launched in the UK in 2002 and are being marketed by Thetford. Several caravan manufacturers are now installing Norcold appliances.

The provision of refrigerators in touring caravans goes back to the early 1970s. In those days this was an optional item in more expensive models – although by modern standards the devices were rather rudimentary. For instance, models like the Morphy Richards Astral had to be lit with a match and the burner could only be reached from an access hatch outside the caravan.

On older fridges, cooling would sometimes cease because an airlock had developed in the refrigeration unit. To solve this, it would be necessary to remove the appliance, turn it upside down for several hours, and then reinstate it. Invariably this temporarily cured the problem but it often involved quite a lot of dismantling and re-assembly work.

In contrast, today's Electrolux refrigerators are supplied with sophisticated ignition and cooling control systems. They also keep the contents cool, even during very hot weather. However, to achieve full efficiency, an Electrolux fridge has to be:

- installed in the manner laid down by the manufacturer;
- used in accordance with the manufacturer's recommendations;
- fully serviced at appropriate intervals.

These points might seem self-evident, but in practice, it is not unusual to find that a caravan manufacturer has not carried out the installation properly. Equally there are many owners who disregard advice contained in the user-instructions. Finally, it is not unusual to find a fridge that hasn't been serviced since the day it left the factory.

The aim of this chapter is to look into these issues more closely; in some cases, readers may note the technical points and want to undertake corrective measures themselves like fitting better wall ventilators, but do not presume that the content is solely directed at the practical person. On the contrary, the final section is included to inform owners what tasks a service engineer should carry out when undertaking a full refrigerator service. The illustrated text demonstrates what is involved and underlines why a refrigerator, like any gas-operating appliance, needs periodic attention.

At no point is it necessary to understand the chemistry of refrigeration. However, a broad grasp of the cooling process is helpful and this is covered first.

Operation and efficient use

A caravan refrigerator is rather different from the appliances fitted in our kitchens at home. It is true that chemicals have to be circulated around a network of pipes – whether it's a fridge at home or in a caravan. Moreover, as the refrigerants circulate, the chemicals change state and draw heat out of the food compartment in the process – but this is where the similarities end.

In a normal domestic appliance, the chemicals are circulated by a compressor whose periodical operation is controlled by a thermostat. You will often hear this spring into life when additional cooling is required although in a busy kitchen at home the noise of a compressor is unlikely to be intrusive.

This is not the case, however, in the close confines of a caravan. A different method is adopted for circulating the refrigerants: heat is used instead of a compressor and this is why a caravan refrigerator is completely silent in its operation.

The manufacturer of this type of appliance refers to it as an 'absorption refrigerator'. These types of refrigerator are not restricted to use in caravans; they are also found in hotel rooms and hospitals.

When an absorption refrigerator is fitted in a caravan, there are usually three sources of heat:

1. A gas burner drawing from the caravan's gas supply.
2. A 230V heating element drawing from a mains hook-up.
3. A 12V supply drawn from the towcar when its engine is running.

Under normal conditions, each of the alternatives will achieve efficient cooling although it's important to point out that the 12V option is not controllable. When operating in this mode, the fridge operates 'flat out' and altering the fascia controls makes no effect whatsoever. This is not the case, of course, when the appliance is run on mains electricity or gas.

It is also important to point out that on some holiday sites, the sheer number of caravanners drawing mains electricity means that the nominal 230V supply can actually drop as low 195V. The tip box on this page adds advice on this point.

Choosing the operating mode

On most caravan refrigerators you have to select the heat source yourself to suit the circumstances. Only the very latest Automatic Energy Selection (AES) refrigerators carry this out without need for owner intervention. Working under a computer monitoring system, the AES fridge has a built-in priority programme. For instance, on site the AES system will automatically choose 230V mains; if this is not available, gas will automatically be selected instead. Furthermore, when you take to the road, it recognises that gas appliances should not be operated during towing. Even if you haven't turned off the gas cylinder control valve, it switches over automatically to 12V operation as soon as the engine is started.

Following this arrangement through further, when entering a petrol station and switching off the engine, the refrigerator will not return to gas operation until a period of twenty minutes has elapsed. This is a safety precaution in case you've forgotten to turn off the gas cylinder.

Although AES refrigerators leave the caravanner with very little to do apart from switching on and setting the cooling level, they are still comparatively unusual. Cost is one of the reasons although they are now being fitted in more expensive models.

Advice to owners

To get the best from a refrigerator, there are a number of measures you can take:

Prior to departure

Before taking to the road, pre-cool the food compartment by running the refrigerator for three hours or more. During this pre-cooling period it is helpful to load some non-perishable items, like bottles of mineral water.

If your caravan is parked at home, it is often possible to couple the hook-up lead to a 13A socket so that the fridge can be operated from a mains supply. However, you will need an adapter and should also fit a portable Residual Current Device (RCD) into the socket as well, in order to provide protection to anyone passing the trailing lead to the 'van. The function of an RCD was described in Chapter 8, *The mains supply system*, and portable units are sold at most DIY stores.

On the road

Always remember to switch to 12V operation when taking to the road. As mentioned in Chapter 10, *Gas supply systems and appliances*, the supply cylinder should be turned off as a safety measure. On a model which has a tiny 'porthole' in the bottom of the food compartment, check here to confirm the gas flame is extinguished.

Do not regard 12V operation as 'second best'. On the contrary, cooling in this mode is just as good as it is under gas or mains. However, there is no thermostatic control and the natural movement of the caravan prevents over-freezing. In the unlikely event that you suffer from over-cooling when towing in cold conditions, fit winter covers on the external ventilators.

On site

Once on site, keep the following tips in mind:

Ignition problems

If attempts to ignite the burner are unsuccessful, this may be because there's air in the gas line. Repeated attempts usually purge the air but if there's continuing difficulty, the appliance is probably due for a service. Cleaning and re-aligning the ignition electrode is one of the servicing tasks.

Cooling fins

The silvered cooling fins at the back of the food compartment draw heat from the interior, so it is most important that these are not covered. Items like canned drink packs should never be pushed hard against the fins. Equally, water droplets or frost on the cooling fins reduce operating efficiency, so remember to cover damp vegetables or put

Handy tip

If your refrigerator is operating on mains electricity on a busy site, you may find the cooling level is disappointing. This often happens because the 230V supply drops as low as 190–195V on account of the large number of caravanners hooked into the system. If this occurs, return to the gas operating mode. This should result in the fridge achieving better cooling.

Avoid over-packing a refrigerator; air must be able to circulate around the contents – this fridge may be too tightly packed.

Covering the silver cooling fins with a drinks pack will seriously affect cooling potential.

135

Stain removal

Sometimes the interior of a fridge gets stained. A broken egg, for example, will leave discoloration from the yolk. To remove a stubborn mark, use a very fine wire wool pad, lubricated liberally with water to reduce its abrasive effect. If used carefully, this will remove stubborn stains without damaging the plastic lining materials.

them in a plastic bag – especially freshly washed lettuce. Similarly, wipe excess moisture from food cartons.

Voltage drops

Take note of the problem of mains voltage drops on crowded holiday parks described earlier.

Packing food

Make sure that plenty of space is left around the items on the shelves. For the contents to cool, air must be allowed to circulate inside the cooling compartment. Also make sure that strong-smelling food like cheese or onions is packed in a sealed plastic bag.

Door use

Open your fridge door as briefly as possible. Regrettably several recent caravan kitchens incorporate a decorative door that hides the fridge completely – including the controls. This means you have to lose cold air just to alter a control or to confirm the red 12V light is working when setting off. It is a poor design feature.

Winter covers

When outside temperatures fall below 10°C (50°F) you are advised to fit 'winter covers' over the

ventilators. Unfortunately some of the 'budget' vents fitted on cheaper models may not have matching covers. Some owners try to overcome this by partially covering the fins with cooking foil. It may help to prevent over-cooling but the arrangement is neither glamorous nor entirely effective.

On arrival home

Remove all food and leave the refrigerator door partially open. Normally there's a door catch with a position which will hold the door slightly ajar. This allows air to circulate.

If it's the end of your caravanning season, Electrolux recommends that the food compartment is cleaned using a weak solution of bicarbonate of soda. A teaspoonful added to half a litre of warm water is recommended. Do not use other cleaners because there have been instances where a reaction with the plastic liner has led to cracking.

Needless to say, if you are not planning to use the caravan for an extended period, consider having the fridge serviced in readiness for the next trip.

Installation

In the opening part of this chapter, it was pointed out that to achieve efficient cooling, a refrigerator must be installed in accordance with manufacturer's instructions. It is most regrettable that over the years, some caravan manufacturers have disregarded several features contained in the Electrolux installation manual. Even 1999 models from some well-respected caravan manufacturers fall short in respect of the ventilation requirement.

Although an appliance with a poorly-formed ventilation facility is certain to achieve a measure of cooling, its full potential is unlikely to be realised. In fact in the heat of summer, its shortcomings will often become apparent.

Self check

To enable the cooling unit at the rear of a caravan refrigerator to operate properly, the rear of a

If the surface above a fridge gets hot, it is likely the appliance has not been fitted correctly.

---

refrigerator should be completely sealed off from the living quarters. There are different ways of achieving this but in most cases aluminium shielding is fitted around the back of the casing. Sealing off the rear of the appliance is necessary because the interior of a caravan can get exceedingly hot when parked in the sun – much hotter inside than out. If this heat reaches the refrigeration unit on the rear of the casing, its operating potential will be significantly reduced.

Furthermore, if the installation has been carried out correctly, cold wind blowing into the wall ventilators will not be able to penetrate the living space. Some caravans can be very draughty inside and in most cases this is the result of deficiency in the shielding arrangement.

Installation inspection

1. On recent ventilators, it is easy to remove the grille.

You can check the installation of your refrigerator as follows:
• If your refrigerator is located below a draining board or work top, put your hand on the surface when it is operating. If it is warm, there's a strong likelihood that the appliance hasn't been shielded off effectively.
• Check for draughts in the kitchen on windy days. Wind blowing through external fridge vents should never reach the interior. This is a sure sign that the shielding system at the rear of the appliance doesn't meet the fridge manufacturer's specifications.
• Look through the outer vents. If your caravan has one of the more recent Electrolux ventilators, you will be able to detach the grille from its frame to see even better. Peering through, you should not be able to see light in the caravan interior, nor inside the kitchen furniture. To seal off the rear of the appliance, aluminium sheet is usually used – with sealant applied around apertures enclosing pipes or cables.
• It may help to remove kitchen drawers when looking from inside your caravan. Once again, the grills should not be visible.
• If you find that a length of sponge or glass fibre quilt has been wedged on top of the casing instead of a metal deflector, this is an unsatisfactory substitute. It is unlikely that this will keep draughts out on windy days because sponge or similar material can compress or become detached.
• To achieve cooling at the rear of the appliance,

2. The flue cover is unclipped and removed separately.

3. Withdraw the upper section of the flue assembly.

4. Detach the complete grille from its support framework.

5. Inside the uppermost vent, a tilting deflector shield should be visible.

When a caravan door is fully opened, check it doesn't touch the flue cover or obscure the ventilators.

ventilators of the specified size are essential. On some caravans you will find them reduced in size; others may be lined with an insect gauze which reduces the effective area quite considerably. In reality, if a fridge has been correctly installed and sealed at the rear, insect gauze is unnecessary. It is essential that air from outside can enter, unhindered, at a low level and then passed back outside above the top of the casing.

• Vents should not be completely obstructed by your caravan door. Electrolux recommends that the distance between the open door and the vents should be at least 50mm (2in). Equally, you should make sure you do not let any part of an awning cover a ventilator. On some caravans, a fully open door obscures the vents – and sometimes it also restricts the outflow of exhaust gases from the flue outlet. This is most unsatisfactory.

• Some owners presume that 'winter covers' are intended as draught excluders. This is certainly not the case; their purpose is to prevent *overcooling*.

If your refrigerator installation fails in any of the

On a badly installed fridge, a tilting deflector shield can sometimes be made from aluminium sheet and fitted as a curative measure.

above respects, the following section gives a brief summary of the key features. Using this information some readers will undoubtedly respond by undertaking corrective measures themselves. Others will prefer to seek the advice of their caravan dealer. However, this is only a summary and to obtain more detailed installation instructions, you should contact Electrolux direct. The address and telephone number are listed in the Appendix at the end of this book.

Key installation elements

When taking all points of installation into account, there are six specific areas of attention:

1. Achieving a level location.
2. Structural fixing.
3. Ventilation.
4. Mains connection.
5. Low voltage connection.
6. Gas connection and flue.

Achieving a level location

The circulation of refrigerant chemicals is hindered a fridge isn't level. So anyone who is refurbishing a older caravan and wants to fit a refrigerator would start by parking the caravan on a level plane. Thereafter, a spirit level is used when installing the appliance so that when the job is completed you know that if the 'van is level, the fridge will be level as well.

On an Electrolux refrigerator, the reference point for verifying a level plane is the shelf in the small freezer compartment. Of course, a very short spirit level is needed to take a reading here. The exception is the RM123 which has a sloping shelf and on this model the spirit level should be placed on the base of the food storage cabinet.

Note: *i) All Electrolux refrigerators manufactured before 1986 had to be completely level to operate. A tilt in excess of 2–3° could impair operation. Since this date, all higher specification models are described as 'tilt tolerant'. Some models will operate at an angle of 3° (e.g. RM122 and RM4206); others operate at 6° (e.g. RM4217, RM4237, and RM4271).*
ii) On the road, a fridge will seldom be level, particularly when driving along a carriageway with pronounced camber. However, as long as a level position is achieved periodically – which is the case on normal roads – chemical circulation will take place and cooling will occur.

Structural fixing

When being towed, a caravan receives a considerable shake-up, especially on bumpy roads, so a refrigerator needs to be carefully secured and Electrolux recommends that wooden blocks are fitted on the floor at the rear of the unit as shown in the diagram opposite. Equally, if the support afforded by adjacent kitchen units is in doubt, blocks can also be fitted on the floor to support the sides of the casing.

In the past, mechanical fixing at the sides has often been achieved by driving screws through adjacent furniture units and directly into the metal casing of the appliance. As long as the fixings penetrated no further than 12mm (½in), the interior plastic lining wouldn't be damaged. However, models like the RM2260 and RM2262 have been manufactured more recently with a projecting flange around the front; this incorporates fixing points.

Even better are the Electrolux fridges made since 1994 which incorporate pre-formed holes in the sides of the food compartment. This means that long screws can be driven from the inside outwards, thereby achieving anchorage from adjacent structures – usually kitchen cupboards. The screw heads are then concealed by a white plastic cap that matches the inner lining of the food compartment.

Overall, a successful structural installation will achieve three objectives:

- The fridge will be in a level position when the caravan is parked on level ground.
- It will not shake loose even when towing on very rough roads.
- The appliance will be easy to remove and reinstate to facilitate servicing.

Ventilation

Some very small refrigerators fitted around ten years ago did not use wall-mounted ventilators. Their food compartment was less than 1cu.ft and nowadays these models are seldom seen. The 'internal venting' employed for these appliances

Older refrigerators were fixed by driving screws through adjacent panels and into the unit's metal casing.

would certainly not meet the requirements of the larger refrigerators that caravanners now expect.

On today's appliances, it is important that the cooling unit on the back of the casing is completely sealed off from the caravan interior. This point has already been mentioned and owners can check the installation using the test procedures given earlier.

Bridging the gap left between the rear of the appliance and the caravan wall is normally achieved with aluminium sheet. To eliminate the need to fabricate this, Electrolux sells a pre-formed frame referred to as the IK1 kit which fits most popular models. This kit, however, may not suit caravans with end kitchen installations on account of the larger-than-usual gap between the wall and the rear of the appliance. Whilst some caravan manufacturers use this item, others prefer to form their own version. On some models, this provision has been overlooked completely.

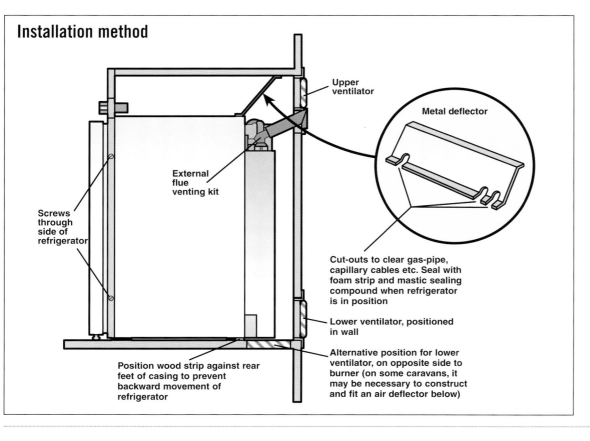

Installation method

Upper ventilator

Metal deflector

External flue venting kit

Screws through side of refrigerator

Cut-outs to clear gas-pipe, capillary cables etc. Seal with foam strip and mastic sealing compound when refrigerator is in position

Lower ventilator, positioned in wall

Position wood strip against rear feet of casing to prevent backward movement of refrigerator

Alternative position for lower ventilator, on opposite side to burner (on some caravans, it may be necessary to construct and fit an air deflector below)

Correct installation is important and the need to fit a metal shield deflector at the rear is emphasised by the manufacturer.

Sections of aluminium sheet are prepared around the fridge so that its cooling unit is completely sealed off when the unit is installed.

Technical Tip

Caravans built after 1st September 1999 have a separate neutral cable specifically for the fridge and this is connected to Pin 7 on the 12S plug/ socket system. Prior to this, all caravan 12V appliances, including the fridge, share a common neutral wire connected to Pin 3, leaving Pin 7 blank. In other words, the 12S socket on your car should be wired to suit the age of the caravan you're towing, as explained in *Chapter 3, Towing matters.*

Once a sealed ventilation path has been created using the shielding, air from outside will be drawn in via a vent. This air will pass across the pipes, burner assembly and other cooling unit components whereupon it will absorb some of the heat created in the refrigeration process. It then rises by convection until it meets a tilting deflector shield that should be mounted on top of the refrigerator casing. The warmed air is thus redirected outside again via the upper vent as shown in the illustration on the previous page. Curiously this important deflector shield is sometimes omitted by caravan manufacturers.

Achieving an unhindered passage of air across the rear of a refrigerator is important and in a correct installation the warmed air will rise naturally. In a correctly installed fridge, there is no need to fit a fan to accelerate air movement. Notwithstanding this advice, some caravanners like to add a 12V operated fan within the sealed section at the back. A fridge fan, for example, is available from PDM Marketing and this is easy to fit to the upper ventilator.

The efficiency of the provision is also influenced by the ventilator units as well. Their size is important. On refrigerators of 2 cu.ft. storage capacity or less, the ventilators should provide at least 240cms^2 of free air space. Models offering more than 2cu.ft. storage require ventilators achieving at least 300 cms^2 free air space. Note that this is reduced if an insect gauze is added on the inside of the grille.

The A1609 and A1620 ventilators made by Electrolux certainly achieve these requirements although they are comparatively expensive. It's for this reason that several manufacturers fit other types – though these versions lack the leak-proof design of Electrolux units and driving rain can penetrate. Equally, some of the less expensive ventilators are not made to accept winter covers, although this problem also occurs with earlier types of Electrolux ventilator, too.

Owners of older caravans often decide to upgrade their fridge ventilators to the A1620 versions since these accept winter covers and integrate the flue outlet neatly within the design. This improvement

work necessitates increasing the dimension of the aperture and you should check there are no obstructions before cutting into the sides.

The position of ventilators relative to the appliance is another issue. The top vent should be located so that its upper edge is at least 55mm (2in) above the casing of the refrigerator. On the other hand, the lower vent can either be positioned in the side wall or in the floor. If the latter option is preferred it should be situated as far from the burner as possible so that draughts don't extinguish the flame. It may also need a deflector plate fixed under the floor so that dirt isn't driven into the vents when the caravan is being towed.

Mains connection

The 230V mains connection is easy to carry out. An Electrolux refrigerator is supplied with a three core flexible cable which needs coupling into the caravan's mains supply. Typically there's a separate spur for the fridge and this is protected by its own miniature circuit breaker on the mains consumer unit. This is described further in Chapter 8, *The mains supply system.* The current rating for the mains connection should be no greater than 5A.

Low voltage connection

Although an Electrolux refrigerator will work well from a 12V supply, its performance is impaired if the actual voltage that reaches the appliance has fallen below this level. It was pointed out in Chapter 7, *The 12V supply system,* that voltage drops occur when a connecting cable is too long and/or too thin. The recommendation of Electrolux should therefore be strictly observed by the fridge installer.

The key features in a supply are shown in the illustration on the facing page and this should be read in conjunction with points covered in Chapter 3, *Towcar preparation* on 12S socket wiring and the Technical Tip box on the left.

The 12V supply that operates the refrigerator's cooling system is usually taken from the vehicle's alternator and this has to be an *ignition-controlled supply* (in other words the current only flows when the engine is running).

However, an additional, *permanent supply* is also needed for the electronic igniter which lights the burner when you switch over to gas operation. At one time a gas burner would be lit by a Piezo crystal spark created when you depressed a red button, but many refrigerators now have electronic ignition instead. It has many advantages although it *does* need a 12V feed. Its current consumption is very small, however, so the supply is normally taken from the caravan's auxiliary battery as shown in the diagram opposite.

Gas operation

Requirements in the gas supply include:
• The need for an independent gas cock in the supply to the fridge. This is usually situated

Key components needed in a 12V cooling system

■ A 15 amp fuse on the fridge supply cable situated as close to the positive terminal on the vehicle battery as possible.

■ A relay – this is an electrically operated switch which activates as soon as the engine is running. Once the engine has started up, it allows current to flow from the vehicle battery to the refrigerator, recognising that the alternator will be charging the battery to compensate for the substantial consumption. A fridge draws at least 8 amps and the rate of consumption is 96 watts or more depending on the model. Suitable relays are available from specialists like Hella, Lucas and Ryder and these are normally fitted in the engine compartment. As soon as the engine is switched off, the relay then automatically arrests the flow of current to the fridge. On arrival at your destination, you then need to switch the fridge over to gas or to hook up to a mains supply.

■ To ensure minimum loss of current, Electrolux recommends the connecting cable to be at least 2.5mm² (21.75A continuous current rating). Cable of this type is supplied as standard if you purchase a Hella fridge relay kit but it is also available from any automotive specialist dealing with car electrical products.

■ Whilst the connection could go directly to the fridge, it is usually routed via a 12V control panel in your caravan. Typically these have a separate switch for the refrigerator supply and there will be another fuse in the box – usually of 10A rating.

■ From the control box, the live and neutral feeds are coupled to a terminal block on top of the refrigerator casing, just behind the control fascia.

■ A 12V feed to the electronic igniter for the gas burner (where this form of ignition is fitted) will be a separate source taken from the leisure battery rather than from the battery that serves the vehicle's engine.

Cable rating

The cable used in cars is made up of a series of copper strands of 0.30mm². To verify the rating of automotive cable, strip away a small length of insulation and count each of the copper filaments in the core. Cable of 2.5mm² has 36 strands. Note: *At one time Electrolux recommended that cable of 2.0mm² rating (28 strands) was used but some installers exceeded the permitted length and voltage drop was commonplace. In the latest installation recommendations, 2.5 mm² cable is now specified.*

12 Volt wiring arrangement

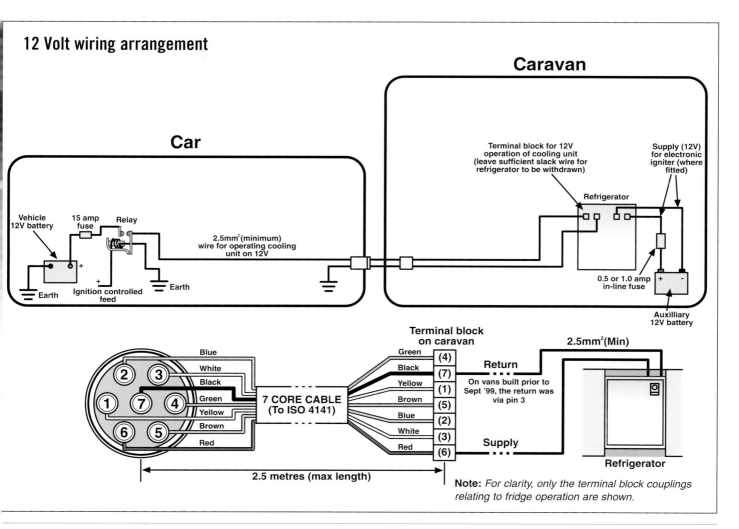

Note: *For clarity, only the terminal block couplings relating to fridge operation are shown.*

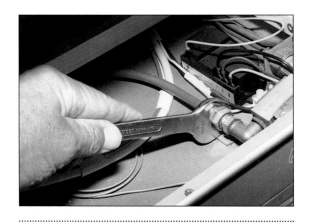

Prior to final removal, the gas supply to a fridge must be disconnected.

adjacent to the appliance in a kitchen cupboard.
• Copper feed pipes of 6mm (¼in) outside diameter (OD). The final connection to the appliance must not be made with flexible gas hose.
• A flue arrangement. This is *entirely different* from the ventilation system described earlier. On the outside of the vehicle, the flue cover plate used to be entirely separate from the ventilator grilles. In 1994, however, Electrolux introduced the A1620 grilles that combined both the flue outlet and the upper ventilation outlet into a single plastic moulded unit.
• An ignition system. In the early 1970s, the gas burner had to be lit with a match. However, push-button ignition in which a Piezo crystal is used to generate a spark soon replaced this system. In the mid 1980s, electronic ignition was introduced and this is now more commonly fitted.
• Gas escape provision must be included when a unit is installed. Accordingly a purpose-formed 'drop-out' hole of 40mm (1⅝in) is normally needed, thus providing a direct outlet to the exterior. In some instances the lower ventilator grill can achieve this objective, but if fitted with one of the older types of winter covers, it then fails to meet the requirement.
• The union for coupling into the caravan's gas supply system is usually situated on the top of the appliance, just behind the control fascia. However, on new fridge freezer models such as the RM4501, the coupling is situated at the bottom rear of the appliance, thus offering access via the lower grill aperture. Whilst it's true that an experienced DIY owner might be able to secure a fridge in its location, the final connection of a gas supply should

be entrusted to a competent gas engineer, as described in the Technical Tip box in Chapter 10, page 126. The joint will be formed using an approved threaded coupling. In a thread-to-thread union, a jointing compound like Calor-tite will be used. There will also be a generous length of excess copper pipe on top of the appliance so that it can be drawn forward from its housing to facilitate removal for servicing.

Servicing

As with any gas-operated appliance, periodic servicing is very important. This not only ensures that the refrigerator operates efficiently; it is a safety element too.

In spite of this, some caravanners *never* have their fridge serviced – and the appliance seems to perform well, season after season. But there's nothing more annoying if it finally fails on holiday, especially when there's a spell of hot weather.

Recognising the different levels of use, Electrolux has recommended that servicing should be carried out every 12 to 18 months to ensure optimum performance. In practice, servicing work is fairly straightforward; the job that often takes a disproportionate amount of time is removing the appliance from the caravan and transferring it to a work bench. Unfortunately caravan manufacturers often fit the appliance early on and then build furniture around it, making its retrieval – and reinstatement – annoyingly difficult.

Since much of the servicing operation demands competence and experience working with gas appliances, it is not a task that a DIY enthusiast should tackle. On the other hand, a labour charge might be saved if an owner were able to remove the refrigerator from its housing. Reinstatement could also be considered, although re-making the gas connection and carrying out a leak test should be conducted by a gas service engineer.

The photographs opposite highlight the key tasks that your dealer should carry out. The work breaks down into the following:

• With the fridge on a bench, the service engineer will remove the flue outlet pipes that are connected to the top of the burner tube. This tube is effectively a chimney clad in an insulating material. Wrapped within its insulation are the heating elements for 12V and 230V operation.
• A baffle is lifted out of the burner tube. This is a twisted piece of sheet metal suspended on a wire and its position within the tube is critically determined by the length of this wire. One servicing task is to clean off all carbon deposits from the baffle.
• At the base of the burner tube, a metal windshield enclosing the burner is removed.
• The burner assembly is disconnected next and pulled away from the base of the burner tube. Using a special wire brush supplied by Electrolux, the engineer will clean all carbon deposit from the tube.
• The burner assembly will be cleaned, too, including the tip of the flame failure probe called the 'thermocouple'.

Thermocouple operation

Gas only flows to the burner when the tip of the thermocouple has warmed up and the operating valve has opened. During the warming-up period, you have to open the valve manually by holding in the gas control knob for a few seconds.

When the tip is heated, a tiny current flows from the thermocouple; it then activates an electromagnet that holds open a spring-operated gas valve. The valve is behind the fascia panel and forms part of the gas control itself. However, the attachment nut that holds the connecting wire in place sometimes shakes loose, thus preventing the current from reaching the electromagnet. In consequence the thermocouple will not hold open the gas valve and the flame goes out as soon as you release the manual override control knob. During a service, the tightness of this nut will be checked.

Servicing a refrigerator

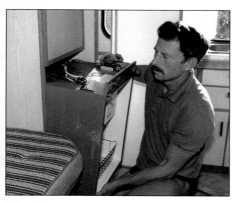

1. In order to carry out servicing work a refrigerator must be removed from a caravan.

2. The sloping 'T' shaped flue section on top of the vertical burner tube should be detached.

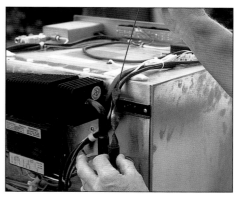

3. The flue baffle is removed and cleaned during a service operation.

4. A protective shield is removed to gain access to the burner assembly.

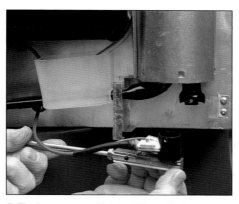

5. The burner assembly should be pulled away from its normal position to prevent soot falling on to it when the flue above is cleaned.

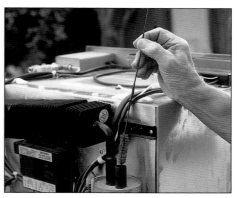

6. A special wire brush is manufactured by Electrolux for cleaning soot from the burner tube.

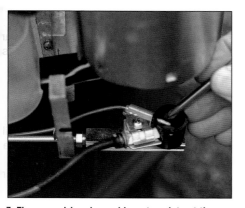

7. The screwdriver is used here to point out the end of the thermocouple; soot on its tip should be removed.

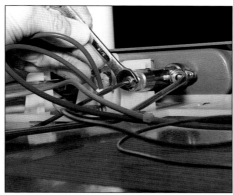

8. The thermocouple connection behind the fascia panel should be checked for tightness during a service.

• The burner is now unbolted in order to gain access to the tiny gas jet. This will be replaced; under no circumstances should the original jet be cleaned since the size of its aperture is critical. Even brushing it with a finger tip can upset the delivery of gas. There are also many jet types to suit different models.
• After re-assembly, the tip of the ignition probe is positioned to achieve the 3mm clearance needed for a spark gap.

• The thermocouple's connecting nut behind the fascia will be checked for tightness. The importance of this is described in the box on page 142.
• After a general inspection of the appliance, a bench test will be carried out to confirm the fridge is fully operational. It will then be re-installed in the caravan and all couplings to gas and electrical supplies will be reinstated and checked.

Improvements and repairs

A caravan can be improved in a number of ways. This selection of projects shows some of the jobs that an owner might like to consider.

Modern caravans feature an extraordinary array of products, and owners of older models are naturally envious. However, it is often possible to upgrade a caravan and this chapter features nine typical improvement and repair jobs.

Many readers will use this for reference and arrange for the work to be carried out at a caravan dealership. Others, however, will tackle the projects themselves. Whichever strategy you follow, there are several points to bear in mind:

• Don't over-spend on upgrades presuming that the full cost of new items will be reflected in a dealer's trade-in price. Adding a thousand pounds of accessories seldom adds the same value to a caravan's resale price.
• Experienced DIY enthusiasts know it is often unwise to do everything themselves. Enlist the help of experts where necessary.
• Note warnings in earlier chapters concerning safety issues. For example, gas and flue

connections must be entrusted to a qualified specialist.
• Remember that caravans have a specified maximum payload and it can be easy to exceed the limit. If additional appliances are installed, the extra weight will take up some of the payload previously available for your personal effects.
• If heavy accessories are added, stability and noseweight may be affected. Fitting a heavy item in a location well away from the caravan's axle can upset weight distribution and towing characteristics.

With these points in mind, remember that fitting a new appliance may be relatively straightforward. With good instructions from the manufacturer, an installation is often achievable by owners who have practical experience and the appropriate tools.

On the other hand, repairing appliances, dismantling assemblies and diagnosing problems is usually much more involved. This type of work nearly always needs a qualified expert.

Structural alterations

Some installations may involve making structural alterations. Revising fixed furniture is not normally a major undertaking but timbers used in the body construction pose a more serious problem.

If you have to form an aperture in an external wall, avoid cutting through a structural member – unless you are able to create alternative

reinforcement. Furthermore, it is important to line an aperture cut in a wall panel using timber inserts. In a bonded wall (as described in Chapter Five), this necessitates cutting away a small amount of block insulant so that battens can be inserted, as shown in the photograph below left.

When a hole is cut in a caravan, a framework of softwood battens is needed to reinforce the aperture and to provide a solid material for fixing screws.

After a metal/timber bonding adhesive has been applied, sections of the timber framework are held in place using G cramps.

Improvement projects

The photographs in this chapter show work in progress. More detailed information is provided in manufacturers' instructions which should be read thoroughly. The times quoted relate to DIY installations; experienced service engineers are likely to complete the work more quickly.

Fitting a Thetford cassette toilet

Comments: *There are many variations on the basic toilet. The side for fitting the cassette retrieval door must be specified, together with the colour of the unit. The flush system can either be manually operated or electrically pumped.*

Before purchase, check there is sufficient space in the shower cubicle; the swivel bowl version may be needed if space is limited.

Instructions are very clear and paper templates make the important job of cutting the wall aperture in the right place quite straightforward. Tasks involved in the job shown here have included cutting and remodelling a plastic shower tray, and fitting a blanking cover over a hole in the cut-out wall section which had previously housed a low level vent.

■ **Time taken: approximately 12 hours.**

Professional guidance

Do not underestimate the work involved and seek help from an experienced caravan service engineer if you have doubts about any of these undertakings. If necessary, consult your caravan manufacturer too, remembering that some of the structural alterations shown here would undoubtedly invalidate a Warranty if the model is a new one.

1. A cassette toilet is supplied with either a white or beige finish and with right or left handed versions according to the position of the access door.

2. Paper plans are provided by the manufacturer for both inside and outside locations. The cutting line is thus marked out with careful precision.

3. The section is cut out using a jigsaw fitted with an appropriate blade. Black insulation tape protects the paintwork from abrasion scratches.

4. The cut section is removed for trimming. Later it will be fitted in the plastic door frame so that it aligns with the coach stripes on either side.

5. Before fitting the access door, a ribbon bedding sealant is applied around the opening to create a water-tight junction.

145

6. The door frame is screwed to the caravan wall using the rust-resistant screws provided with the fitting kit.

7. This model features a motorised flush rather than a manual pump so a 12V supply has to be connected into the caravan's 12V circuit.

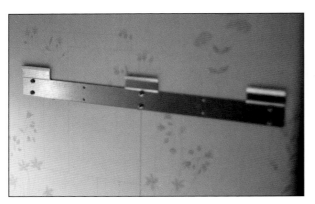

8. To anchor the toilet to the wall of the shower cubicle, a galvanised strip with attachment clips is fitted.

9. In this project, the original shower tray had to be trimmed down and modified to make space for the toilet.

10. Once silicone sealant had been applied around all the joins between the toilet unit and the interior walls, the installation was complete.

146

Toilet repairs

Replacing a split plastic pipe

Comments: *Occasionally repairs are needed and Thetford stocks a wide range of kits. The customer service department is very helpful and staff from the British operation attend major exhibitions to answer caravanners' questions. Demonstration components are shown too, like a cut-off cassette lid to show the location/fitting of components like fuses, rubber gaskets and magnetic level floats.*

These repairs show:

The replacement of a split plastic pipe – an improved rubber component is now supplied as shown in the photographs. Long arms are an asset and removing the original joint sealant from connections can pose a challenge.

■ **Time taken: 30 minutes**

How a water level indicator is unclipped and a replacement fitted.

■ **Time taken: 10 minutes.**

1. Flexible plastic pipe in earlier Thetford cassette toilets is sometimes inclined to split near the level inspection tube.

2. A replacement part has a modified design and is made of a more flexible compound.

3. Before fitting the replacement part, all remnants of the original sealant must be removed from the socket in the flushing reservoir.

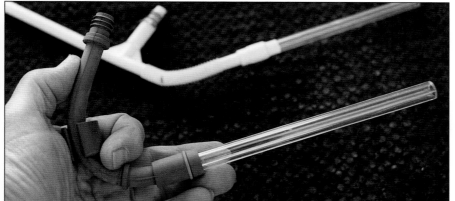

Replacing the water level indicator

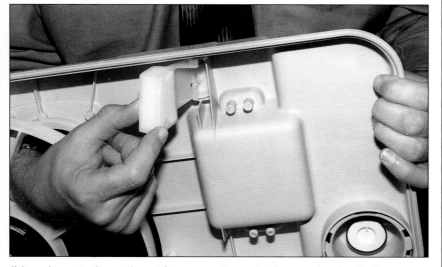

Using a demonstration section cut from a cassette section, the procedure for clipping a replacement level float is shown.

Installing an Electrolux GY20 roof ventilator

Comments: *Perhaps the hardest part of fitting a component to a caravan roof is constructing a safe work platform in the first place. Access staging can be hired, together with scaffold planks. If the planks are laid double thickness to limit flexion and lashed to the staging, a rigid structure can be created.*

If a roof light gets damaged, most types fit into a standard size aperture and it is easy to fit a replacement.

The Electrolux GY20 unit shown here, however, offers permanent ventilation on account of its weather-proof design. This is useful – especially when a caravan is laid-up for an extended period. As wind blows across the dome, turbulence draws air from inside the caravan.

Installation necessitates cutting through the roof panels, but not any structured reinforcement timbers. Wood spacer pieces will also have to be inserted into the void. The job shown here was carried out on a glass reinforced plastic roof.

■ Time taken: 3½ hours

1. The lower section of the vent is mounted on the ceiling; the upper section with its clear plastic rain deflector is fitted to the roof outside.

2. A jigsaw fitted with a blade for cutting through GRP was used to prepare the hole in the roof.

3. The timber spacers fitted in the void were screwed from underneath and trimmed to shape using a barbed wood rasp.

4. Even though a rubber insert is fitted to the base of the outside section, some Carafax ribbon sealant was added as well.

5. The lower collar was fitted from the inside by driving rust-resistant wood screws into the timber spacer inserted around the aperture.

6. Stainless steel screws were used to attach the domed outer cover to the roof.

Installing a Remis mesh door screen

Comments: *Many caravans are now fitted with fly screens on windows whereas the door is often left unprotected. The screen from Remis was first fitted in British caravans in 1996. It can also be added to many models as an improvement project – provided the doors are a standard 650mm (25½in) width and 1800mm (71in) height.*

Unlike many screens, the Remis product needs a very small amount of free space around the door for its mounting – 15mm (⅝in) at the sides and 35mm (1⅜in) beyond the top and bottom rubber of the surrounds.

The kit comprises a framework and the unusual feature is that the section containing the blind and roller is not fastened to the wall – which is why less space around the door is needed. When drawing the screen, the cassette is pulled across the opening instead, unrolling as it goes.

■ **Time taken: 1½ hours**

1. Each part of the framework is laid out and identified.

2. In a practice assembly, the upper nylon guide wheels are inserted into the track.

3. The guide peg at the bottom of the cassette is inserted into the groove in the base frame section.

4. After practising the assembly operation, installation commences by fitting the bottom section of the surround.

5. Other sections are added, accuracy is checked at the corners with a try square and the guide peg is located in the bottom track.

6. The completed installation is checked to confirm the operation and to see that all openings are closed off by the sealing frills.

Television aerials

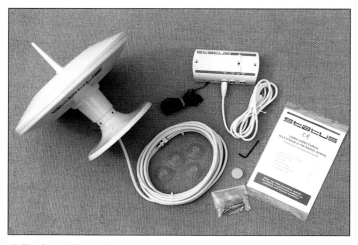

1. The Status TV aerial is supplied as a complete kit of parts.

Comments: *The Status omni-directional aerial from Grade (UK) is fitted to many new caravans. It includes an FM radio aerial and a battery-driven sound amplifier. When stopping near a transmitting station, there is also a signal reducing control as well.*

An 'omni-directional' aerial receives TV signals without having to be adjusted in any way. In contrast, a 'directional aerial' has to be turned so that it points towards the local TV transmitter – a job that has to be repeated on arrival at every site. However, a directional aerial normally captures a stronger signal.

Most omni-directional aerials are fixed permanently to the roof but removable versions with suction pads and a trailing connection cable are available. Many caravanners merely trail this through a roof light or window. If you prefer a removable aerial it is much more satisfactory to mount one of the weather-proof cable couplings used on motorcaravans and cabin cruisers. These are available from **Index Marine** whose address appears in the Appendix at the end of the book.

Whichever type you decide to install, make sure the aerial cable is not strapped alongside other cables in the caravan; this can cause interference. If you find that a fluorescent light causes interference, suppressors are available from **Lab Craft** that can be fitted inside the offending unit.

■ Time taken: 1½-4 hours, depending on the type installed.

2. Using the hexagonal spanner provided, the base can be tilted to suit a sloping roof installation.

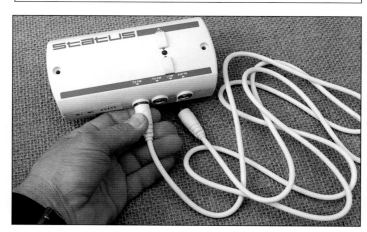

3. The 12V amplification and signal control unit is fitted at a convenient point inside.

When correctly orientated, directional aerials usually provide a better signal than omni-directional models.

Rather than cutting a cable hole in the roof, you can use a model with suction pads.

One way to lead the cable inside is to fit one of the weather-proof couplings used on boats.

Coupling head friction stabilisers

Comments: *This type of stabiliser is especially convenient since there is nothing additional to couple-up. However, with the exception of the Winterhoff unit – seldom seen in Britain – coupling head stabilisers only reduce unwanted lateral movements. Vertical pitching cannot be controlled.*

The system relies on pads bearing against the tow ball and it is essential that the contact surfaces are completely free of grease. The ease of articulation is thus suppressed and an inexpensive test device from The Stabiliser Clinic will confirm that lateral movements are being correctly damped down.

These friction systems should not be confused with the Roll Safe 'Trapezium' coupling head stabiliser that uses a clever principle of changing geometry to assure good stability.

Stabilisers are designed to resist instability from uncontrollable outside forces like side winds. They are not curative measures for inherently unstable outfits where a bent chassis or a badly loaded caravan is causing irregular movements.

The SSK Mk II is an example of a coupling head stabiliser. It is simple to fit and its Teflon-coated friction pads are easily replaced as well. The product is currently imported and distributed by Bulldog as part of its stabiliser range.

■ Time taken: Fitting 1 hour; pad replacement ½ hour.

The coupling head stabiliser test kit from The Stabiliser Clinic includes a dummy ball and an indicator torque wrench to check resistance to movement.

The SSK stabiliser

1. Since caravan towing tubes differ in diameter, reducing collars are included with a fitting kit.

2. A clamp system operates the pressure levers that press the friction pads against the tow ball.

3. On both the SSK and the AL-KO Kober coupling head stabilisers, the friction pads apply pressure on either side of the tow ball.

4. To replace the friction pads, the lever retaining spring is unclipped.

151

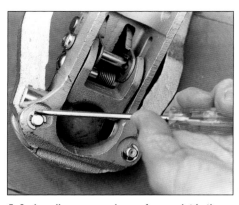

5. Spring clips are eased away from a slot in the retaining bolts – don't let the clip 'ping' into long grass.

6. The bolts which hold the operating levers in place are now withdrawn.

7. The levers are pulled outwards together with the friction pad unit.

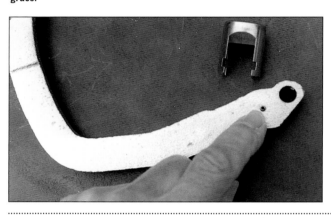

8. When re-assembling the stabiliser, note that a pin in each lever has to locate in the grooves of the friction pad unit.

Single leaf stabilisers: Scott friction disc replacement

1. With the stabiliser held firmly in a vice, the central nut on the friction turntable is removed.

Comments: *The Scott stabiliser was one of the first of these types to be introduced but many others like the Bulldog, Mowbray and SAS models are also popular today.*

Most stabilisers of this type reduce pitching movement too, because the blade is a single leaf spring that exerts downward pressure on the caravan attachment bracket.

Instructions with products describe the installation procedures but these devices are only effective if the friction system is adjusted to resist sideways pressure. On a Scott Halley model, for example, no rotation on the friction turntable should occur until a load of 27kg (60lb) is applied at the end of the blade.

Note: *It is believed that many stabilisers fail to achieve this because adjustments are never made by the owner – so thousands of products in use are virtually ineffective.*

In addition, lateral resistance is affected if the friction discs are worn. Replacements are available for most stabilisers and a specialist called The Stabiliser Clinic carries out a refurbishment scheme. Periodically, Bulldog offers a similar service to owners of their units.

Checking resistance can be done by pushing the extreme end of the blade against the weighing plate of bathroom scales which you hold sideways. Alternatively The Stabiliser Clinic can supply an inexpensive test device.

The illustrations here show replacement pads being fitted to a traditional Scott Halley model. It is also possible to upgrade this older type of stabiliser by fitting a quick release mechanism.

■ **Time taken:** ¾ hour.

2. The smaller nut at the rear is also removed; check how all the sections fit together.

3. The assembly components on a traditional Scott are shown in sequence.

4. Friction surfaces on the right hand plate are covered by a deposit which hinders operation.

5. If pads are bonded to the steel plates, they can be detached with a knife.

6. Subject to the manufacturer's approval, the surface of the friction plates may be cleaned with an angle grinder. Safety goggles must be worn.

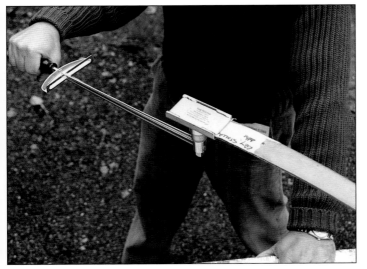

7. After re-assembly, the torque wrench tester from The Stabiliser Clinic checks the setting to confirm that the turntable bolt has been sufficiently tightened.

8. Older types of stabilisers can be fitted with a quick-release mechanism that make it easier to locate the blade in the caravan bracket.

153

Carver Cascade water heater installation

Comments: *Since their original introduction, Carver's storage water heaters have undergone steady improvements. Early models took a long time to drain down whereas recent improvements have led to the addition of a pressure relief valve control to speed-up the emptying process.*

Originally the Cascade only offered a gas heating system; now there are units with a mains 230V heating element as well. Kits are available to add this mains facility to an older gas-only appliance.

Fitting a Carver Cascade is an involved job but the installation instructions are very thorough in detail. Templates also ensure the wall aperture is cut accurately. Many experienced DIY owners fit these units successfully or upgrade older models. However, the point is re-affirmed that coupling up the gas supply is one part of the job that must be entrusted to a qualified gas engineer as defined in Chapter 10, *Gas supply systems and appliances*.

The photographs show a new gas/electric unit being fitted in place of an original gas-only models. Although the aperture in the side was already formed and the plumbing in place, the complete job took quite a long time because a new mains supply lead had to be wired-up.

■ Time taken: 5 hours.

1. The original unit is removed and old sealant cleaned off from around the aperture.

2. In the bed box, the hose and the gas connection are disconnected.

3. A mains switch with a warning light is installed and coupled into the existing 230V circuit.

4. Having placed ribbon sealant around the flange of the new heater, the unit is offered-up.

5. A front-mounted drop flap in the bed box affords access to the electrical connection points.

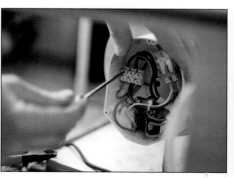

6. The earth, live and neutral cables are connected up to a connecting block in the housing mounted on the inner end of the tank.

7. The gas engineer connects up the gas feed to the union located alongside the burner assembly.

8. The outer cover plate is screwed into place. The gas system is then leak tested before the unit is put into commission.

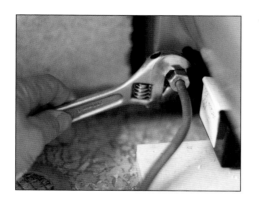

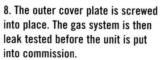

Fitting a Carver space heater

Comments: *Integrating a 230V mains heating unit into gas-operated space heaters has become an increasingly common practice. On the first Carver Fanmaster Mk1 units for example, a mains heating element was built into the casing housing the air distribution fan; this in turn was fastened on the rear of the gas heater. However, on the latest Fanmaster space heaters, the mains elements are now inside the main casing and adjacent to the heat exchanger, thus leaving the 12V fan as a separate item.*

A further change relates to space heater installation. Previously Carver fitted the heating components of an appliance on a floor plate and some of the servicing operations had to be carried out from underneath the caravan. On many 1999 heaters, like the 4000 model shown here, the unit is completely self-contained in its casing, which enables a service engineer to withdraw the appliance quickly – as a total unit – and to transfer it to a bench to carry out servicing or repairs.

Note that on these new heaters, there is still a floor aperture – but this is to provide an air intake for the combustion air.

Fitting involves general woodworking skills and Carver's instructions are clearly written. Moreover, if a caravan has not had warm air ducting previously fitted, this is a job that a competent DIY enthusiast might tackle. On the other hand, fitting a mains supply to serve models which incorporate a 230V heating element might be entrusted to a qualified electrician. With regard to the gas and flue connections, all DIY installers should get a qualified gas engineer to complete these jobs – and to carry out a system test before the unit is put into commission.

■ **Time taken: 5½ hours or more, depending on the ducting needed.**

1. Removing an original heater is fairly straightforward but care should be taken with the flexible flue duct which has sharp, jagged edges.

2. When the decorative front cover is removed, the heat exchanger and gas control on the right is easily identified.

3. The unit is offered up to check the fit. Access from a wardrobe above is beneficial since the ducting has to be coupled up to the fan.

4. The gas engineer will feed the flexible stainless steel flue pipe to the coupling point on the bottom of the heat exchanger.

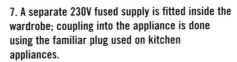

5. The flexible sealing ring for the flue is made from a more heat-resistant material than the type used on earlier appliances.

6. The gas engineer will direct the copper feed pipe towards the union which is located near the under-floor air intake.

7. A separate 230V fused supply is fitted inside the wardrobe; coupling into the appliance is done using the familiar plug used on kitchen appliances.

8. Covers are available in a wide range of colours. When clipped in place the appliance is discreet in design yet smart in appearance.

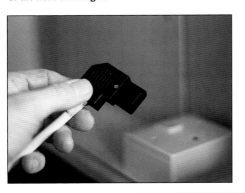

13
Contents

Servicing

Pre-storage
tasks

Pre-season
tasks

Servicing and seasonal preparation

Like any other road-going vehicle, a caravan has to be serviced regularly. There are seasonal tasks to carry out too, particularly if a caravan is unused for long periods.

The need to keep a car serviced regularly is never questioned. It is, therefore, rather surprising that some caravanners do not realise that their caravan should be serviced as well.

Servicing

Many jobs might be included under the heading of 'servicing' but some stand out as particularly important. For instance, it is essential that safety items like the brakes are periodically adjusted; the operation of road lights needs checking, too. It is also essential to carry out regular damp checks to confirm there are no leak points in a caravan's bodywork – a subject discussed in Chapter 5.

Then there are the appliances and if a refrigerator, a heater, an oven or a hob are never serviced, there could be more than a risk of malfunction. An unchecked fault here might lead to the release of carbon monoxide.

So it is most important that a caravan is regularly serviced. This raises two questions – what needs to be done, and who should carry out the work?

Servicing specialists

A disturbing feature is that some 'specialists' who claim to carry out service work, charge £100 or more for their labour, yet fail to provide any documentation to clarify what has actually been done. On closer inspection it often transpires that many jobs have been overlooked.

In sharp contrast, other specialists conduct the work in a thorough and professional manner. A detailed service schedule is supplied with comments on matters like brake shoe condition, tyre wear and so on. Dated certificates are also provided to verify that the gas and mains supply systems have been checked by qualified persons and are found to be safe. In some instances a damp test report is provided, accompanied by a drawing indicating where all the checks have been

taken with the test meter. This exemplifies the way a service should be conducted.

Anxious to achieve this level of customer care, The National Caravan Council in partnership with The Camping & Caravanning Club and The Caravan Club introduced *The Approved Caravan Workshop* programme in November 1999. Workshop capability is independently assessed by Jones Venning Inspection Agency and the scheme enables an owner to have his or her caravan serviced, maintained or repaired in a workshop conforming with a uniform set of standards. In addition, the scheme ensures that all customers are treated fairly.

Who should carry out the work?

As the subsequent section shows, the scope of a service is wide. Without doubt, some routine jobs can be easily carried out by an owner; tasks like lubricating hinges and greasing corner steadies are obvious examples.

Looking at more involved jobs, some DIY practitioners could equally service brakes and

Applying a light film of grease to the corner steady spindle is a job which many owners could tackle.

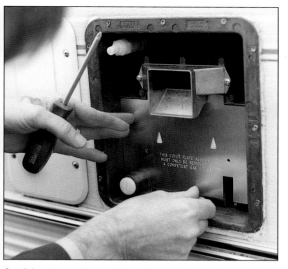

Servicing gas appliances like a Carver water heater must only be undertaken by a qualified gas engineer.

Using an air line, the service specialist will remove dust from the burners of gas appliances.

undertake maintenance work on chassis components following the guidance in Chapter 4, *Caravan chassis and running gear*. However, achieving safe access is crucial and service centres equipped with a caravan ramp are at a clear advantage here.

Whereas brake servicing might be tackled by a competent owner, any work involving the gas system and gas appliances must be entrusted to a qualified engineer. This point was emphasised in Chapter 10, *Gas supply systems and appliances*, and the matter of qualification was clarified in the Technical Tip Box on page 126. Equally the wisdom of having a mains electricity supply checked by a qualified electrician and an inspection certificate issued was discussed in Chapter 8, *The mains supply system*.

Since the respective background experiences and professional qualifications of caravan owners are all different, there is no simple answer as to what part of the servicing work we could or could not tackle ourselves. As a caveat, however, it must be emphasised that during a Warranty Period, a caravan manufacturer would require all work to be undertaken at an approved dealers and warranty documents signed, dated and stamped accordingly.

Refrigerator servicing

The importance of having a fridge serviced regularly is clearly stated by Electrolux and the procedures are described and illustrated in Chapter 11, *Refrigerators*. Curiously, however, this is a job seldom included in a basic schedule. In a standard service, the engineer usually only checks that the appliance is working.

If you want to have your fridge serviced in accordance with Electrolux instructions, the work is normally an 'optional extra' which has to be

Well-equipped service centres have a ramp which affords excellent access to the underside of a caravan.

(Photograph courtesy of Crossley Coachcraft)

To check a gas supply system is leak-free, many gas engineers use a purpose-designed air pump fitted with a gauge.

157

requested when the caravan is booked in at the dealers. It is rather disappointing that this isn't made clearer by caravan manufacturers and servicing specialists alike. Many people have their caravan serviced but do not realise that service work on the fridge has not been included.

Service schedule

Clearly it is most important to know what work should be carried out when a caravan is booked for a service. Moreover, the importance of working to a strict schedule is self-evident. However, there is no doubt that some items are more critical than others. For instance a periodic check of door mechanisms, window catches and blind recoil operation is desirable; but this is not as important as checking, adjusting and correcting any element that relates to safety on the road.

In recognition of this, some centres offer different levels of service – including separate damp checks, and basic road-going checks which cover safety items like brakes, tyres, chassis components and road lighting. This makes good sense, especially if owners want to carry out the more straightforward jobs themselves.

Abbreviated servicing aside, the schedule opposite covers jobs that should be included in a major servicing operation, together with two 'optional extras'. Readers are advised to use this as a basis for discussion when booking-in a caravan at a dealers. It becomes especially important if you are planning to have work done by a service provider whose workshop documentation is either poor or non-existent. In addition, the list also provides an aide memoire for the DIY enthusiast.

Charges

Apart from labour charges, there will also be a charge for parts. For instance, on older caravans the brake drum retention nuts are held with replaceable split pins; on newer models the 'one-shot' nuts have to be renewed every time the drums are removed as described in Chapter 4, *Caravan chassis and running gear*. These would be 'charge items'.

It is also appropriate to point out that some

service centres will carry out small repairs during the course of the work without adding an extra labour fee. For instance if the gas system is found to have a small leak at a coupling, the tightening of the connection is often carried out 'there and then'. Typically a fluorescent tube in a lamp unit will be changed if it is obviously faulty. You should establish the policy adopted when booking-in your caravan, bearing in mind that any parts fitted will be costed out on the invoice.

More serious jobs, of course, might also appropriately be done while the 'van is in the workshop. However, if something like a new water pump needs to be fitted, a service centre would be expected to contact an owner before embarking on this type of repair. Pumps can be costly items. This is another procedure to check with your dealer.

Owner servicing

Even though some servicing jobs should be left to qualified persons, a number of readers will wish to carry out many tasks themselves. Reference to the earlier chapters will provide the information required.

The accompanying photographs also provide further insight into the work involved. In some

If you plan to service the over-run system, a grease gun is an essential tool.

Sometimes a hub puller is needed to remove a difficult brake drum.

If a gas leak is detected during a service, it is often remedied there and then.

Typical Standard Service Schedule

Make: .... **Model:** .... **Year:** .... **Chassis number:** .... **Vehicle Identification no.** ....

Section 1: Chassis and Running Gear

Comments

1. Check coupling head; lubricate as necessary ☐ ....
2. Lubricate over-run piston using grease gun ☐ ....
3. Check hand brake operation and adjust ☐ ....
4. Check breakaway chain/cable. ☐ ....
5. Check and lubricate jockey wheel ☐ ....
6. Check and lubricate corner steadies. ☐ ....
7. Remove wheels/drum assembly. Remove dust ☐ Shoe condition ....
8. Check tapered bearings, clean, re-grease ☐ ....
9. Adjust brakes, commencing at drum ☐ ....
10. Replace split pin or 'one shot' stub axle nut ☐ ....
11. Torque 'one shot' nut to manufacturer's data ☐ ....
12. Replace wheels and torque check nuts/bolts ☐ ....
13. Check tyres, remove stones, check pressures ☐ Tyre condition ....
14. Check operation, grease spare wheel rack ☐ ....

General report: ....

Section 2: Gas

Comments

1. Carry out pressure test on system ☐ ....
2. Replace washer on butane regulator ☐ ....
3. Replace flexible hose; fit new hose clips ☐ ....
4. Fridge: Light and test for cooling ☐ ....
5. Cooking appliances: Light and verify operation ☐ ....
6. Check space heater operation; clean burners ☐ ....
7. Check water heater operation, clean burners ☐ ....
8. Certificate of Gas System Check appended ☐

Report on gas appliances: ....

Section 3: Electrical

Comments

1. Check RCD and MCBs on central unit ☐ ....
2. Test 13 amp mains sockets ☐ ....
3. Test 12V sockets ☐ ....
4. Check integrity of wiring and fuses ☐ ....
5. Check operation of all interior lights ☐ ....
6. Check road lights, reflectors, awning lamp ☐ ....
7. Certificate of Mains Check appended ☐

Report on the electrical system: ....

Section 4: Water systems

Comments

1. Check operation of water pump, clean grit filter ☐ ....
2. Check waste & fresh water system for leaks ☐ ....
3. Flush through with purifying cleaner ☐ ....
4. Change charcoal water filter, if fitted ☐ ....
5. Check toilet flush and blade operation ☐ ....

General comments on water systems: ....

Section 5: Body-work and General Condition

Comments

1. Carry out damp and seepage tests. ☐ ....
2. Look for poor sealant/potential leak points. ☐ ....
3. Confirm window operation; lubricate if needed. ☐ ....
4. Check/oil door lock; oil hinges. ☐ ....

Comments on bodywork/general condition: ....

Section 6: Fire warning systems

Comments

1. Check fire alarm operation/ battery ☐ ....
2. Check expiry date on extinguisher ☐ ....
3. Check fire blanket location/fixing ☐ ....

Work completed by: .... Date: .... Official stamp:

Statement of Standard Labour Charges £ ____ : ____

Statement of Parts Required £ ____ : ____

SUB-TOTAL £ ____ : ____

Value-Added Tax £ ____ : ____ TOTAL: £ ____ : ____

Additional Service Options: Service refrigerator in accordance with Electrolux instruction; check/lubricate furniture catches and hinges, check blind operation.

Note: The schedule proposed here was drawn up after studying NCC Service Centre reports, and taking into account recommendations by manufacturers including AL-KO Kober, Electrolux, Carver and Truma. Additions were also added by the author such as Section 5: Fire Warning Systems.

As regards service intervals, the use of a caravan cannot be easily gauged in miles. In the case of average use, a caravan should be serviced every 12 months. However, anyone who uses a caravan regularly and extensively should submit it for servicing more often.

© John Wickersham

instances special tools will be needed. A grease gun, for example, is one of the essential items. You may also need a 'puller' to withdraw a stubborn brake drum.

Pre-storage tasks

If you are not going to use your caravan for several months, certain tasks have to be carried out. This is especially true when laying it up for winter.

Outdoor tasks

❑ Select a suitable location
Make sure the caravan is parked in a place where damage cannot be caused by falling branches, slates or tiles. Even a conker can cause a dent on an aluminium roof panel. Remember too, that trees leave a green algae deposit during a long storage period.

❑ Remove the awning
Make absolutely certain that your awning is dry before packing it away for winter. Brush off bird lime and clean the plastic skirts if necessary. If the awning has been left dirty or if it has been used under trees which exude sticky substances, a thorough wash is needed. Often it's best to re-erect it for cleaning and there are products you can use such as *Awning Cleaner* from Camco. Tent cleaners sold in outdoor activity shops can also be helpful. Finally, check that damp hasn't found its way into any of the pole sections.

❑ Chock the wheels so you can leave the handbrake off
Over an extended lay-up, handbrake mechanisms sometimes seize up, leaving the brakes locked on. If you can park on level ground, chock the wheels, lower the corner steadies, and disengage the handbrake. Bear in mind that even on a mild slope, some of the plastic chocks sold in caravan accessory shops have a nasty tendency to slip on smooth, hard surfaces.

Tie a fabric bag over a gas supply hose to keep out spiders and insects during a period of storage.

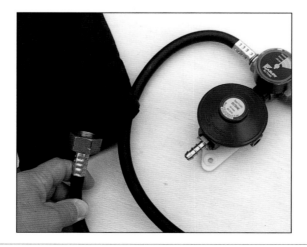

❑ Decide whether to remove the wheels, substituting axle stands
Tyre walls can sustain damage if a caravan is left unmoved for a long period – especially if they're exposed to sunlight. Storing the wheels avoids this and also makes theft more difficult. Winterwheels from PGR can be put in place of removed wheels, although axle stands are better because they also relieve the suspension system. The stands used must be robust and have a wide base.

❑ If you decide against removing wheels, consider security clamps
Thefts of laid-up caravans are all too common. Fit at least one security device. A close fitting wheel clamp is an excellent deterrent, but use a heavy duty version. Remember that electronic systems are of no use when the battery is flat.

❑ Protect the coupling head
Fit a loose-fitting plastic cover to protect the coupling head and to allow air to circulate around it.

❑ Remove the gas cylinders and transfer to a safe, ventilated store
Transfer gas cylinders to a lockable, well-ventilated shed. If you leave cylinders in a caravan locker box, they may get stolen and could be a fire risk. Never store cylinders in a cellar or a location where leaks of this heavier-than-air gas would be unable to escape.

❑ Cover a gas pipe outlet with a fabric bag and an elastic band
If spiders decide to nest in an exposed length of flexible gas hose, you might suffer from gas blockages when the caravan is put back into commission. Avoid using a plastic bag since this will retain any dampness.

❑ Remove battery to a place where it can be periodically charged
A battery will soon be ruined if left in a discharged condition. Transfer it to a garage or workshed where you can monitor its condition and re-charge when necessary.

❑ Spray 12N and 12S plugs with a moisture repellent like Tri-Flow
Brass pins and sockets get coated with a deposit that affects their electrical contact. Spray them with a moisture repellent like Tri-Flow; this won't damage the plastic part of the plug.

❑ Block off water supply inlets
Keep out spiders and insects. A water inlet, or outlet, provides a pleasant home for them in winter – and blockages later.

The pins on connection plugs and sockets should be sprayed with a moisture repellent like Tri-Flow.

❏ Replace the water filter

Arguably this could be left until Spring, but doing the job in late Autumn means you can get 'off the mark' quicker when the new season arrives. What's more, the price of the filter might be higher next season.

❏ Drain off a water heater

Repairing a frost-damaged water heater is costly and drain-down procedures will be given in the Owner's Manual. Typically you need to open all the taps first and then remove a drain plug. Until Carver's revised 1996 water heater was launched with a pressure-relief control, draining down could take an hour or more.

❏ Empty the flushing water from a cassette toilet

If you own a Thetford cassette toilet, check the vertical tube clipped inside the access door that shows water level. Pull it from the clip and fold downwards to drain off the remaining water. Then empty the top-up bowl as well.

❏ Polish out serious marks on exterior bodywork

Remove body stains under fitments or guttering before the onset of winter. Several products are

Drain down a water heater well before the arrival of frost.

now available which will do this and cleaning work was discussed in Chapter 5. If time permits, apply a coating of polish for additional seasonal protection.

Indoor tasks

❏ Consider removing residual water in pipes by disconnection

Many water supply systems have a non-return valve near the point of entry. This ensures water doesn't drain back to the water container whenever taps are turned off but residual water in the pipes can freeze. Plastic hose sometimes copes with the expansion, but it is always advisable to disconnect a low level pipe to drain off the water. Better still – fit one of the drain-down taps shown in Chapter 9, *Water systems*.

❏ Remove any interior stains before they set for good

Stains should always be removed as soon as possible. If left too long, they will become permanent. Guidance is given in Chapter 6, *Interior maintenance and improvements*, on stain removal and the cleaning of furnishings.

❏ Leave the fridge door open using the second catch position

If you shut the fridge door completely, the interior will start to smell unpleasant. Start by wiping out the interior using a weak solution of bicarbonate of soda as described in Chapter 11, *Refrigerators*. Then leave the door ajar using the second catch position.

❏ Clean appliances

Degrease the oven and hob with a proprietary cleaner. Remove dust from the burners using a stiff brush, but don't be tempted to use a wire brush – this can easily damage a jet.

Clean off the black streaks which often form below body fixings.

Remove the rust and dust from your hob using a stiff brush.

Where a fixed pump is fitted, shake out any residual water from its casing.

❏ Put plugs in the sink and basin to keep out waste pipe smells

On most caravans, the waste pipe is only a convoluted hose which may hold residual water where it sags under the floor. Insert plugs to prevent waste pipe smells entering the caravan.

❏ Shower heads

Make sure no residual water is left in the shower head. If you have a submersible pump, check similarly that no water is trapped in its casing.

❏ Toilet

Double-check that the holding tank has been emptied and flushed out. Clean the rubber seal using Thetford Bathroom Cleaner or a luke warm diluted solution of washing-up liquid. Never use a household cleaner – this can irreversibly damage the seal. Dry thoroughly and then apply either olive oil or Thetford's Toilet Seal lubricant. Never use any other type of vegetable oil or Vaseline. Leave the blade open throughout the storage period; this prevents it from becoming stuck in the closed position.

Pre-storage work on a toilet cassette

1. Clean around the seal using Thetford Bathroom Cleaner or a diluted mix of washing-up liquid.

2. Dry the seal completely with a cloth.

3. A special maintenance spray is available to protect toilet seals.

4. An alternative seal lubricant is olive oil. Once applied, leave the blade *open* throughout the storage period.

❑ Remove mattresses and cushions, or cover rusting bed box hinges

Ideally, transfer mattresses indoors. If left in the 'van, damp may cause hinges on bed boxes to leave rust marks on the underlining. Alternatively cover the hinges temporarily with sticky tape or lay old towels under the mattresses.

❑ Make list of repair jobs for Spring recommissioning – or do them now!

If you need any parts, order them at the end of a season. Delivery is quicker in winter.

Pre-season tasks

After a long lay-up period – especially during the winter – a caravan will need some preparatory work before it is ready for your first trip away in the new season. It is often surprising how quickly the exterior and interior surfaces bear the marks of an extended storage period.

Pre-season tasks include:

❑ Check the tyres

Check the tyre pressures, including the spare; and carry out a visual check of the side walls; look carefully at both sides to confirm there's no sign of cracking or premature failure. Make a further tyre check after your first trip.

❑ Check the handbrake

Make sure the brake operates freely by pulling/releasing the lever several times.

❑ Reinstate furnishings

Replace the cushions and any other soft furnishings that have been transferred to a warm storage base.

Reinstate the leisure battery having checked its charge with a voltmeter.

❑ Services

Carry out a run of all the services. Couple-up a gas cylinder and make sure the gas appliances are working. Note that it may take several moments for air to be purged from the supply pipes. Reinstate the leisure battery – take a reading with a voltmeter if you own one.

❑ Water filter

If the system has a cartridge fitted and you didn't replace it at the end of the previous season, fit a new one.

❑ Sterilise water system

It is wise to start the season by running a sterilising solution through the water pipes. A product like Milton is often used which is available from any good chemists. Milton is the product widely used for sterilising babies' feeding bottles.

❑ 12N and 12S couplings

Check the connections are sound by coupling up and testing both the road lights and the internal 12V systems. It is not unusual for grit and damp to get inside the car sockets during the winter. If the systems seem wildly at fault, this is often a sign that the earth return connection needs attention.

❑ Clean the caravan

Use a brush to remove webs, insects, and dust from around the doors and locker lids. Similarly clean the awning channel; a purpose-made brush is available from W4 Accessories which can be inserted into the channeling to scour the inner trackway completely.

❑ Servicing

If you didn't complete the season with a service, be certain to arrange this in good time. If you are intending to book-in your 'van at a dealership, do this at the earliest possible opportunity. It can be especially hectic at the start of a season. Now enjoy the caravanning season ahead in comfort and safety!

It is always advisable to flush a water system, using a sterilising fluid like Milton, before the season begins.

Establishing the age of a caravan

Although cars have a Vehicle Registration Document, there is no obligatory form of registration to accompany a caravan. It can therefore be quite difficult to establish a caravan's age. Chassis plates, for example, are not always helpful and there's no doubt that some second-hand models offered for sale are older than the seller suggests. The following notes record changes that have occurred and these act as helpful clues for anyone trying to establish when a caravan was manufactured.

1970s caravans

■ Caravans of this period are heavy and are built very differently from post 1980 models.
■ Bargain buys for around £500-£800 exist and sometimes provide a pleasant introduction to caravanning – but be careful if you're not prepared to carry out repairs or improvements yourself.
■ Spares can be difficult to obtain for earlier models – particularly spare parts for appliances, fittings for furniture, chassis items and coupling components.
■ Locker boxes to house gas cylinders – previously clamped to the draw-bar and open to the weather – became common after 1971.
■ Refrigerators like the Morphy Richards models of the early 1970s had to be lit using a match and often failed to provide cooling because of an air lock.
■ Chassis made by firms like B&B, Peak, and CI need periodic painting.
■ The running gear of the period employed spring suspension and shock absorbers; damaged items may be difficult to replace.
■ To reverse a 1970s caravan, you usually need to operate an over-ride catch on the coupling head before starting the manoeuvre. This is an annoying chore.
■ In the early 1970s, fluorescent lights became popular but gas lamps were often fitted too, in order to provide back-up lighting.
■ In the early 1970s, water pumps were usually foot or hand-operated devices.
■ Bodywork construction comprised a framework made of wood. This skeleton structure was clad with aluminium sheet on the outside and a coated hardboard or plywood wall on the inside.
■ Insulation was poor on most 1970s 'vans. Usually fibreglass wool was placed in the void between the wall panels – but this eventually slumps, leaving cold spots.

■ Floors were made from plywood with supporting joists underneath and seldom had any form of insulation.
■ Windows were single glazed and glass was used. However, in November 1977 it became obligatory for new caravans to be fitted with safety glass.
■ In response to legislation, the industry introduced acrylic single-glazed windows comprising a frameless moulded pane. Aluminium frames were discontinued overnight.
■ Not long afterwards, double glazed versions of these 'plastic' windows became the standard fitting.
■ From 1st October 1979, it became mandatory for all new caravans to include a rear fog lamp. Absence of a fog lamp suggests a 'van is a pre-1978 model.
■ From 1978, a double socket system was used – the 12N socket for caravan road lights; the 12S socket was reserved for internal supplies.

1980s caravans

■ A new approach to building was introduced using pre-manufactured bonded sandwich floors and wall panels; most manufacturers soon adopted the system.
■ New computer-designed lightweight chassis were introduced around 1980.
■ On lightweight chassis, the coil springing system together with its shock absorbers was replaced by a rubber-in-compression suspension system.
■ As late as 1984, some chassis were still painted, but galvanising was more usual now as a standard finish.
■ In April 1989, all caravans manufactured had to have auto-reverse brakes; a manually operated lever fitted to the coupling head became obsolete. Automatic brake disengagement mechanisms were now built into the drums.
■ More and more low voltage appliances appear in caravans including electric pumps, reading lights, fans and stereo systems. Now a separate 'leisure battery' becomes an essential item.
■ Fused distribution panels were introduced so that low voltage circuits could be separated and fused independently.
■ In the mid-1980s, caravans lost their symmetry and became wedge shaped using sloping fronts to achieve better fuel economy.
■ From 1986, virtually all gas storage lockers were built into the body itself. A separate locker box mounted on the draw bar was no longer fitted.
■ From the mid-1980s many caravans were equipped with water heaters and the Carver

Cascade storage heater was the most popular of these appliances.

■ Around 1987, the cassette toilet arrived, revolutionising bathroom design and vastly improving emptying arrangements.

■ From 1st May 1989 smoke alarms had to be fitted to all new caravans and all second-hand 'vans sold by a dealer.

1990s caravans

■ Road lights set high on the sides (marker lights) became obligatory on caravans manufactured after 1st October 1990.

■ Combustion Modified (CM) Foam became mandatory in caravans built after 1st March 1990.

■ From April 1991, all fabrics have to be a fire-resistant type.

■ Hardly any caravans have been sold in the 1990s that haven't been wired for mains electricity by the manufacturer.

■ In the latter part of the 1990s, reeded and stucco surfaces were used less and less on external walls. Smooth aluminium finishes became popular again.

■ In 1992, AL-KO Kober announced that their latest lightweight chassis must not be drilled – even for mounting a stabiliser bracket on the draw bar.

■ The CRiS (Caravan Registration and Identification Scheme) was introduced in 1992 and UK-manufactured caravans were issued with a Vehicle Identification Number (VIN). This is documented with owner information recorded at CRiS headquarters and the number etched on windows.

■ Since 1994, flame failure devices have been fitted on stoves.

■ Around 1992, BPW chassis and running gear featured maintenance-free sealed bearings.

■ The AL-KO Euro-axle with sealed bearings appeared in 1994 ranges. The sealed bearings are well engineered, but to inspect the brake shoes an expensive torque wrench is needed to remove/replace the 'one-shot' nut which holds the drums in place.

■ In Spring 1995, the Abbey Domino was launched with GRP impact-resistant sheet on its side walls instead of aluminium sheeting. Other models have followed using this easy-repair material.

■ From 1st January, 1996, gas appliances have had to bear a CE mark to indicate they meet European standards.

■ In caravans manufactured from 1997 onwards, a small 'tamperproof' tag containing the Vehicle Identification Number is hidden within the body-work and this can only be identified using a CRiS 'reader'.

■ AL-KO Kober introduced a 'universal' chassis with bolt together main members in Spring 1999. This meant that models of different lengths in a manufacturer's range could be accommodated using the same chassis components.

■ In Spring 1999, AL-KO Kober introduced the Euro Over-Run Automatic Self-adjusting Brake. This detects movement when a 'van is parked on a backward facing slope and will re-apply a slipping brake automatically.

■ A CRiS Scheme was launched in 1999 in which caravans manufactured before 1992 can be retrospectively CRiS registered and tagged.

Note: *If planning to purchase a CRiS registered caravan, you can have the age of the 'van confirmed together with verification that it has not been reported as stolen by 'phoning CRiS on 01722 413434*

Standards, legislation and legal issues

In Appendix A, *Establishing the Age of a Caravan*, reference is made to some of the regulations which have altered the design and specifications of caravans over the last 30 years. For example, a rear fog lamp became mandatory on caravans constructed on or after 1st October 1979. Manufacturers were also required to fit a smoke alarm in new caravans from 1st May 1989 onwards.

References to legislation, British Standards and Codes of Practice are also included throughout the text of this book. For instance, changes in the law regarding towing brackets are mentioned in Chapter 3, *Towcar preparation*.

In recognition of these earlier references, the intention here is simply to provide a broad overview of more recent changes that have taken place. At present, legislation, standards and Codes of Practice are undergoing radical amendments. In fact by the time you read this, further changes may have taken place and you should always seek guidance about the current situation.

Members of the two major caravan clubs are able to obtain advice from their respective Technical Departments. Information also appears in the caravan magazines. And although the National Caravan Council (NCC) is principally a trade organisation, the council's attendance at major indoor exhibitions provides members of the public with further opportunity to obtain guidance.

Standards and legal requirements

Bear in mind that certain elements covered in British and European Standards often become embraced within the law. For instance, the subject of European Type Approval tow bars forms part of Directive 94/20/EC. However, after the Directive was approved, an amendment was then made in the Road Vehicles (Construction & Use) Regulations 1986. Compliance with this Directive then became a legal matter in Britain, taking effect from 1st September, 1998. Fuller details on the subject are covered in Chapter 3, *Towcar preparation*.

However, many recommendations under the broad heading of 'Standards' do not reach the statute books. Nevertheless, manufacturers in this country have worked closely in line with relevant British Standards for many years irrespective of whether their implementation carries a legal mandate.

In addition, most British manufacturers are also members of the NCC and their products are built in accordance with further requirements that go above and beyond British and European Standards. Moreover, the NCC has a Code of Practice that encompasses all relevant legislation and which forms part of a Certification Scheme. Caravans manufactured by NCC member-companies and which meet the requirements of this Certification Scheme carry a badge to denote approval. Below is a summary of the British and European standards covered by the NCC Certification scheme:

Touring caravans

BSEN1645/1	Habitation Requirements relating to health and safety
BSEN1645/2	User payload
BSEN1648/1	12V d.c. extra low voltage electrical installations
BSEN721	Safety ventilation requirements
BSEN60335-1	Specification for safety of electrical appliances
BSEN60335-2-29	Specification for safety of battery chargers
BSEN60529	Specification for protection by enclosures
BSEN60742	Requirements for isolating transformers
BS5482 Pt2	LPG installations
BS6765 Pt4	Specification for undergear
BS5446-1	Specification for self-contained smoke alarms
BSEN 1949:2002	Specification for the installation of LPG systems in caravans.
BSEN 12864:2001	Standard relating to regulators used in touring caravans.

In the past, some caravans – especially models imported from abroad – do not carry the NCC badge. There is no doubt that many imported caravans are well built, but one feature that hasn't met the NCC Code of Practice is the position of doors. A door on an imported caravan is usually on the opposite side to a door on a British model. In other words in this country, where cars are driven on the left, when an imported caravan is parked on the nearside, its door opens directly on to the road.

European Standards for Caravans

The introduction of common standards throughout member countries of the European Community has many merits. Even though there may need to be small detailing differences in Export Models, e.g. door position as mentioned above, the new situation means that a caravan made in one country doesn't have to undergo further approval tests in the country which imports it.

The implementation of a European Standard structure also creates a situation of free trade between partner countries. This undoubtedly helps British Caravan manufacturers who export to several of our European partners.

Other benefits include the fact that vehicle manufacturers cannot insist that you only fit their own design of towing bracket. The whole principle behind free trade means what it says – as long as products on sale fulfil the relevant standards.

As regards the main changes from British Standards to European Standards these are currently showen below.

To summarise, we are in a situation of change and a helpful booklet on the subject is entitled *European Standards for Caravans* by John Lally, NCC Technical Manager, and is available from Caravan Business Magazine, 7 Marennes Crescent, Brightlingsea, Essex, CO7 0RX. The booklet costs £5 which includes postage.

Another useful booklet is *Towing and the Law* published by The Society of Motor Manufacturers and Traders Ltd. This is currently available at £3, direct from the publisher: SMMT, Forbes House, Halkin Street, London, SW1X 7DS.

These are points of reference to the standards and laws that underpin the manufacture and use of 'trailer caravans'. The position is different in respect of 'motor caravans' and 'holiday homes'. Suffice it to say, if you buy a product made by a respected and accredited caravan manufacturer, you can be assured that it will offer high standards in terms of both comfort and safety.

The European Standard	Former standard
EN 1645-1 Caravans: Habitation requirements	BS4626 Specification for trailer caravans
EN 1645-2 Caravans: User Payloads	Payload requirements were formerly included within BS4626
EN 27418 Vocabulary	BS6760 Vocabulary
EN 1648-1 12v DC ELV Electrical Installation in Caravans	Previously 12V DC ELV requirements were embraced in Code of Practice 201 with reference to BS6765 Pt 3
EN721 Ventilation requirements in Leisure Accommodation Vehicles	BS5601 Pt1 Ventilation in caravans
EN 1949 LPG Installation in Leisure Accommodation Vehicles	This has replaced BS5482 Pt 2

European Norms (ENs) 12864:2001 and 1949:2002 both have the status of British Standards (BS). However, it should be noted that these are "standards", NOT "regulations". Unless there is a change in UK Law there is no legal obligation for these ENs to be implemented. Nevertheless, the advisability of adopting a standardised gas system in European caravans was acknowledged by the National Caravan Council (NCC). Accordingly, all caravan manufacturers in membership of the NCC were required to implement the system in UK caravans manufactured on and after 1st September, 2003. In effect these are models in the 2004 ranges and adherence to the new standards was added to the "check items" in the NCC "Approved Badge Scheme". In practice a few imported caravans on sale in the UK had this new system already installed in models sold in the summer of 2003.

Appendix B Continued

Revised Gas Standards

Cylinder-mounted gas regulators described in Chapter 10 have been in use for many years and will continue to be available for use in caravans. However, the fact that there are so many different gas cylinder couplings in use throughout Europe has prompted the introduction of two new standards: BS EN 1949:2002 and BS EN 12864:2001. These standards have also addressed some practical issues concerning the use of butane and propane.

In the past, owners wanting to run their caravan on butane and propane have been required to purchase two regulators: one to suit butane cylinders; the other to connect to propane cylinders. However, in most 2004 and later caravans this is no longer the case because a new type of regulator has been developed which will accept gas from both butane *and* propane cylinders.

Under the new standards the purchase and installation of a regulator is no longer the responsibility of persons buying new caravans; the new combined butane/propane regulator is now a standard fitment in the latest models. These products are normally mounted permanently in the gas cylinder locker by the caravan manufacturer. The only item that an owner now has to purchase is the short coupling hoses to suit the cylinders that he or she wishes to use.

A benefit of this facility is that during trips abroad, the cylinders sold in the countries you are visiting can now be used as long as you purchase connecting hoses with the appropriate couplings. The notes which follow summarise the implications of these revised arrangements.

Notes on the implications of the BS EN revisions:

■ Technical literature distributed by Calor Gas Ltd and supported by the NCC clearly states that new butane/propane regulators should NOT be installed retrospectively in pre-2004 caravans i.e. those model fitted with the former supply system. The Company reported: "The gas pressures of the new regulator and your existing installation are NOT compatible". (Leaflet published February 2003 New Requirement for LPG in Caravans).

■ In Chapter 10 (Technical Tip, Page 124) it was pointed out that previously fitted cylinder-mounted regulators were rated at 28mbar (butane) and 37 mbar (propane). In contrast, the new regulator which operates in conjunction with both butane and propane delivers gas at a standard pressure of 30 mbar.

■ Three manufacturers of regulators launched products which fulfilled the new requirements, namely GOK (supplied by Truma), CLESSE (from Comap) and RECA (from the Cavagna Group).

■ The gas appliances installed in caravans fitted with this revised system also have to be manufactured to run at a standard pressure of 30mbar and this has t be clearly shown on a label affixed to the product.

■ The hose which connects the regulator to the supplying cylinder MUST: a) carry a High Pressure rating, b) be marked accordingly on the side, and c) be supplied with factory-fitted couplings on both ends Under no circumstances should low pressure hose and conventional hose clips be used on the revised system; the unregulated gas being drawn from the cylinder is emitted at a high pressure.

Three regulator specialists have products for supply to UK caravan manufacturers. The regulators are the GOK (supplied by Truma), CLESSE (from Comap) and RECA (from the Cavagna Group).

On this 2005 Bailey caravan, a GOK regulator is installed on the bulkhead wall in the gas locker. Note the closeness of the brackets for securing the gas cylinders; their couplings have to be near the regulator inlet.

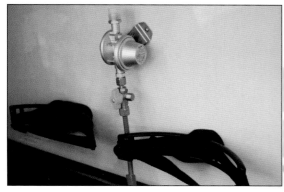

On caravans built after 1st September 2003, the owner only has to purchase a hose with factory fitted couplings to suit his or her choice of cylinder.

■ The overall length of the new coupling hose must not exceed 450mm (about 18in) and many different versions are sold so that a UK caravanner can purchase one to suit the connections on cylinders sold in the European country being visited. (Longer hose up to a maximum length of 750mm is permitted where cylinders are mounted on a pull-out tray arrangement).

■ In Britain it was decided that the new universal butane/propane regulators would be wall-mounted in caravans' gas lockers, a practice followed in several countries in mainland Europe. It was surprising, therefore, that some German caravans built in 2004 for sale in that country were exhibited with an unmounted universal 30 mbar dual gas regulator, apparently for direct cylinder mounting.

■ In view of the many types of different couplings on portable gas cylinders, it has been decided not to sell coupling hoses to suit every possible pattern of connections. Adaptors have been made to suit several types of cylinder; examples include adaptors for the clip-on couplings used on Calor 7kg and 15kg butane cylinders.

■ The specification of flexible hose has to be stamped on its side. It is NOT rubber; it is a special compound resistant to damage by LPG and its colour does NOT signify its high or low pressure rating. For instance there are examples of black Low Pressure hose and black High Pressure hose – hence the importance of checking the markings on the side.

■ Under the new system, a factory-fitted regulator forms part of a supplied caravan's fixtures and fittings. It therefore receives a manufacturer's soundness check together with the rest of the installation before it leaves the factory.

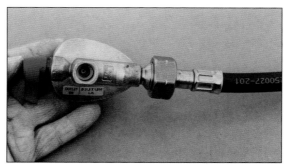

It seems unlikely that coupling hoses will be manufactured to match every type of cylinder sold throughout Europe and sometimes adaptors have to be purchased. This one is for Calor 7kg and 15kg clip-on butane cylinders.

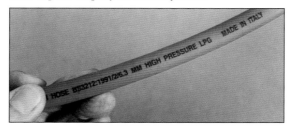

Under the new system the coupling hose must be of a high pressure designation and marked on the side. The connectors on both ends have to be pre-fitted by the component manufacturer.

Conclusion

Standardising the gas supply systems in European caravans makes good sense. British caravanners travelling abroad recognise that Calor cylinders are only available in the UK and although the Campingaz 907 cylinder is sold in many parts of mainland Europe, its modest "fill" of 2.72kg of butane is quickly consumed during winter trips. In addition, propane versions of Campingaz cylinders are not available and this is the preferred gas for use in very cold conditions.

Being able to use the cylinders supplied in other countries abroad is a benefit to the caravanner which is long over-due. It's very helpful, for example, if you want to spend a long winter sports holiday in the French Alps because you merely need to buy a coupling hose to suit the French cylinders. However, there is a matter to bear in mind which affects caravanners who want to tour from country to country. You have to ensure that you don't start collecting an array of different cylinders because there would be no space to store them all safely in your caravan.

Gas blockages

Gas starvation has occasionally been reported in caravans fitted with wall-mounted 30mbar regulators and built since 1st September, 2003. Investigators have found an 'oily substance' in faulty systems which could affect the regulation and flow of gas. The substance is thought to be condensation which forms initially in the high pressure connecting hose and which then absorbs the plasticising agents present in the flexible material. The resulting 'oily liquid' could undoubtedly upset regulator operation and, in turn, lead to irregularities in the flow of gas.

A fuller description of the problem and the necessary remedial measures are given in an information document published by The National Caravan Council (NCC). This was made public in January 2007 and copies can be accessed from the website www.thecaravan.net or obtained from the Council direct. (See Appendix C)

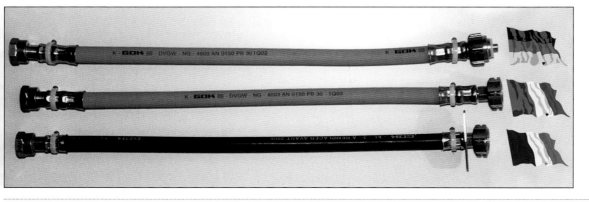

Coupling hoses are made to fit cylinders used in many countries throughout Europe although the union for coupling to the regulator itself has been standardised.

Contact addresses

This address list was correct at the time of going to press. It includes specialist suppliers and manufacturers whose products and services have been mentioned in this book. Several of the firms have web sites and these are easy to locate using search engines.

Abbey Caravans –
See The Swift Group

A.B. Butt Ltd,
Frog Island,
Leicester,
LE3 5AZ
Tel: 0116 251 3344
(Solar Systems and inverters)

ABI Caravans Ltd,
(ABI ceased manufacturing touring
caravans in summer 2001. Information or
supply of parts and warranty repairs
currently unvailable)

ABP Accessories,
27 Nether End,
Great Dalby,
Leicestershire,
LE14 2EY
Tel: 08700 115111
(Importer of Camco products)

Adria Concessionaires Ltd,
Hall Street,
Long Melford,
Sudbury,
Suffolk,
CO10 9JP
Tel: 01787 378705
(Importers of Adria caravans)

Airflow (UK) Ltd,
Crown House,
Faraday Road,
Newbury,
Berkshire,
RG14 2AB
Tel: 01635 569569
(Airflow trickle battery charger)

Air Muscle Ltd,
(Flexator leveller and Rolljack)
At time of reprint, the Company
appears to have ceased trading.

Alde International (UK) Ltd,
A3 Regent Park,
Booth Drive,
Park Farm South,
Wellingborough,
Northamptonshire,
NN8 6GR
Tel: 01933 677765
(Central heating systems, Gas leak
detector, Kitchen systems)

Al-Ko Kober Ltd,
South Warwickshire Business Park,
Kineton Road,
Southam,
Warwickshire, CV47 0AL
Tel: 01926 818500
(Chassis, running gear, stabilisers,
wheel carriers)

Apollo Repair Chemicals,
Leisure Plus,
Unit 3,
Airfield Industrial Estate,
Hixon,
Staffordshire, ST18 0PF
Tel: 01889 271692
(Wholesaler distributing Apollo
delamination kits)

Ashley Banks Ltd,
5 King Street,
Langtoft,
Peterborough, PE6 9NF
Tel: 01778 560651
(Supplier of tow car spring assisters,
MAD systems, Monroe)

Assembled Supplies (Electrical) Ltd,
Albany Road,
East Gateshead Industrial Estate,
Tyne and Wear,
NE8 3AT
Tel: 0191 477 3518
(Manufacturer of electronic wiring systems)

Auto Glym,
Works Road,
Letchworth,
Hertfordshire,
SG6 1LU
Tel: 01462-677766
(Caravan and car interior and exterior
cleaning products)

Autovan Services Ltd,
32 Canford Bottom,
Wimborne,
Dorset, BH21 2HD
Tel: 01202 848414
(Major body repair and rebuilding work)

Avondale Coachcraft Ltd,
Carlyon Road,
Atherstone,
Warwickshire, CV9 1JE
Tel: 01827 715231
(Manufacturers of Avondale caravans)

Awning World,
Dave Barron Caravans,
Chapel Lane,
Coppull,
Chorley,
Lancashire,
PR7 4NE
Tel: 01257 793008
(Display and sale of awnings)

Bailey Caravans Ltd,
South Liberty Lane,
Bristol,
BS3 2SS
Tel: 0117 966 5967
(Manufacturers of Bailey caravans)

Bailey & White Ltd,
2 Corn Kiln Close,
Cogenhoe,
Northampton,
NN7 1NX
Tel: 01604 890686
(Centinel Security Devices)

A. Baldassarre,
Upholsterer and Coachtrimmer,
103, Coventry Road,
Queens Park,
Bedford,
MK40 4ES
Tel: 01234 359277
(All types of upholstery work
and soft furnishings, foam
supplied to order. Edge finishing
of removable carpet pieces)

BCA Leisure Ltd,
Unit H8,
Premier Way,
Lowfields Business Park,
Elland,
North Yorkshire,
HX5 9HF
Tel: 01422 376977
(Manufacturers of Powerpart mains
kits, the Power Centre & Powerpart
Mobile)

Belling Appliances,
Talbot Road,
Mexborough,
South Yorkshire,
S64 8AJ
Tel: 01709 579902
(Belling cookers, hobs and water
heaters)

Bessacarr Caravans – See The Swift Group

Blue Diamond Products,
Unit 13,
Bottoms Mill,
Rouse Mill Lane,
Batley,
Yorkshire, WF17 5QB
Tel: 01924 420048
(Awning spares and accessories)

BPW Ltd,
Legion Way,
Meridian Business Park,
Leicester, LE3 2UZ
Tel: 0116 281 6100
(BPW chassis and Winterhoff stabilisers)

Bradleys,
Old Station Yard,
Marlesford,
Suffolk,
IP13 0AG
Tel: 01728 745200
(Mail Order supply of ABS repair kits
and paint products for plastic)

Brink UK Ltd,
Unit 7,
Centrovell Industrial Estate,
Caldwell Road,
Nuneaton,
Warwickshire,
CV11 4NG
Tel: 01203 352353
(Towbars)

British Car Auctions Ltd,
Sales & Marketing Department,
Expedier House,
Portsmouth Road,
Hindhead,
Surrey,
GU26 6TJ
Tel: 01428 607440

**British Rubber Manufacturers'
Association Ltd,**
6 Bath Place,
Rivington Street,
London, EC2A 3JE
Tel: 020 7457 5040
(Trade Association for the tyre
industry)

BRK Brands Europe Ltd,
Fountain House,
Canal View Road,
Newbury,
Berkshire, RG14 5XF
Tel: 01635 528080
(First Alert smell-sensitive gas alarm)

**Buccaneer Caravans –
See The Explorer Group**

Bulldog Security Products Ltd,
Units 2, 3, & 4,
Stretton Road,
Much Wenlock,
Shropshire, TF13 6DH
Tel: 01952-728171/3
(Bulldog stabilisers, SSK stabiliser importer,
security devices and posts)

C.A.K. Tanks,
Caravan Accessories (Kenilworth) Ltd,
10 Princes Drive,
Kenilworth,
Warwickshire,
CV8 2FD
Tel: 01926 854271
(Water accessories, air conditioners,
furniture fittings)

Calor Gas Ltd,
Athena Drive,
Tachbrook Park,
Warwick,
CV34 6RL
Tel: 0800 626626
(Supplier of butane, propane and
LPG appliances)

The Camping & Caravanning Club,
Greenfields House,
Westwood Way,
Coventry,
CV4 8JH
Tel: 02476 694995

The Caravan Club
East Grinstead House,
East Grinstead,
West Sussex,
RH19 1UA
Tel: 01342 326944

Camco Products – See ABP Accessories

Camping International Superstore,
Clock Tower House,
Watling Street,
Gillingham,
Kent,
ME5 7HS
Tel: 01634 577326
(Display and sale of awnings)

Campingaz
Coleman UK Inc.,
Parish Wharf Estate,
Harbour Road,
Portishead,
Bristol,
BS20 9DA
Tel: 01275 845024
(Supplier of Campingaz butane and
LPG appliances)

Caralux Upholstery,
(The Company is no longer trading)

Carafax Ltd,
Rotterdam Road,
Sutton Fields Industrial Estate,
Hull HU7 0XD
Tel: 01482 825941
(Cartridge sealants)

Caralevel,
Springhill Farm,
Great Horwood Road,
Little Horwood,
Milton Keynes,
MK17 0NZ
Tel: 01296 713476
(Electrically operated automatic
levelling system)

The Caravan Centre,
Unit 3A,
Gilchrist Thomas Industrial Estate,
Blaenavon, NP4 9RL
Tel: 01495 792700
(Specialist breakers supplying
caravan/motorhome products)

Caravanparts.net,
Unit 5,
Grovehill Industrial Estate,
Beck View Road,
Beverley,
East Yorkshire,
HU17 0JW
Tel: 01482 874878
(Supplier of caravan parts and
the Henry-GE water heater)

The Caravan Seat Cover Centre,
Kings Road,
Brislington,
Bristol,
BS4 3HH
Tel: 0117-9770797
(Re-upholsterer, loose covers,
and foam supplier)

Carcoon Storage Systems Int. Ltd,
Orchard Mill,
2 Orchard Street,
Salford,
Manchester,
M6 6FL
Tel: 0161 737 9690
(Power & Charge System: Mail Order direct)

Carlight Caravans Ltd,
Church Lane,
Sleaford,
Lincolnshire,
NG34 7DE
Tel: 01529 302120
(The Company has ceased full scale
production; repairs still undertaken)

**Carver product spares –
See Truma (UK) Ltd**

CEC Plug-In-Systems,
Contact your caravan dealer
(12V control components, water level sensors,
gauges, electronic alarm)

Coachman Caravan Co Ltd,
Amsterdam Road,
Sutton Field Industrial Estate,
Hull,
HU7 0XF
Tel: 01482 839737
(Manufacturers of Coachman caravans)

**Compass Caravans Ltd –
See The Explorer Group**

Cosmic Car Accessories Ltd,
Sadler Road,
Brownhills,
Walsall,
West Midlands,
WS8 6NA
Tel: 01543 452626
(Accessory supplier including
"Big Foot" corner steady base)

Creative Resins Distribution,
7, The Glenmore Centre,
Eurolink Industrial Estate,
Castle Road,
Sittingbourne,
Kent,
ME10 3GL
Tel: 01795 599880
(Mail Order for 'A' Glaze Caravan Total
Surface Protection)

CRiS
Dolphin House,
New Street,
Salisbury,
Wiltshire,
SP1 2PH
Tel: 01722 413434
(Caravan Registration & Identification
Scheme)

Crossleys,
Unit 33A, Comet Road,
Moss Side Industrial Estate,
Leyland,
Lancashire,
PR5 3QN
Tel: 01772 623423
(Major body repair and rebuilding
work)

**Crown Caravans –
See The Explorer Group**

B. Dixon-Bate Ltd,
Unit 45,
First Avenue,
Deeside Industrial Park,
Deeside,
Clwyd,
CH5 2LG
Tel: 01244 288925
(Towing accessories including cushioned
towball units)

W. David & Sons Ltd,
Denington Industrial Estate,
Wellingborough,
Northamptonshire,
NN8 2QP
Tel: 01933 227186
(David's Isopon resin, filler paste and
U-Pol branded versions)

**D.J. Russell Sales –
See Miriad Products Ltd
Dometic Ltd,**
99 Oakley Road,
Luton,
Bedfordshire,
LU4 9GE
Tel: 01582 494111
(Air conditioners, refrigerators, Seitz
windows – formerly Electrolux
Leisure)

Driftgate 2000 Ltd,
Little End Road,
Eaton Socon,
Cambridgeshire,
PE19 3JH
Tel: 01480 470400
(Manufacturers of XCell Mains
inverters)

Elecsol Europe Ltd,
47 First Avenue,
Deeside Industrial Park,
Deeside,
Flintshire,
CH5 2LG
Tel: 0800 163298
(Elecsol batteries)

Electrical Contractors Association (ECA),
3 Buenavista Gardens,
Glenholt,
Plymouth
Tel: 01752 700981
(Mains supply system checking)

**Electrolux Leisure Appliances –
See Dometic Ltd.**

Elddis Caravans – See The Explorer Group

Elsan Ltd,
Elsan House,
Bellbrook Park,
Uckfield,
East Sussex,
TN22 1QF
Tel: 01825 748200
(Manufacturers of toilets and chemicals)

Eriba Ltd,
The Priory,
A417 Faringdon Road,
Lechlade,
Gloucestershire,
GL7 3EY
Tel: 01367 253452
(Importers of Eriba caravans)

Europa Specialist Spares,
Fauld Industrial Park,
Tutbury,
Burton upon Trent,
Staffordshire,
DE13 9HR
Tel: 01283 815609
(Vehicle trims, light clusters, and specialist
vehicle parts)

Evode Ltd,
Industrial Division,
Common Road,
Stafford,
ST16 3EH
Tel: 01785 257755
(Manufacturers of Evo-Stik Adhesives)

Exhaust Ejector Co Ltd,
Wade House Road,
Shelf,
Nr. Halifax,
West Yorkshire,
HX3 7PE
Tel: 01274 679524
(Replacement acrylic windows made to order)

Exide Leisure Batteries Ltd,
Gate No. 3,
Pontyfelin Industrial Estate,
New Road,
Pontypool,
NP4 5DG
Tel: 01495 750075
(Exide Leisure Batteries)

The Explorer Group,
Delves Lane,
Consett,
Co Durham,
DH8 7LG.
Tel: 01207 503477
(Caravan manufacturer of Buccaneer, Elddis,
Compass, Crown and Herald models)

Farécla Products Ltd,
Broadmeads,
Ware,
Hertfordshire,
SG12 9HS
Tel: 01920 465041
(Caravan Pride acrylic window scratch remover
and GRP surface renovator)

Fiamma water pumps and water tanks
Contact your motorcaravan dealers for
Fiamma products.

Flavel Leisure,
Clarence Street,
Leamington Spa,
Warwickshire, CV31 2AD
Tel: 01926 427027
(Flavel cookers and hobs)

Fleetwood Caravans Ltd,
Hall Street,
Long Melford,
Sudbury,
Suffolk, CO10 9JP
Tel: 01787 378705
(Manufacturers of Fleetwood caravans)

FFC (Foam for Comfort) Ltd,
Unit 2,
Wyther Lane Trading Estate,
Wyther Lane,
Kirkstall,
Leeds,
LS5 3BT
Tel: 0113 274 8100
(New foam supplier, composite bonded
foam specialist)

Franks Caravan Supplies,
16/27 Wigmore Street,
Stopsley,
Luton,
Bedfordshire,
LU2 8AA.
Tel: 01582 732168
(Former breakers now specialising in caravan
products)

Freedom Caravans,
Lichfield Road,
Stafford,
ST17 4NY
Tel: 01785 222488
(Importers of Freedom caravans)

Gardner of Wakefield Ltd,
76 Wakefield Road,
Flushdyke,
Ossett,
West Yorkshire,
W5 9JX
Tel: 01924 265367
(Portable showers, protective covers
for components)

Gaslow International,
The Manor House,
Normanton-on-Soar,
Leicestershire,
LE12 5HB
Tel: 0845 4000 600
(Gas leak gauges, refillable cylinders,
LPG components)

Gobur Caravans Ltd,
Peacock Way,
Melton Constable,
Norfolk,
NR24 2BY
Tel: 01263 860031
(Manufacturers of Gobur folding caravans)

Grade UK Ltd,
3 Central Court,
Finch Close,
Lenton Lane Industrial Estate,
Nottingham,
NG7 2NN
Tel: 0115 986 7151
(Status TV aerials and accessories)

Gramos Repair Kits, Mail Order,
Kingdom Industrial Supplies Ltd,
6/10 Bancrofts Road,
Eastern Industrial Estate,
South Woodham Ferrers,
Essex,
CM3 5UQ
Tel: 01245 322177
(Kits for repairing ABS plastic)

Grayston Engineering Ltd,
115 Roebuck Road,
Chessington,
Surrey,
KT9 1JZ
Tel: 0181 9741122
(Tow car spring assister kits)

Hammerite Paints
Available from DIY stores and
automotive specialists.

Häfele UK Ltd,
Swift Valley Industrial Estate,
Rugby,
Warwickshire,
CV21 1RD
Tel: 01788 542020
(Furniture components and hardware)

HBC International A/S,
Fabriksparken 4,
DK9230 Svenstrup,
Denmark
Tel: +45 70227070
(Professional system for repairing aluminium
body panels)

Hella Ltd,
Wildmere Industrial Estate,
Banbury,
Oxfordshire,
OX16 7JU
Tel: 01295 272233
(Hella towing electrical equipment)

**Herald Caravans –
See The Explorer Group**

Hodgson Sealants,
Belprin Road,
Beverley,
North Humberside,
HU17 0LN
Tel: 01482 701191
(Manufacturers of caravan
sealants)

Jablite insulation
Available from
Builders' Merchants

Johnnie Longden Ltd,
Unit 24,
Dawkins Road,
Poole,
Dorset,
BH15 4JD
Tel: 01202 679121
(Caravan Accessories including
components for older caravans)

Kenlowe Ltd,
Burchetts Green,
Maidenhead,
Berkshire,
SL6 6QU
Tel: 01628 823303
(Radiator cooling fans and automatic
transmission oil coolers)

**Knott (UK) Ltd –
See Miriad Products Ltd**

LabCraft Ltd,
228 King Street,
Saffron Walden,
Essex,
CB10 1ES
Tel: 01799 513434
(Lighting units)

Peter J Lea Company Ltd,
Peterlea Works,
Shaw Road South,
Shaw Heath,
Stockport,
SK3 8JG
Tel: 0161 480 2377
(Manufacturers of the
Scott Stabiliser)

Leisure Accessories Ltd,
Britannia Works,
Hurricane Way,
Airport Industrial Estate,
Norwich,
NR6 6EY
Tel: 01603 414551
(POSIflow, FLOking
water pumps)

Lunar Caravans Ltd,
Sherdley Road,
Lostock Hall,
Preston,
Lancashire,
PR5 5JF
Tel: 01772 337628
(Manufacturer of Lunar caravans)

**MAD tow car spring assisters –
See Ashley Banks Ltd.**

Marlec Engineering Ltd,
Rutland House,
Trevithick Road,
Corby,
Northamptonshire,
NN17 5XY
Tel: 01536 201588
(Wind and solar systems)

Magnum Mobiles and Caravan Surplus,
Unit 9A,
Cosalt Industrial Estate,
Convamore Road,
Grimsby,
DN32 9JL
Tel: 01472 353520
(Caravan surplus stock)

Maxview,
Common Lane,
Setchey,
King's Lynn,
Norfolk,
PE33 0AT
Tel: 01553 810376
(Maxview TV aerials)

Merlin Equipment,
Unit 1, Hithercroft Court,
Lupton Road,
Wallingford,
Oxfordshire,
OX10 9BT
Tel: 01491 824333
(PROwatt Inverters)

Mer Products Ltd,
Whitehead House,
120 Beddington Lane,
Croydon,
Surrey,
CRO 4TD
Tel: 0181 401 0002
(Distributor of Mer Car Care products)

Miriad Products Ltd,
Europa House,
Wharf Road,
Burton-upon-Trent,
Staffordshire,
DE14 1PZ
Tel: 01283 531541
(UK distributor of Knott running
gear & BPW chassis)

**Monroe tow car spring assister systems –
See Ashley Banks Ltd.**

Morco Products Ltd,
Morco House,
59 Beverley Road,
Hull,
HU3 1XW
Tel: 01482 325456
(Instantaneous Water Heaters)

Munster Simms Engineering Ltd,
Old Belfast Road,
Bangor
BT19 1LT
Northern Ireland.
Tel: 01247 270531
(Whale semi-rigid pipework system
& all plumbing accessories)

The National Caravan Council,
Catherine House,
Victoria Road,
Aldershot,
Hampshire,
GU11 1SS
Tel: 01252 318251

National Inspection Council for Electrical Installation Contracting,
(NICEIC)
Vintage House,
36-37 Albert Embankment,
London,
SE1 7UJ
Tel: 020 7564 2323
(Certification to confirm a caravan is correctly wired for mains electricity)

National Trailer and Towing Association,
1, Alveston Place,
Leamington Spa,
Warwickshire,
CV32 4SN
Tel: 01926 335 445
(Trade association with accreditation scheme for towbar fitters and list of member installation specialists)

O'Leary Spares and Accessories,
314 Plaxton Bridge Road,
Woodmansey,
Nr Beverley,
East Yorkshire,
HU17 ORS
Tel: 01482 868632
(Retailer of surplus stocks purchased from caravan manufacturers)

**Peitz axle, chassis and over-run couplings –
See Miriad Products**

PGR Products Ltd,
16 Crofton Road,
Lincoln,
Lincolnshire,
LN3 4NL
Tel: 01522 534538
(Sectional TV mast, wheel clamps, winter wheels)

Protimeter plc,
Meter House,
Marlow,
Buckinghamshire,
SL7 1LX
Tel: 01628 472722
(Caravan moisture meters)

Pyramid Products Ltd,
Unit 1,
Victoria Street,
Mansfield,
Nottinghamshire,
NG18 5RR
Tel: 01623 421277
(Patriot wheel clamp and accessories)

Remis UK,
(Blinds for caravans – Order through dealer accessory shops)

RoadPro Ltd,
Stephenson Close,
Drayton Fields Industrial Estate,
Daventry,
Northamptonshire, NN1 5RF
Tel: 01327 312233
(Suppliers of chargers, inverters, satellite TV systems, electrical accessories)

RT Marshall,
Woodside Industrial Estate,
Bayton,
Kidderminster,
Worcestershire, DY14 9NE
Tel: 01299 832533
(Satellite TV systems)

Ryder Towing Equipment Ltd,
Mancunian Way,
Ardwick,
Manchester, M12 6HW
Tel: 0161 2735619
(Electrical towing equipment & 'The Practical Guide to Towbar Electrics')

Safe and Secure Products Ltd,
Chestnut House,
Chesley Hill,
Wick,
Bristol, BS30 5NE
Tel: 0117-937 4737
(SAS stabilisers, security devices, posts & Dart spare wheel carrier)

Sargent Electrical Services Ltd,
Unit 39,
Tokenspire Business Park,
Woodmansey,
Beverley,
Hull, HU17 0TB
Tel: 01482 881655
(Electrical control systems and low voltage panels)

Scotch Gard Upholstery Products
Available from DIY Superstores e.g. B & Q

Selmar Guardian Chargers
Tadmod Ltd,
Galliford Road,
Malden,
Essex,
CM9 4XD
(Selmar stage chargers, sold Mail Order direct from M.A.C. Tel: 01621 859444)

Sew 'n' So's,
42 Claudette Avenue,
Spalding,
Lincolnshire,
PE11 1HU
Tel: 01775 767 633
(Bespoke awnings, cover systems, bags and generator covers)

SF Detection Ltd,
Hatch Pond House,
4 Stinsford Road,
Nuffield Industrial Estate,
Poole,
Dorset,
BH17 0RZ
Tel: 01202 665330
(SF330 Carbon monoxide detector)

Shurflo Ltd,
Unit 5,
Sterling Park,
Gatwick Road,
Crawley,
West Sussex, RH10 2QT
Tel: 01293 424000
(Shurflo diaphragm water pumps)

Sika Ltd,
Watchmead,
Welwyn Garden City,
Hertfordshire, AL7 1BQ
Tel: 01707 394444
(Sikaflex Cartridge Sealants)

The Society of Motor Manufacturers and Traders,
Trade Sections Department,
Forbes House,
Halkin Street,
London,
SW1X 7DS
Tel: 020 7235 7000
(Publishers of SMMT booklet Towing and the Law)

Solar Solutions,
Unit 1,
565 Blandford Road,
Hamworthy,
Poole,
Dorset,
BH16 5BW
Tel: 01202 632488
(Suppliers of solar panels)

Sold Secure Trust,
5c Great Central Way,
Woodford Halse,
Daventry,
Northamptonshire,
NN11 3PZ
Tel: 01327 264687
(Test house conducting attack tests to verify the integrity of caravan security devices)

The Stabiliser Clinic,
Holme Grove,
Bypass Road,
Garstang,
Preston,
Lancashire,
PR3 1NA
Tel: 01995 603745
(Stabiliser test kits and complete overhaul service)

Stain Devils Information Service,
107-111 Fleet Street,
London,
EC4A 2AB
Tel: 020 7353 4499
(Guidance on stain removal)

Sterling Caravans – See The Swift Group

Stoves plc, *Company name now changed to:*
Glen Dimplex Cooking Ltd,
Stoney Lane,
Prescot,
Merseyside, L35 2XW
Tel: 0151 426 6551
(Grills, Hobs, Ovens)

Superpitch,
Conduit Road,
Conduit Industrial Estate,
Norton Canes,
Cannock,
Staffordshire,
WS11 3TJ
Tel: 01543 270987
(Superpitch motorcaravan
conversion accessories)

Swift Group Ltd,
Dunswell Road,
Cottingham,
Hull,
HU16 4JX
Tel: 01482 847332
(Manufacturer of Abbey, Bessacarr,
Sterling & Swift caravans)

Tetroson brake and clutch cleaner
Available from automotive factors.

Thetford (UK) Spinflo,
4 -10 Welland Close,
Parkwood Industrial Estate,
Rutland Road,
Sheffield, S3 9QY
Tel: 01142 738157
(Norcold refrigerators; Thetford toilets and
treatments; Spinflo Grills, Hobs, Ovens)

Thompson Plastics (Hull) Ltd,
Bridge Works,
Hessle,
East Yorkshire,
HU13 0TP
Tel: 01482 646464
(Manufacturer of acrylic-capped ABS
caravan components)

Tockfield Ltd,
Pitt Lane,
Shirland,
Nr. Alfreton,
Derbyshire,
DE55 6AT
Tel: 01773 834968
(Re-upholsterer and foam supplier)

**Tri-Flow Suppliers –
See WYKO Industrial Services**

Towsure Products Ltd,
151-183 Holme Lane,
Hillsborough,
Sheffield,
S6 4JR
Tel: 0870 60 900 70
(Accessory supplier and towbar manufacturer)

Truma UK,
Park Lane,
Dove Valley Park,
South Derbyshire,
DE65 5BG
Tel: 01283 586020
(Space and water heating systems, gas
components, water systems; BP GASLIGHT
gas cylinders)

Trylon Ltd,
Unit J,
Higham Business Park,
Bury Close,
Higham Ferrers,
Northamptonshire,
NN10 8HQ
Tel: 01933 411724
(Resins, glass and guidance on glass
reinforced plastics)

Tyron Safety Band (UK) Ltd
Available from all good caravan dealers;
for more information Tel: 0845 4000 600

Vanmaster Caravans,
Unit 57C,
Bradley Hall,
Bradley Lane,
Standish,
Wigan,
WN6 0XQ
Tel: 01257 424999
(Manufacturer of Vanmaster caravans)

Vanroyce Caravans,
(No longer in manufacture; contact
Auto-Trail V.R. Ltd
Tel: 01472 571000)

Varta Automotive Batteries Ltd
Broadwater Park,
North Orbital Road,
Denham,
Uxbridge,
Middlesex,
UB9 5AG
Tel: 01895 838993
(Gel-type, non-spill leisure batteries)

V & G Caravans,
107 Benwick Road,
Whittlesey,
Peterborough,
Cambridgeshire,
PE7 2HD
Tel: 01733 350580
(Replacement replica panels in
GRP)

W4 Ltd,
Unit B,
Ford Lane Industrial Estate,
Arundel,
West Sussex,
BN18 0DF
Tel: 01243 553355
(Suppliers of 230V kits, double-pole
switched sockets, socket testers, and
ribbon sealants)

WAECO International,
Unit G1,
Roman Hill Business Park,
Broadmayne,
Dorset,
DT2 8LY
Tel: 01305 854000
(Battery chargers, inverters and
electrical accessories)

Watling Engineers Ltd,
88 Park Street Village,
nr. St. Albans,
Hertfordshire,
AL2 2LR
Tel: 01727 873661
(Designer/manufacturer of towing
brackets)

West Riding Leisure,
Unit 19,
Perseverance Mills,
Lockwood Scar,
Lockwood,
Huddersfield,
HD4 6BW
Tel: 01484 451760
(Specialists in repairing ABS panels
and caravan repair work)

**Whale Products –
See Munster Simms Engineering Ltd,**

**Winterhoff coupling head stabilisers –
See Miriad Products Ltd and
BPW Ltd**

Witter Towbars,
Drome Road,
Deeside Industrial Park,
Deeside,
CH5 2NY
Tel: 01244 284500
(Towbar systems and cycle
carriers)

Woodfit Ltd,
Kem Mill,
Whittle-le-Woods,
Chorley,
Lancashire,
PR6 7EA
Tel: 01257 266421
(Hinges, fittings, hardware, wire storage
baskets and catches)

WYKO Industrial Services,
Amber Way,
Halesowen,
West Midlands,
B62 8WG
Tel: 0121 5086000
(For address of nearest WYKO branch
retailing Tri-Flow moisture inhibitor
spray)

ZIG Electronics Ltd,
Saxon Business Park,
Hanbury Road,
Stoke Prior,
Bromsgrove,
Worcestershire,
B60 4AD
Tel: 01527 577800
(Low voltage control components,
chargers, and gauges)

Index

Acknowledgements

This manual touches on many technical subjects and to ensure accuracy in words and illustrations, a large number of specialists proof-read either the entire manuscript or particular specialist sections.

The author and publishers would like to thank the following:

Specialist sections:

Ken Ashby (Hella Ltd)
Martin Baker (Calor Gas Ltd)
Gordon Carson (Munster Simms Engineering Ltd)
Keith Colder (Witter Towing Brackets)
John Corbett (Carver Products)
Keith Fox (Evesham College)
Gordon King (BCA Leisure Ltd)
Hugh Lamberton (Electrolux Leisure Appliances)
Peter Leivers (Truma Products)
Richard Miller-Mead (M-M Services)
Mike Pantrey (National Caravan Council Ltd)
David Ryder (National Trailer and Towing Association)
Martin Spencer (Technical Officer, The Caravan Club)
British Rubber Manufacturers' Association Ltd

Photographs and illustrations:

Front cover photograph: Janette Lavery
Title page photographs courtesy of The Swift Group and Lunar Caravans
AL-KO Kober
Carlight Caravans
Crossley Coachcraft
John Harbron
Hella
Andrew Jenkinson
Leisure Accessories
Paul Tanswell
Plug-in-Systems
Sika Ltd
Zig Electronics